PIECE
by
PIECE

PIECE
by
PIECE

Selected Prose

RACHEL HADAS

PAUL DRY BOOKS
Philadelphia 2021

First Paul Dry Books Edition, 2021

Paul Dry Books, Inc.
Philadelphia, Pennsylvania
www.pauldrybooks.com

Copyright © 2021 Rachel Hadas

ISBN: 978-1-58988-155-6

Printed in the United States of America

Library of Congress Control Number: 2021937200

CONTENTS

ACKNOWLEDGMENTS

Special thanks to the following publications for essays that originally appeared in them:

Able Muse, Bellevue Literary Review, The Hopkins Review, Hotel Amerika, The Los Angeles Review of Books, Literary Matters, New England Review, Parnassus: Poetry in Review, Southwest Review, The Agni Blog, The American Scholar, The Hudson Review, The New Criterion, The Times Literary Supplement, and *The Threepenny Review.*

FOREWORD

THIS SELECTION from my recent and not so recent prose pieces (the earliest piece here was written in about 1994, the most recent in 2019) has gone through several iterations. Originally it included too many book reviews. Many of these, though not all, have been replaced by more personal pieces. Poised between the cloudy genres of essay and mini-memoir, these mostly brief selections were often occasioned by something I'd read. But others originated elsewhere—a place, a dream, a conversation. A classroom in Corfu or Kumasi, an art gallery in Accra, a soak in a spa in Truth or Consequences, New Mexico, a waiting room for prospective jurors down at New York City's law courts, my mother-in-law's gift of a hat and scarf—any of these might start a train of thought.

As I look over these pieces a few themes present themselves. First and last is reading, mostly but not solely reading poetry. Writing a book review, it turns out, is only one way, and rarely the most interesting way, to engage with what one has read. I'm more interested in what happens to that book as time passes—the obliterations and transformations of memory. What and how did I recall what I'd read, sometimes many years before? How, at different times in my life, did books help me?

There are memories outside books, as well. As time passes, and more and more of one's experience is relegated to memory, more and less recent memories tend to present themselves shoulder to shoulder rather than in the chronological order of whichever decades they originated in. My mother, who died in 1992, and my father, who died in 1966, are more vivid presences to me now than they were fifteen or twenty years ago. The first section of *Piece by Piece*, "Close to Home," looks at my own early years through the lens of my parents. Both my parents were teachers, and so am I; teaching, too, is a constant.

Books, teaching, writing—all are ways of passing on what one has received. I've always loved, even when I was too young to understand it as well as I do now, the passage in *The Book of Ephraim* where James Merrill writes:

> Hadn't—from books, from living—
> The profusion dawned on us, of languages
> Any one of which, to who could read it,
> Lit up the system it conceived?

But what to do with this profusion? Over a lifetime the question posed in my poem "Piece by Piece," which opens this volume, becomes more pressing: What to keep? What to let go? What to give away? There's limited time: "It is time / to be packing." But I sometimes think there's unlimited space. It helps that I can and do send boxes of manuscripts, drafts, and correspondence to my archive at Alexander Library at Rutgers University—New Brunswick. I could and did have the piano, untouched since my late husband's death, shipped to my son in North Carolina. And the space of memory, if more capricious, is also much more capacious. Neil Gaiman once said of writing fiction that unlike with the film industry, one's special effects budget is unlimited. What we remember is something that we can keep, for our lifetimes, and pass on at the same time. The sections "Storage and Retrieval," "Translations and Transitions," and "Poetic Knowledge" all concern some kind of handing on. And speaking of storage and retrieval, I'm aware that the pages that follow repeat a few facts or passages that were evidently so crucial in my memory that they turned up more than once, in more than one context. I apologize for any redundancy.

The kind of bookish person I am may be a dying breed. I think of my childhood friends Missy Roberts and Lydia Davis, both of whom grew up in homes at least as saturated with books as mine was. We're all in our seventies now. It's time, one way or another, to pass on what we know. Of course, this is what we've been doing all along—in the classroom, on the page, and sometimes at home. I remember my delight when some years ago my son, visiting the apartment where he grew up and where I still live, glanced up at a light cord and casually quoted T. S. Eliot's poem "The Old Gumbie Cat": "The curtain-cord she likes to wind, and tie it into sailor knots." No one had forced that poem down Jonathan's throat; he absorbed it.

When my poem "Piece by Piece" was accepted for publication by *Gettysburg Review*, the thoughtful editor, Mark Drew, persuaded me to cut the final line. I resisted, but just a little. He was right; it was in keeping with the spare, stern tone of the poem to end it with the challenging question: "What is there I will not let go?"

I want to reinstate that deleted final line here. The poem as published ends with that question, but originally its final line answered the question: "You, my beloved. I need you." *You* is my dear husband Shalom Gorewitz, who since 2013 has cherished me in ways I had never imagined. In the safety and joy and attention of the life we share, I've been able to look back, to reflect, and to begin to let go. But a person one loves is a keeper.

PIECE BY PIECE

All you grasp will be thrown away.
All you hoard will be utterly lost.

—Tao Te Ching, 44,
translated by Ursula K. Le Guin

I've practiced the poetics of space,
but there's a sequel: empty spaces
have a resounding poetry.
I'm standing, skimming through the B's.
On the shelf near Bachelard,
Keith Basso: *Wisdom Sits*
in Places. Sits in empty places.
While it's easy, study the hard.
We've heard about the art of losing;
passing on is also choosing.
Things are in motion, fast or slow.
Clouds keep sailing through the sky.
Holding on makes nothing stay.
Give things permission to go.
Touch with gentleness, release,
and rooted objects will break loose,
a landslide that gathers speed
and leaves a brightness in its wake,
a lacy layer of memories
like foam lines scribbled on a beach.
This was Vermont. And here was Greece.

For the time left, what do I need?
What to take? What not to take?
Little by little, page by page,
let me give myself away.
Each addition to one's age
asks for subtraction. It is time
to be packing. Travel light.
What is the final appetite?
What is there I will not let go?

I

Close to Home

MATER SAGAX

Wʜᴏ ᴡᴀs ᴍʏ ᴍᴏᴛʜᴇʀ? I'll quote two paragraphs from my sister Beth's afterword to *Ferdinandus Taurus*, our mother's 1964 translation into Latin of Munro Leaf's 1936 classic, *The Story of Ferdinand*. *Ferdinandus* was reissued by David R. Godine in 2000; my sister and I each contributed a kind of postscript. Beth writes:

> Elizabeth Chamberlayne Hadas (1915–1992) was a teacher, a reader, a translator, a mother. Those activities were not separate parts of her life. She was the most bookish person I have ever known [which, I might add, is saying quite a lot; Beth has been an editor for about half a century]. She read aloud to my sister and me long before we could possibly understand what she was reading to us, and it is not an accident that both of us have devoted our lives to books, one of us as an author and the other as a publisher. . . .
>
> Elizabeth Hadas was brought up to teach. Her father, Lewis Chamberlayne, a professor of classics, died when she was a very small child. Faced with raising two daughters, her mother, Bessie, took a job teaching at St. Catherine's School in Richmond, Virginia. Bessie and her little girls lived on campus, presumably in exchange for supervising the boarding students. From St. Catherine's, Elizabeth went to Bryn Mawr, and after graduation she went on to teach Latin at St. Timothy's School. Eventually she developed an interest in seeing the world beyond girls' schools. She moved to New York during the war years, married Moses Hadas, had two daughters, and stayed at home with us until 1959, when she went back to teaching Latin at Spence, another girls' school. She spent the rest of her career there.

Beth covers the main points deftly and crisply; her very concision means that much has been elided. A great deal could be said about the distinguished men, both professors of classics, in my mother's life: her father, Lewis Parke Chamberlayne (1879–1917), and my father, Moses Hadas (1900–1966). (Can a father who dies when his child is two years old be said to be in that child's life? Yes and no.) But I want to try to stick with my mother.

The dead keep their own counsel. But my mother was exceptionally good at keeping her own counsel even during her lifetime. Furthermore, although, as my sister notes, our mother was one of the most bookish people imaginable, Elizabeth Chamberlayne Hadas didn't leave much of a paper trail. That's not quite true; think of the dozens of detailed report cards (more like essays) she wrote over the course of a quarter of a century for her Spence students. Think of the letters she wrote (now mostly lost). Still, for such a supremely articulate woman, it's a meager record.

What are books, I ask my students, if not a person talking to you who is no longer able to talk to you? When my father died in 1966, I turned to his books to hear his voice. There was nothing terribly personal there, but as my memories of him in life receded, the written record was precious. More than forty years later, when I was the age my father had been when he died, my new love and I found ourselves comparing notes on our departed fathers—their shared affection, for example, for bow ties, Groucho Marx, Gilbert and Sullivan—and I returned to my father's writings. But here I am writing about Moses again. As my old friend Lydia Davis notes, "of course it was your father who received more attention, who seemed to collect the energy in the room into himself. Not that she seemed fazed by that—she seemed very accepting, very unruffled." But today, Mother's Day 2017, a week before the twenty-fifth anniversary of my mother's death, I am turning my thoughts to her, and she is more elusive.

As my sister's account suggests, it is possible to see the twenty-one years of my mother's marriage to Moses Hadas—they were married in 1945—as a kind of island in the midst of various girls' schools. (It should be added that Elizabeth put in two stints as a librarian, first at the Library of Congress and then at the New York Public Library.) When she retired from the last of these schools, Spence, in 1984, my mother became a pretty much full-time grandmother to my son Jonathan, her only grandchild, who had been born earlier that year. She died when Jon was eight years old. What does he remember? He writes:

My memories of Lizzie are sparse: her presence in the house in Vermont (making "great speckled pancakes" or bacon in the even-then ancient electric frying plan), her reading Tolkien to me on the sofa in the Riverside Drive apartment, or feeding me cube steak and milk. I remember the apartment with its grandfather clock (unless I'm making that up?) and exercise bike. Her cats . . . meanwhile Lizzie's own presence seems to have been so discreet as to be vanishing—light footprint indeed.

Some aspects of that somber, first-floor Riverside Drive apartment are captured by Lydia Davis in her 1986 story "Five Signs of Disturbance." Lydia and her family were friends of my family; Lydia spent some time in the apartment one summer:

> In the dining room she pushes upright the heavy books that have been leaning far over to one side on the shelves and sprawling open for so long now that their covers are warped out of shape. There is another bookcase in the living room, with glass doors, and on top of it a clock that hisses every time the second hand passes a certain point. [Can this be the grandfather clock Jonathan thought he remembered?] Now she walks down the hall, straightening more books as she comes to them. The hall is long and dark, with many angles, so that around every bend more hallway opens out and this hallway seems to her, sometimes, infinitely long.

Cindy Quimby, whose friendship with me dates back to summers in Vermont in the 1950s, writes, "It's interesting what images stay fixed in memory, isn't it?" The feeding and the reading Jonathan recalls, the food and the book: these (unlike that grandfather clock, which was a figment) ring true. Later Jonathan said that he thought he remembered his grandmother reading him the chapter about Beorn in *The Hobbit*. One of my own (vanishingly few) memories of my mother's mother, Elizabeth Mann Chamberlayne, is her reading me Edward Lear's "The Owl and the Pussycat" in her Virginia accent and a wonderfully growly voice.

When I think about my mother and my son together, I remember her carrying him as a baby around the garden in Vermont and naming flowers. A little later, I remember walking down the dirt road with her, Jon on my shoulders or on hers—he ruffled her white hair. "Amma's hair," he said. Or, touching her glasses, "Amma's asses." Earlier still, she was carrying him down the long hall of our West End Avenue apartment when Jonathan, looking up over his grandmother's shoulder at the light fixture on the ceiling, said his first word: Ite! Ite! Jon inherited my mother's flawless spelling, her interest in gardening, and her love—the family love—of books. Books! There's no end to the memories here. *Ferdinand*; *The Princess and the Goblin*; *The Young Visitors*; *The Hobbit*; *A Little Princess*; *The Racketty-Packetty House*. Books she didn't read me but loved, and that I came to love too: *Kim*. Books she read me that I later read and reread: *Pride and Prejudice*. Beth remembers being read *Alice in Wonderland*; I don't. It was our father, not our mother, who especially enjoyed performing Dickens's fairy tale *The Magic Fishbone*. But books were the lingua franca of the household.

My mother was primarily a reader of books, not a writer. After translating *The Story of Ferdinand*, she spent some time translating some of Aesop's Fables into Latin. That this project was never finished may mean that it was interrupted by my father's death in 1966. Earlier, in 1960, she edited *The Life of Christ*, a rich little book (it really should have been a capacious coffee table tome) which combined Gospel passages and works of art to tell the story.

I wish my mother had written more. Given the right prompt and within her range of subject matter, chiefly literature (not only the classics) and art history, Elizabeth was extremely knowledgeable. She always seemed to know the answer to every question. My sister Beth inherited this trait—it's no accident that Beth aspires to go on *Jeopardy*, where everyone in the family is sure she would perform brilliantly and where, in many categories, Elizabeth would have done very well too.

Reminiscing about my mother, Cindy Quimby brings up her salient quality of being able to answer questions: "to me it seemed that [Elizabeth] always offered innately sound, informed, and logical answers to all questions. She seemed to be an oasis of calm and competence." (Cindy adds "and her light southern accent was calming, too.") I think of the charming line in *Ferdinandus*: "Quod erat mater sagax, etsi vacca." Sagacious: a good word for Elizabeth. Debbie Hadas, daughter of Elizabeth's stepson David, unknowingly echoes this adjective: "If I had a problem, [Elizabeth] would offer sage (and confidential) advice."

The conversations Cindy is recalling took place in the summers of the late 1950s and early 1960s, in the cramped kitchen of our house in Vermont, where my mother would be making dinner for our family of four, for her stepson David's family of four, and for our friends the Quimbys, another family of four. "Cooking for twelve is no easy thing!" Cindy notes. My mother wasn't brought up to cook; I think my father taught her. I seem to remember a running joke between them about the initials S.C.; she had been born in South Carolina, but Moses, as I recall, insisted that S.C. stood for sour cream.

To be cooking for twelve people, six of them children and two of those very small children, with both one's stepdaughter-in-law (David's wife Hannah) and my mother's beloved friend Mary Jo, Cindy's mother, in and out of the small kitchen, and simultaneously to carry on any kind of conversation at all, let alone a calm and logical one—this feat (as complicated as this sentence is becoming) may not have been exactly what I had in mind when I wrote, in my afterword to *Ferdinandus Taurus*, that "my mother never made heavy weather of any task." But it's the same kind of accomplishment. Lydia Davis calls Elizabeth "calm and quiet"; but she was also indefatigable and focused even in the midst of multi-tasking. That multi-tasking included, for most of my childhood, not only running a household and raising two daughters, but also teaching Latin at an excellent school. My mother's scores of students over the years could and probably would like to write their own tributes to her. It's as a teacher that she touched the most lives; but it's also true that most of the younger people she encountered outside the classroom—that is, her family—learned from her. Debbie writes that Elizabeth "didn't hesitate to encourage me to improve my spelling, or my character. I remember a letter pointing out I'd misspelled the word 'tomorrow,' and also her pointed missives reminding me of the importance of thank you letters."

Part of my mother's sagacity lay in her unerring sense of which book to give a child, and at what age. (I like to think I have inherited this gift, though in a much diluted form.) Among the books she gave me that made a lasting impression were two poetry anthologies: Louis Untermeyer's *The Magic Circle* and John Hollander and Harold Bloom's *The Wind and the Rain*. I was then around eleven or twelve. Did my mother know I liked poetry? Clearly. That I was on my way to becoming a poet? Possibly. But these were also books, or poems, she had enjoyed herself and thought I'd like too. The luminous figure of the (great great great) grandmother in *The Princess and the Goblin* explains to little Princess Irene, her namesake, that a name is one of those things you can give away and keep at the same time. The same is true of books. It occurs to me now that as Robert Frost wrote in "The Figure a Poem Makes," "the figure is the same as for love." You give it; you pass it on; you also get to keep it.

It may be that Elizabeth's sense for precisely which books to give children only applied when those children were girls. Her father had died when she was two; she had no brothers. Her world, as Beth suggested, was largely one of girls' schools. Beth recalls our mother saying "I don't know what I would have done if you all had been boys." (I'd amend this to "youall," a southernism that better captures her inflection.) Our father, fifteen years my mother's senior, had no appetite for throwing balls or for active sports, and I knew he too was glad Beth and I were girls. David's son Edward writes: "[Elizabeth] did not really know what to do with boys—my father suggested that, and it made sense."

But whether she knew what to do with boys or not, it was to Elizabeth that Edward turned at a difficult juncture of his boyhood:

> When my parents split up, I wrote a long letter to her. I don't remember at all what I said, but I remember I put my heart into it, whatever was in my little boy, would-be man heart. I somehow thought she was the most upright and unconfused person in the world, and that was somehow a comfort. She had that effect on me for as long as I was in contact with her. In retrospect, that judgment seems vastly exaggerated. She was as baffled by the problems of life as anyone, I suspect. But she wasn't like anyone in my life then. She wasn't Jewish, she wasn't tormented, she wasn't crude or excited. She wrote me back something polite and calm. I remember being a little comforted and a little hurt that she didn't seem to understand what I was saying (whatever it was). But calm was something she did very well.

Eddie's sister Debbie writes: "Lizzie was my grandmother who somehow seemed to understand me when no one else did. Her kindness to me in my teens and twenties cushioned me through those difficult years."

Edward and Debbie were Elizabeth's step-grandchildren. And now that I too am a step-grandmother, I realize that the latest child who can be thought of as my mother's heir is my step-granddaughter. This little girl, born in January 2017, is named Camilla. I suggested the name; we knew that the child would be a girl and that the name had to begin with C, since her mother's name does—a custom of the country in her father's native Guyana. The suggestion met with approval. Camilla, now four months old, has been repaying me ever since I suggested her name. She has sent me back to the *Aeneid*, where there's a warrior maiden named Camilla; and ever since, I've been reaping the rewards of close attention (I've been on sabbatical and have had the time) to this timeless poem, whose darker reaches I hadn't properly plumbed.

To date, I've written twenty-seven poems that all refer to lines from the *Aeneid*. I'm going to call the resulting little book *Poems for Camilla*. Catullus writes *cui dono lepidum novum libellum*—"To whom shall I give this pretty little booklet?" To Camilla, that's who. Our time together may be brief; she may not remember much about me; but she'll be able to read the poems. I wish my mother could read them too. But part of growing into a writer is coming to terms with the fact that you're no longer writing for your parents. I wish my father and mother could read the verse translations of Euripides' Iphigenia plays I recently completed. But although I may have undertaken these translations in my father's shadow, in his tradition, through him, or my Camilla poems in the tradition, in the lineage, of my Latin teacher mother, through my mother, through isn't the same thing as for.

Mother, grandmother, stepmother. The latter term comes with cultural baggage attached. At my mother's memorial service in 1992, David, my half-brother and my mother's stepson, recalled that when he first met my mother, he was prepared to dislike her because he knew she had made his own mother unhappy. But it proved impossible for him to dislike his father's second wife: "As a wicked stepmother, Lizzie was a miserable flop."

Elizabeth excelled at giving books or answering questions, but she rarely volunteered opinions or information unless she was asked. Edward recalls Elizabeth correcting his sister Debbie "about some phrase which D. had used wrongly—Lizzie looked very frustrated—that surprised me. She usually had great equanimity." But what was the wrongly used phrase? For that matter, when Cindy Quimby recalls my mother's sound, informed, and logical answers, what were the questions (is this a game of Jeopardy?)? What were those conversations in the crowded Vermont kitchen about? What did those letters in what Debbie accurately calls Elizabeth's "beautiful neat handwriting" say? Gone with the snows of yesteryear.

Still, a couple of answers my mother gave me do remain etched in my memory. In both cases, I'd overheard her talking on the phone and badgered her with questions afterwards. The easier question (though still not all that easy) came when I'd heard her make some excuse for not being able to attend a social event with my father. I didn't know that they had other plans for that evening, and as soon as she got off the phone, I asked her about this. A thoughtful pause; and then my mother told me the truth: "Honey, it was a social lie." My much harder question, after I'd heard my mother talking, perhaps in hushed tones, to her brother-in-law, my Uncle Clinker, was "Mommy, what happened to Aunt Mary?" Again that pause; again the truth. "She hanged herself," answered my mother. I might have been twelve years old. What stands out here: the honesty; the clarity; the lapidary concision.

My mother never said much about her feelings for her troubled older sister Mary—or she didn't say much to me. And when her beloved husband died, she didn't say much about her grief. Edward remembers "seeing her cry discreetly once shortly after Moses died." And he tries to imagine his way back to a much younger Elizabeth, when she and Moses (who had been her Latin prose composition teacher at Columbia Summer School in 1942) were first together: "I often think now what she must have been like with Moses when she was young and he was married [to his first wife]—not all that reserved, I presume."

Unreserved: among Cindy Quimby's memories of Elizabeth is an unexpected and intimate, almost dreamlike vignette from about 1963. Only three years before my father's death, my mother retains some of her youthful glow: "I can still picture her with long braids wrapped around her head. I once saw her and your father in bed at your apartment on Riverside Drive. They were reading the newspaper and drinking coffee, and she looked radiant—it was the only time I saw her with long hair flowing freely. The two of them presented such a beautiful domestic image."

I can remember playing paper dolls with Beth on the floor of our shared room on Sunday mornings while our parents slept in. But coffee in bed? Did she make the coffee and then take it to Moses in bed and climb back in? Hard to imagine, but that's how it must have happened. As often happens with memories from our childhood, my sister may recall this scene more clearly than I do. I'll have to ask her. On the other hand, it may be something Cindy witnessed and never forgot, which Beth and I, absorbed in our paper dolls or later our homework, simply never noticed.

Elizabeth lived for twenty-six years after Moses died: teaching Latin, summering in Vermont, a kind and hospitable hostess to Eddie when he was a student at Columbia, always welcoming Debbie on visits, in touch with both their father and his new wife and with their mother; and finally, a devoted grandmother to Jonathan for the eight brief years she and he coincided. I like to think her stoical equanimity was a constant resource over what must often have been lonely years. She and I spent lots of time together during these years; my family and I lived only a mile or so south of 460 Riverside Drive. But my most poignant memories of her are earlier ones—not only from my childhood, but from the time of my father's death. Not surprisingly, one of these memories is connected to a text. Soon after my father died, my mother sent me a passage, in both Latin and English, from Tacitus's *Agricola*, a tribute to the historian's father-in-law. I am struck, rereading Tacitus's wise and consoling words all these years later, by several things. First, that my mother was in need of consolation herself; she offered me something that had helped her, but she didn't advertise her own emotions at all. Second, that it is probably pretty unusual for a mother to send her seventeen-year-old daughter a passage from a Roman historian. And third, that this passage is now at least as applicable to my mother as it was to my father. She was a role model I'm happy to try to emulate. As I near the age of seventy, and now that I'm a grandmother (or step-grandmother), I have much more in common with Elizabeth in her later years than did the anguished adolescent to whom she sent these words.

In Latin and then in English, with a few adjustments for gender, here is the passage.

Si quis piorum manibus locus, si, ut sapientibus placet, non cum corpore extinguuntur magnae animae, placide quiescas, nosque domum tuum ab infirmo desiderio et muliebribus lamentis ad contemplationem virtutem tuarum voces, quas neque lugeri neque plangi fas est. Admiratione te potius et immortalibus laudibus et, si natura suppeditet, similitudine colamus: is verus honos, ea coniunctissime cuiusque pietas. Id filiae quoque uxori praeceperim, sic patris, sic mariti memoriam venerari, ut omnia facta dictaque eius secum revolvant, formamque ac figuram animi magis quam corporis complectancur; non quia intercedendum putem imaginibus quae marmore aut aere finguntur, sed, ut vultus hominum, ita simulacra vultus imbecilla ac mortalia sunt, forma mentis aeterna, quam tenere et exprimere non per alienam materiem et artem, sed tuis ipse moribus possis.

—Agricola 46

If there is any mansion for the spirits of the just, if, as the wise aver, great souls do not perish with the body, quiet, O Mother, be your rest! May you call us, your household, from feeble regrets and unmanly mourning to contemplate your virtues, in presence of which sorrow and lamentation become a sin. May we honor you in better ways—by our admiration, by our undying praise, even, if our powers permit, by following your example. That is the true honor, the true affection of souls knit close to yours. To your daughter . . . I would suggest that she revere the memory of a mother by continually pondering her deeds and sayings, and by cherishing her spiritual, above her physical, presence . . . The image of the human face, like that face itself, is feeble and perishable, whereas the essence of the soul is eternal, never to be caught and expressed by the material and skill of a stranger, but only by you in your own living.

When I began to feel I was coming into my own as a poet, I sometimes had the sense that the profound familiarity with and love of literature my mother instilled in me was analogous to some superior ingredients which I, a chef, had been provided with, and which I then somehow processed into poetry. This notion of the raw and the cooked now seems condescending and presumptuous to me. The essential qualities of my mother's soul—her patience and discretion, her generosity and, yes, her sagacity—weren't raw ingredients. Rather they are traits I'm fortunate to have inherited, to the very incomplete degree that I have indeed inherited any of them (the patience not so much). I didn't cook them—I, or nature, recombined them somewhat differently. (Isn't that what DNA does?)

I like Tacitus's reminder that images of the physical presence, like that presence itself, are "feeble and perishable." In a poem written not long after my mother's death, here is how I expressed this idea of the tangible versus the imperishable parts of what we inherit:

As for my mother's legacy,
it can't be told as quantity,
piled up or counted or assessed.
If right this moment I should divest
myself of all that can be seen
in what she left me, there'd remain
hours upon hours of gentleness:
her reading voice's calm caress,
the realm of books she opened to
my young attention as I grew
and let me roam in, safe and free,
with a whole world for company
of voices I can always hear
whenever no one else is near

or when I'm reading to my son
and so can hand affection on
in the same shape as what I took
so happily from her: a book.

    (from "The Double Legacy," in
    The Empty Bed, Wesleyan University Press, 1995)

HUMBLE HERB IS RIVAL TO PROZAC

AN ITEM in *Science Tuesday* caught my eye. A woman in Germany—and it seems that she is only one of many—who has been drinking several cups a day of the flower/herb St. John's Wort dried and brewed into tea reports that "The fear that everything good would disappear has stopped."

Pause. Parse. Taste each piece of this, phrase by phrase: The fear. That everything good. Would disappear. Has stopped. The fear has stopped.

I lift my eyes from the page and see something shiny and peeling. It's elderly Scotch tape, no longer translucent, no longer strong enough to keep the little sprigs in place, to hold them flat on the page, to maintain the shape of wild flowers picked and pressed under something heavy, say between the pages of a big book. Not pressed quite long enough to be really flat, as flat as the maple leaf I found when I paged through an old Bible we'd bought at an auction somewhere. Even at five years old I probably found that time was moving too slowly—"Those flowers must be all pressed flat by now!" Maybe I scooped the pressed flower out before it was wholly flattened. But it's hard to flatten out a flower.

Pressed, anyway, and dried, and then taped into the pages of a small-ish spiral notebook, which bulges with its cargo of flower after flower.

Open the notebook. Turn the freighted page. Here they are: butter-cup; daisy; clover; yarrow, brown with age or else (or simultaneously?) almost pellucid. Either way, they're fragile. Time has not only thoroughly discolored the pages of this makeshift album; it has begun the task of disassembling. Delicate petals have lost their tint; they're amber-veined and clear. Tough little stalks now show their pith. The tiny, no longer yolk-gold tubelets that combine to form the eye of the daisy, have begun to come apart. And as they've separated from one another, one by one they have escaped the sagging tape, which can no longer confine them, and now meander down the page unanchored, like stray eyelashes, like fluffs of lint.

Black-eyed Susan; Queen Anne's lace—found, picked, pressed, taped, and labeled. Aster; devil's paintbrush; everlasting; St. John's Wort.

Even then I knew, or think I knew, that this last-named flower was rarer than the others. Knew it how? How did I know anything? Because my mother showed me the reliably fivepetalled, pale gold blossom. I had to be taught every flower's name. Or did I think that Solomon's seal, vetch, mullein, and morning glory were my birthright? All the names of flowers came to me through her, who guided my unsteadily printing pencil in the summer of 1953. Her death in 1992 didn't make me fear that everything good would disappear. It teaches me, if anything, a lesson I must relearn each year—a lesson of renewable epiphany, of the cycle of loss, recovery, loss, recovery. The loss is inevitable. And the recovery? Its provenance isn't always so predictable.

The little notebook, its pages an eye-ease greenish tint, with my staggering penciled captions labeling every blessed thing, each flower picked and pressed and taped down to the page, contains more than specimens of wildflowers from a Vermont meadow. It encloses the first summer I remember. My mother's full skirts, longish, well below the knee—their cotton prints, the florals and batiks I can still see clearly; me clinging at knee level, or her bending over to pick a flower, or leading me across the dirt road to the cow field, where clover and thyme attracted hordes of noisy bees. Her showing me where this and that flower grew, teaching me their names and how to spell them, enlisting me in the whole enterprise of naming and writing.

To press a summer flat between the pages of a heavy book: what storage! What retrieval! What an arc from something tiny as a daisy's eye to something too vast and nebulous to name, let alone hold onto or write down—call it the trail from recollection to invention, blazed and reblazed out of invention's mother necessity, since memory can take us only so far before it lets us down.

That bulgy little spiral notebook vanished years ago. I no longer care whether or not I find it. Probably it's gathering (even as it turns into) dust somewhere. No matter. The laws of leaf and stem and petal hold. What seems sheer desiccation unlocks its stored power into this brew, this brimming mug whose steam (yes, Proust knew this) wreathes the lonely air: *Courage. Nothing good will disappear.*

CLASSICS

And then the massive volume of the world
Opens again.

—James Merrill

I.

Mʏ ᴇᴀʀʟʏ ᴍᴇᴍᴏʀɪᴇs of Riverside Drive, Riverside Park, and the Columbia campus are monumental rather than cozy. On campus, pigeons clustered around the huge stone urns—my father called them sugar bowls—that adorned the Low Library plaza and the stairway outside Dodge Hall. Did pigeons really build nests inside these vast opaque vessels? Or (since they were too tall for me to peer into) were the vases mere giant ashtrays, deep in cigarette butts? It was a mystery. We had some fairly monumental ashtrays at home, imposing, seldom (but not never) used: of cut crystal, clear or green or black or bubbled glass, mostly gifts from people my father had married. As an ordained rabbi, he was licensed to perform the marriage ceremony; as a Jew married to a non-Jew, he presumably sympathized with, and was in demand by, people seeking to secure a similar union. *"By the authority vested in me by God and the state of New York,"* he would intone, *"I now pronounce you husband and wife."* I was present, I think, at only one of these ceremonies. I used to hope that he would one day marry me.

The pigeons and I weren't the only creatures on Morningside Heights to make ourselves a habitat inside a monument. There was also Alma Mater's celebrated owlet, all but hidden in the folds of her bronze robe, peering discreetly out for those who knew where to look. When, years later, my son learned of the existence of this owl, he assumed it was a live bird, cleverly concealed, nesting in Alma Mater's skirts.

A more recent local bird would be the falcon I heard about one snowy morning a few years ago. Jeffrey, a frantic neighborhood character I have known for about as long as I can remember (as happens when you live in one place long enough), accosted me the day after a blizzard to tell me about a predator he had found roosting on his windowsill. Wingspread like *this*, talons like *that*—but then, he qualified soberly, "the falcon was my mother." That was the winter the entire neighborhood, according to Richard Howard, was "in the grip of falcon attention." Richard's students, according to him, had recently gathered in Hamilton Quad to watch a hawk—maybe it was the same one Jeffrey had seen—dismember and devour a squirrel.

Pigeons and stone sugar bowls; the fostering mother with the owl tucked into the bronze folds of her robe; the brooding nude Thinker outside Philosophy Hall (seated, as Auden writes, "in the posture / Of a man at stool"); the quads; the big fountains—these artifacts and monuments and fauna constituted the combined public and private landscapes of my childhood. Because I still live in much the same neighborhood I grew up in, in one sense I have never had to rediscover these primary elements of my experience. Safe from the wrecker's ball, they never budged, even if other things did. Buildings were demolished, others were built, people grew up, moved away, came back, aged, died. Live long enough and New York, like any place but maybe more than any place, becomes a perpetual dance of losses and recognitions, reunions and recoveries.

Imagining what it would be like to revisit a scene from his childhood, George Orwell writes in his essay "Such, Such Were the Joys" that his reaction would be *How much smaller everything has grown, and how great is the deterioration in myself.* Around the time my mother's fatal illness was diagnosed, I had a dream in which the pots and pans in our kitchen at 460 Riverside Drive were the size of dolls' dishes. Going back to my college years two decades earlier, I found (and have since lost again) a poem in which the pedestrians on the Drive have shrunk. Only last year, not in the old neighborhood but in midtown, in fact across the street from the purportedly monumental St. Patrick's Cathedral, I was taken aback by what seemed the sudden narrowness of the sidewalk; there was barely room for the crush of walkers. And yet, on a rainy afternoon two days after the turn of the millennium, there didn't seem to be that many people on the street, despite some leftover holiday tourists milling around. The problem was that the street had contracted.

More important than this shrinkage is what seems to me now the sheer strangeness of the past. Even if nothing else has moved, time has passed, and people have changed. Although the Upper West Side is not exactly a small town, I've often had the uncomfortable feeling that Nabokov has someone like me in mind—someone who lived much of her life in the same neighborhood—when he writes with elegiac disdain, in *Speak, Memory*, about the kind of continuity his own life signally lacked:

> I wonder . . . whether there is really much to be said for more anaes-thetic destinies, for, let us say, a smooth, safe, small-town continuity of time, with its primitive absence of perspective, when, at fifty, one is still dwelling in the clapboard house of one's childhood, so that every time one cleans the attic one comes across the same pile of old brown schoolbooks, still together among later accumulations of dead objects.

Possibly, though this is not what Nabokov means, even a metropolis turns provincial if one stays put long enough. But I protest against the charge that my destiny has somehow been "anaesthetic." As the years go by, we are all exiled from our own pasts, whether or not we move a mus-cle. The writer Lydia Davis, my contemporary and also once a Columbia faculty brat, evokes with sympathy and precision what it is we keep and lose as we age. The crucial distinction isn't between displaced aristocrats and small-town bores but between present and past, the living and the dead. Davis observes:

> It is sure that the dead . . . live in memory, in the recesses of the mind. But seem to be outside the mind. Just as a childhood landscape remem-bered seems to be outside, as it was really outside at the rime. That landscape was outside me at the time, but is inside me now. No one sees it but I.

II.

Ground floor apartments have an aura all their own, and it has been my lot to know them well. My first husband Stavros and I shared a tiny flat on Kleomenous Street, high on the slopes of Mt. Lykabettos in Athens, an interior space whose only natural light came from a courtyard and whose bluepainted walls made the place seem even gloomier. The first year I knew my second husband, he was living in a ground floor apart-ment at 21 Claremont Avenue, the building where countless Columbia faculty children including my sister and me had gone to nursery school (George's apartment was in the rear of the ground floor and looked out over a courtyard; the nursery school, in front, had a view of Claremont Avenue). In that group of little children were Missy Roberts and her brothers John and Hugh, Freddy and Catherine Stern, Beth and I . . . and Jim Trilling? I don't think so.

Like Alma Mater's owl, this nursery school hasn't budged in the ensuing decades. The day in late summer 1976 when George's scanty furniture was being moved into his new apartment—indeed, just as his piano was being edged around a tight corner in the lobby of 21 Claremont—back from some excursion came a troop of Tompkins Hall nursery-school tots and their teachers. Ignoring the piano teetering over their heads, the group marched through the lobby of the building and into their school, whose door happened to be right across the hall from the open door of George's apartment. "Make way for ducklings," was his comment. I felt right at home in that building, and no wonder.

Books lined the walls of the dining room of the ground floor apartment at 460 Riverside Drive where I grew up. From this room it was sometimes possible to see across the courtyard the two Trilling cats sitting on the windowsills of their owners' ground floor apartment on Claremont Avenue; the back windows of their apartment faced ours. My family, however, lacked the Trillings' special reason for living on the ground floor. I can't remember a time when I didn't know that Mrs. Trilling was afraid of elevators. My family, I assumed, lived in a ground floor apartment because that was what had been available to them when, after the war, my parents moved to New York from Washington, DC, where my sister had been born.

We used to have a snapshot of Jim Trilling blowing up a balloon in Riverside Park. The photo was black and white, but the balloon itself, I remember, was green. It, Jim's distended mouth, his eyes, his whole head, his plump stomach—all were variations on the same long elliptical shape. The occasion for this photograph was someone's birthday party, perhaps Jim's—he had a July birthday. Born in November 1948, I was a few months younger; Missy Roberts followed me in March 1949. I remember several birthday parties in the park, including at least one in honor of Missy, who was my best friend. At another of her parties, when she and I were about ten years old, the guests were taken to a wonderful Peter Sellers movie, *The Mouse That Roared*, and two weeks later we all came down with measles.

When I was eight or nine, I was invited over to Jim Trilling's house to play. The term *playdate* wasn't current in the fifties, nor do I remember that as children Jim and I were especially chummy. (Years later, in college, we did go out a few times.) When I try to reconstruct it, this childhood occasion, which as far as I can remember took place only once, it now feels more like a gender-reversed enactment of Pip being summoned to Miss Havisham's house to play than anything else I can compare it to. At home I played endless games of paper dolls with my sister—talking, talking, talking all the while. Missy Roberts and I, best friends from the age of three, also played together endlessly, sheltering under an umbrella as an orphaned brother and sister who lived on black raspberry soda, or making a house out of an empty cardboard packing crate, or learning from my big sister Beth how to make cookies, or comparing the virtues of Louisa May Alcott and Lois Lenski, or (a little later) acting out the Pyramus and Thisbe playwithin-a-play from *A Midsummer Night's Dream.*

But how did one play with a boy? Sitting on the floor in Jim's ground floor bedroom, he and I played with his toy soldier collection by lamplight (these ground floor bedrooms, as I had good reason to know, were conspicuously dark). Later we were summoned to the kitchen for refreshments: we drank 7-Up, which I'd never had at home and didn't much like, and ate delicious ladyfingers. Or perhaps Mrs. Trilling had brought in the food on a tray and we then returned our empty plates and glasses to the kitchen. It must be my memory of this occasion that provides the only image I can still grasp of the Trillings' kitchen, where Mrs. Trilling was beating eggs and sugar in a bowl. I admired the colors. "Yes," she answered gravely, "yellow and white are my favorite color combination."

Did we ever invite Jim over, just around the corner from Claremont to Riverside? Not that I can remember. Was I reluctant, or was it my mother who was? Don't know. I imagine that my father and Lionel Trilling regularly tipped their hats to one another when they met on the street, but I don't know whether they often, or ever, conversed. To the mild buzz surrounding Jim Trilling's recent memoir in *The American Scholar,* in which he tentatively diagnoses his father as having suffered from Attention Deficit Disorder, I have nothing of substance to add. I remember Lionel as dignified and distant, but then such behavior would have been what I expected of most fathers—not that I knew very many. My friend Justine, who lived in Washington Heights with her mother and grandmother, had no visible father; Corinna Gaster's father was tall and fat and foreign and pompous. Freddy Stern's father, and to a greater extent, Missy

Roberts's, seemed to me delightful. I'm sure I understood at a young age that very few fathers could be expected to be as enchanting as Henry Roberts, who rubbed balloons against the dog's coat to generate static electricity so that they would stick to walls; who, in the country, made fascinating plaster casts of animal tracks (I remember a beautiful fox track over the mantelpiece), and who had sculpted an animal by adding legs to a twisted piece of metal he had found and captioned the resulting quadruped "Alert or Grazing" (depending on which end of the thing one faced). My own father appeared to me busy and tired—Missy recalls he was the only grownup she knew at the time either to have a beard or to take naps, and both of these characteristics filled her with awe—but not distant, not exactly. I never doubted he was loving.

Of the wide range of responses to Jim's article which appeared in subsequent issues of the *Scholar*, the one that struck me most was one apparently sympathetic comment, from whom I can't now recall, to the effect that Jim didn't get much affection and he doesn't return much. This assessment is surely an oversimplification, but I find myself taken by its uncondemning tone. Also, it reminds me of those early ground floor years and of how much affection I myself took for granted—affection, above all else, from my mother.

These are murky waters, though. It sometimes irked me that, during my mother's many years of widowhood, living in our book-filled apartment and, as my sister has written, one of the most bookish people either of us ever knew, she never wrote a book—about herself, her husband, her children, some scholarly topic, anything. But in fact my mother did write reviews and essays about children's literature in connection with her work for an organization called, I believe, the Child Study Association. In addition, she edited a book of Renaissance paintings of episodes in the life of Christ, paintings carefully chosen to illustrate relevant Biblical texts. Alas, I cannot now lay my hand on her *The Life of Christ*, although I still vividly recall it: a small paperback with a shiny black cover and Christ's mournful thorn-crowned head (after a Durer drawing?) in gold. And in 1964 her translation into Latin of the children's classic *The Story of Ferdinand* was published, with its dedication *Meo marito, sine quo fieri non potuisset.*

Wrapped by then in the cocoon that envelops most adolescents, perhaps I was embarrassed by *Ferdinandus* or assumed that as real books went, somehow a translation did not count. Children are merciless. If in her later years my mother disappointed me by failing to be a formidable literary figure and cultural spokesperson like Diana Trilling, when I was younger I used to wish that she were as tender, funny, and utterly accepting as Missy Roberts's wonderful mother, Debbie. At that young age, I did, however, have the sense not to want a mother like Diana—a memory brought back to life for me by Jim's memoir, which has as much to say about his mother as it does about his father.

Of course, it is only because Diana Trilling was a writer that I can now turn back to her retrospective account of her marriage, *The Beginning of the Journey*, published in 1993. The section on parenthood is fairly brief. I've never forgotten the remarkable phrase used in connection with Jim's conception: "I became pregnant that evening"; and I am still touched by the evocation later on of the experience she and her husband shared as the parents of an infant:

> Often Lionel and I spoke of how strange it was that none of our friends who had had children had told us of the extraordinary joy of being parents. No one had told us of the incomparable beauty of an infant waking in the night, flushed with sleep, or of the wrench of aching love with which one saw one's child reach out his trusting hand for help. No one spoke even of the wonder of a child's growth: the first step, the first word, the first assertion of an independent self, a self on its own in the world. These friends of ours had of course supposed that we would never have children. They were sparing us the knowledge of what we missed.

It would be easy—much too easy—to juxtapose this lyrical reminiscence with some of Jim's more painful childhood memories as expressed in *his* memoir, but to do so would be misleading and beside the point. I believe in the sincerity of the emotion expressed in the mother's passage; like most mothers, I imagine, I myself share it. I also believe Diana Trilling's claim that Lionel was a devoted father, heading out to the sandbox with Jim on Saturday mornings or staying up nights by the sleepless boy's bedside. At the same time, I have no trouble believing in the sincerity of Jim's memories of his childhood rages, fears, frustrations, and the sense that his parents were at a loss to know how best to cope with these.

All three Trillings were, or were to become, writers; how should their subjectivities not clash? Perhaps, it now occurs to me, my mother's profound discretion spared me this kind of confusion, these rival claims. Rival claims not only to the personal truth of an experience but also to a loved one's concentrated attention, indeed to that loved one's unbroken physical presence. As soon as Jim Trilling's memoir sent me back to Diana's book, I was reminded of another memoir by another child of writers—Reeve Lindbergh's beautiful *Under a Wing*, which appeared in 1998. In this book, Reeve—my country friend and neighbor for many years—sets down, as writing makes it possible for us to do, much that she doesn't usually talk about, including her response to the death of her two-year-old son. But the part of *Under a Wing* I was drawn back to when I began thinking about writers both as parents and children was Reeve's pondering in middle age what her mother's being a writer had meant to her as a child:

> I don't know at what age I learned that my mother was a writer, beloved by millions of readers around the world. I think I was very young, certainly too young to read or write myself. It wasn't until many years later that I became reconciled to her profession, and it was later still when, to my surprise, I made this same profession my own. In the beginning, though, her literary work was only an inexplicable interruption in the mother-child relationship—a sad cross for a sensitive child to bear.
>
> What I disliked most about her writing was that it separated her from me physically, by means of a closed door. When she was in her "writing room" in the house in Connecticut, we children were forbidden by our father to disturb her. I often did this anyway, if I thought I could get away with it, usually at a time when my father was outside chopping wood, or was himself engrossed in his own writing project in his own office, downstairs. Nobody would think of disturbing *him* when the door was closed and he was tapping away with two fingers on his old Royal typewriter, working on *The Spirit of St. Louis*.
>
> I had no interest in my father's flying or his writing career, but I thought that surely my mother did not *really* want to be shut away for a whole afternoon with a pen and a pad of paper, without seeing my face, hearing my thoughts, inspecting my bruises, or in some other way affirming for both of us the extraordinary importance of my presence in her life.
>
> I knew this was true because if I knocked on my mother's door, she always answered, and if I entered the room, she never seemed to mind. She would put down her pen immediately, and smile gently, and ask what I wanted. (See? She *was* concerned about my needs, above all else, I thought triumphantly. What did my father know? *Nothing.*)

. . . My father, however, was an uncannily perceptive man. No matter how far away I had thought he was, he would inevitably show up at my mother's writing room door at just about this time, looking extremely displeased. He would take me away from my mother's pleasant nest. . . . He would shut the door behind us, and he would lecture me once again about my mother's creative gifts, about her need for privacy in order to exercise such gifts to their fullest extent, and about my obligation to respect this aspect of her life. Each time I heard his lecture I nodded, and apologized, and told him I understood what he was saying and would try to do better in the future.

I didn't mean a word of it. How could I?

A wonderfully honest account of a child's need, greed, quenchless thirst and hunger for a mother's physical presence, particularly if that mother is at work in the same house as the child, is what one reads between the lines of Diana Trilling's brief description of her experience as a mother who wrote, a writer who worked at (or close to) home:

> For a short period when Jim was little I felt that I needed more quiet than he permitted me and I rented a room in the apartment adjacent to ours and tried to work there. He was only two, and I supposed that he would not know where I went when I shut the door behind me. But he soon figured out that we were divided only by a wall. He beat a tattoo on the wall until I came home. I gave up the rented room and in one way or another, largely by improving my concentration, I learned to work at my living-room desk, whatever might be going on around me.

As the child of a mother who was not, or who seemed not to be, a writer, I myself was spared such scenes. But this absence of conflict was also owing partly to the fact that—as I recently had occasion to remember when I wrote my half of the Afterword that my sister Beth and I contributed to the reissued *Ferdinandus Taurus*—my mother never made heavy weather of any task. Translating into Latin, correcting endless grammar homework assignments for her Spence students, writing equally endless letters of recommendation for their college applications, she always seemed to have attention to spare.

I first read Jim Trilling's memoir in Vermont, in late June, during a prolonged dry spell, sitting in a ragged deck chair on the parched lawn of our summer house. After I'd finished reading, I poured what was left of my tepid coffee onto the yellowing grass at my feet. For a little while the liquid simply lay there in a small convex puddle before seeming to gather its forces and sink into the baked earth. The ground was far too dry to be immediately absorbent; earth, like a sponge, needs to be moist before it can soak up what it needs.

A mind is like that, too. Books and attention, books as attention, conversation, books as conversation—endless attention and attentiveness are required. I and the children I knew growing up, children whose parents were readers and writers, were not always ecstatically happy by any means, but it seems to me that we were sufficiently moistened to soak up as much as we could, swelling to make room for each successive drop. "Take you me for a sponge, my lord?" Rosencrantz or Guildenstern asks Hamlet in a wounded tone, and Hamlet scornfully assents. Missy and Jim and Lydia—and Reeve, too, though I didn't get to know her until we were both grown up—we all soaked up as much as we could hold. Later, as parents, as writers, we would ourselves be wrung out to moisten the soil each succeeding generation needs for growth.

III.

Books do furnish a room. And in the world I lived in as a child, rooms were built for books; whole buildings, indeed, were built for books. Facing Alma Mater across the quad was Butler Library, across whose facade marched a stone frieze of ancient writers' names. Homer, Herodotus, Sophocles, Plato—each name in this sequence (I think I used to find this mildly mystifying) represents both the person and the oeuvre. Notoriously, many names are missing, among them that of Euripides, who in his play *Helen* explores the confusion generated by the relation between a name and a person's identity. Half a dozen years ago, I translated this romance (it is not a tragedy), often working on Saturday mornings in the waiting room of the National Academy of Design building just off Fifth Avenue and Eighty-Ninth Street, while my son took a drawing class upstairs. Throughout the play, Helen keeps trying to explain to anyone who will listen that a name is not necessarily a self. *The name is not the creature, not the thing! Only my name ever went to Troy!* The doubleness associated with Homer, Herodotus, Thucydides, or Demosthenes was quite a different matter. Public personages whose names I seemed always to have known simply from seeing them up on Butler Library, they were also characters I lived among: our household words.

Inside Butler Library one was greeted by a mural. Clad in some sort of diaphanous evening gown, a glamorous Athena raised an aegis (whose shiny scales were made of some real metal) in a gesture at once proud and defensive, warding off the naked, bald, grimacing green men, human in shape but clearly demons, who writhed and leered angrily on either side of her. These figures represented spirits of hatred, ignorance, prejudice, violence, fear . . . Whether I grasped their significance straight from the allegory visible before me or from the accompanying little legend that explained it, the meaning was crystal clear. Past the mural, on the landing as one climbed the stairs to the Reading Room, one saw President Eisenhower (in his academic regalia as president of Columbia) on the righthand landing and President Nicholas Murray Butler on the left. Both these paintings, though massive, were disappointing in their lack of myth and mystery—no livid, twisting limbs, no flashing aegis, no pale, fierce face of the goddess, only elderly flesh and academic gowns. Perhaps Nabokov would sneer that my memories of Butler Library are a classic instance of a life spent tamely in one spot, in which case these paintings and that mural would presumably constitute "the same pile of old brown schoolbooks." In the light of my own experience, I persist in thinking that the same old books tell us different things each time we open them.

When did I learn the Greek alphabet? I used to be nonplussed by people's assumption that I had been born knowing Ancient Greek—that my father, like Montaigne's, had raised his children to speak ancient tongues. Alas, acquired characteristics have to be acquired all over again in each generation. Greek was never either my mother or father tongue. In fact, I came late to Ancient Greek and never knew the language at all well. My Latin, which was once firmer than my Greek, is now so rusty I can barely help my son Jonathan with his homework, particularly if it's prose (whether in Greek or Latin, I always did better with poetry).

Before I could *read* a word of Greek, I think I *saw* the language; the letters of the alphabet were something I could learn by copying. (When I was in kindergarten, a teacher corrected me: "Remember, Rachel, you're supposed to be writing, not drawing.") I'm a bit reminded now, thinking about a system that fascinated me before I came to understand it, of the tantalizing diagrams of the female anatomy, cross-sectioned and clearly labeled, that some years later in my growing up came in every box of my sister's Tampax. I studied the names and locations and made sure I could find the equivalent openings in my own body so as to be ready when my turn arrived, all the while wondering, in my competitive littlesisterly way, if it ever would.

When I began to read, what I read was certainly not Homer, Herodotus, and the rest of the crew from the monumental Butler Library frieze; it wasn't Greek at all. What did I read? Early on, George MacDonald's *The Princess and the Goblin,* and a bit later Frances Hodgson Burnett's *A Little Princess*—both of these books over and over again. A little later still, I took out from the library of Hunter College Elementary School an elegant small book, also by Burnett, about a family of dolls, entitled *The Racketty-Packetty House.* When I wanted to renew the book for the third or fourth time, the librarian gently advised me to read more books that were more—"realistic" may not have been the word she used, but I understood (and resisted) the implication of her advice. This was long before the phenomenon (now familiar from the Harry Potter books) of adults applauding a child who is intent on reading anything, including fantasy.

Around the time I was becoming an avid reader, my mother, who didn't return to teaching high school Latin until I was in seventh grade and thus out of the house all day, was active in the Child Study Association. My understanding was that either the association as a whole, or the committee my mother was on, specialized in children's books, and it may have been in this capacity that she sometimes queried my sister and me about our reading preferences. (At the time, I probably just assumed this interest was, in Reeve Lindbergh's words, an affirmation "for both of us of the extraordinary importance of my presence in her life.") Whatever their provenance, such questions from our mother seemed to me peculiar, even disingenuous; surely our taste in books derived from hers?

Once, for example, when she and I were crossing Broadway at 116th Street, heading west, so that the gates of College Walk were behind us (lofty, elaborately wrought iron gates, flanked by two tall stone figures, one male, one female, gazing ahead with unseeing eyes)—she turned and asked me why it was that I liked fairy tales so much. I was flattered to be asked and I wanted to help her, but the answer I came up with struck me even then as lame, unconvincing if not actually inaccurate. "Because," I said, "all fairy tales are so much alike." My thought at the time may have been that if I liked one fairy tale and they were all alike, it followed that I liked them all. But what I think of now is the commanding first line of Robert Graves's poem "For Juan at the Winter Solstice": *There is one story and one story only.*

Was it that single central story that appealed to me, or the repetition and similarity among its offshoots? Certainly I was partial to the familiar, the predictable; I shared the predilection of hobbits for large books filled with facts (or fiction) already known to everyone. Even new furniture jarred me. When my parents invested in new dining room chairs, my furious rejoinder, "We didn't buy this house to make changes!" became a family joke. Books stay blessedly put; they echo one another, they grow with us, but they don't disappear. (Maybe Nabokov's right after all—I do keep pawing through the same old stuff in the attic.) Perhaps I should have told my mother that one story was all I could handle. The names might change; that didn't matter. As the omniscient and omnipotent grandmother in my beloved *The Princess and the Goblin* says, a name is something you can give away and keep at the same time. So is a story.

Before Greek myths, then, I encountered fairy tales. But Greek literature, when I got there, did something for me that fairy tales couldn't. Even through—no, especially through—translation, Greek literature shaped my idea of lyric poetry in a very specific way, and I believe that this is why:

In translating some of the plays of Euripides in the 1930s, my father and his collaborator, John McLean, had opted for plain if dignified prose for the dialogue portions. To render the choruses, theirs was a clever solution: "The lyric portions are in a different mood and a different idiom," they write in the Preface to their 1936 *The Plays of Euripides*. "We have tried to make the distinction easy for the reader by the device of employing italic type for lyric passages." For at least one young reader, the distinction was not so much easy as it was magical. The typeface was a shortcut, a signal—a coded path to a wholly different texture and mood, a mode at once quicksilvery and somber, conveying a kind of embedded intensity words alone in regular typeface seemed to be incapable of getting across. And henceforth that, for me, would always be what *lyric* meant: crystalline, knotted, flowery, or obscure, but always special, always other, always intense. These were not necessarily qualities that could be heard. The italics signaled them so that you could see them; but the essence of lyric resided also in what could not be seen.

It may have been a bad way to convey (and hence for me to learn about) poetry; it was certainly an odd way, this attempting an end run around the recalcitrant medium of words, lazily letting a typeface do the poet's work. All my life, for better or for worse, when reading poetry I have looked for words to burn with the strange fire that flickered through the italics of those choral odes, the weird light proclaiming that however ordinary the diction of the choruses, theirs was no ordinary speech. What difference did it make if I often couldn't quite make out what the choristers were getting at? Their words did not advance the action but expressed feeling. Even as it faithfully stayed on the page, their poetry—prose through the prism of italics—strained to escape the time and place of the drama. The sad women of the Chorus in *Hippolytus* yearn to fly up and away, yet, like all tragic choruses (comedy is something else again), they stay on earth, patiently waiting in the frail, durable shelter between the pages.

Sitting in a dim corner of the living room on a little cherrywood love seat, upholstered in red, that one of my mother's few surviving relatives had sent up from Virginia, I'd open a fat orange volume: *The Plays of Euripides*, translated by Hadas and McLean. Later it was Lattimore's *Oresteia*—a slim aqua paperback in the University of Chicago Greek tragedy series, where the choruses were not in italics. But the pull of the choral poetry was similar in both books, and it was to the choruses that I used to turn, puzzling over the pages in a small pool of lamplight before flipping to the more prosaic, grumpy, faintly realistic give-and-take of stichomythia, the factual logjam of a prologue, the shriek of a climax.

"Don't read in the dark, you'll ruin your eyes," my father used to say. In fact, as I now know very well, children's eyes do fine in semi-darkness, while we grownups need floodlights to read by. What I couldn't understand I could read again and again, intrigued by the very obscurities I was learning by heart. There was no need to move on—not from the little love seat in the corner, nor from a yellowing page of choral lyrics in magic italics. Poetry suspends the stern laws of narrative—laws which, when they're in full force, subject us to another kind of reading altogether, a galloping, slavering, panting, voracious attack on the pages. Poetry is not a page turner. Italics, which look as delicate as lace, weigh as much as memory.

Where, while I was reading there on the love seat, were my mother and father? Probably working in the dining room, which doubled as my father's study. My sister usually did her homework in the little bedroom (originally a maid's room) halfway down the hall. I oscillated between my own room and the less private but brighter and more sociable dining room, which was pretty much filled up by its enormous table. I've said that when I started seventh grade, in 1959, my mother went back to teaching Latin, which had been her job before her marriage. Henceforth in the evenings, sitting at that table, she would correct Latin grammar exercises or compose report cards or college recommendations which required not merely grades but myriad synonyms for *promising, industrious, immature, distracted*. . . . My father, knowing everything, rarely seemed to prepare for class, except by putting the tiny homemade bookmarks he used to cut from matchbook covers into his books to mark passages he needed to note for the next day's lecture. Is there a gene for such cutting up of stiff paper for this purpose? I now use index cards.

He mostly used the dining room table for other, paraacademic tasks, such as grading the Greek College Boards. One year all the boys from a certain Catholic high school who took the Greek Boards translated an essentially untranslatable Homeric particle as *at the same time*, so that poor Lykaon's plea to Achilles in Book 21 of the *Iliad* and Achilles's beautiful, heartless answer lost all their poignancy in a weird spate of simultaneity: "at the same time spreading wide both his hands," for example, or "And Achilles answered him at the same time." I had never read the *Iliad*, but I was allowed to look at these translations, blue book by blue book—versions, suspiciously alike, of an infinitely remote, grand, and authoritative original.

IV.

Since our apartment was on the ground floor, some noise, especially during the warm months, came through our living room windows from the normally peaceful Drive. Sidewalk conversations, traffic sounds— these I don't remember as being very obtrusive; it was more bothersome to know that passersby could look right it into our living room if they so desired. On the other hand, I loved the view across the street to Riverside Park and, beyond it, the Hudson River.

More immediate and much louder noise than street sounds used to blast through our living room wall from the lobby. Earl, the chief doorman, would play the radio, sneeze thunderously, or greet tenants as they went in and out. But as I think of him now, what stands out most vividly is the way he polished our doorknob. Regularly—daily? Weekly? Surely it was more than once a month. Wearing his uniform, white gloves and all, and standing on the top step of the three marble stairs which led up to our front door from the level of the lobby floor, Earl would grasp and rattle the brass knob of our front door, twisting its long neck this way and that as, with a coffee can of smelly brass polish and a rag, he vigorously buffed it. Visitors in our living room must have been nonplussed to see and hear the doorknob twisting jerkily back and forth, apparently of its own accord, on our side of the door. We in turn may have reassured them (surely we should have, but I don't remember our doing it) that the disruption signaled neither a frustrated burglar nor Marley's ghost, but only Earl doing his job.

Whenever anyone, but especially a child, opened that door and went down the three steepish marble steps to the lobby, Earl would warn them, "Don't fall down, now!" Why, I wondered, should anyone fall? There was a small brass railing (which he also polished tirelessly) for the fearful to clutch at. Once one was safely down the three stairs, it was out through the small marble-paneled lobby and through a first set of glass doors to the narrow space where the buzzers were (and a crucial radiator), then a second grander, heavier set of glass doors, these with wrought iron decorations, that led to the granite stoop and the Drive and the icy winds blowing in from the river. If one were entering the building from the Drive, of course, the order of these steps was reversed. The wind blew so hard it was often difficult to pry the doors open, and the hot smell and hiss of the radiator was reassuring.

I am grateful to live now in a third-floor apartment, at a discreet distance from the street. Doormen at this West End Avenue building are paid for by tenants (I'm one of those who does the collecting); these doormen come and go, ununiformed, gloveless, polyglot, defiantly human. Ilya, a grandfather who runs in the marathon and recently became an American citizen, likes to practice his English orthography and often buttonholes passersby to ask them to check his grammar or spelling. Steve has been getting a degree in physical education at LaGuardia Community College for at least twenty years; his mother died only last year. She was never very friendly, or maybe it was just that her English remained sketchy for thirty years after she arrived in New York from her native Hungary. But once she learned that her son and mine had the same birthday, she used to smile beatifically whenever I passed her in the lobby.

Whether through Earl's ministrations or for some other reason, I never did fall down when leaving the apartment at 460 Riverside, though I remember running on College Walk, up on the Columbia Campus, tripping, and falling on the bricks with their handsome herringbone pattern. My father called the resulting lump on my forehead a pigeon's egg—

related perhaps to one of the pigeons that roosted in the stone urns he called sugar bowls. Roller skating down the Drive, or on the broad plaza in front of Grant's Tomb, I don't remember ever falling. My sister fell off her bike in the park once, and her knee healed with a black seam of dirt sealed into the scar, which is still visible if you know where to look. In Nabokov's *Pnin*, the speaker recalls consulting Pnin's eye-doctor father about a speck of dust in his eye, and he finds himself wondering where that speck of dust is now.

When I was growing up, it seemed to me that Columbia-owned buildings such as the one I lived in were full of widows. They probably still are. Otto Luening's widow lives on in 460, and so does Edith Hazen, widow of a university librarian and mother of a son named Allen and nicknamed Cricket with whom I vaguely remember going out (to the theater? a musical? Gilbert and Sullivan?) once or twice; he is now a professor of philosophy in Australia. Diana Trilling, who lived on until her death in the late nineties in her ground floor apartment on Claremont Avenue, fitted the widow pattern, as did my mother, who outlasted her husband in 460 Riverside for more than a quarter of a century. It was May 1992 and our doorman Earl had long been dead when my husband helped my mother down the three stairs from our apartment for the last time.

These days, my walks with my friend Eleanor often take us north through Riverside Park, east at the Interchurch Center and back south via Claremont to Broadway. Sometimes, though, we walk north on the Drive instead, so I get to go right past 460. I remember perfectly the layout of the apartment, from the approach past the hissing radiator in the lobby and the wiggling front doorknob on through the rooms, the books, the furniture, the smells. The building is still there, the apartment is still there, or they seem to be; but where are they really now? As Lydia Davis wrote of one's dead, they seem to be outside but are really inside me. Or in this case they are both outside and inside. I don't know who is living in the apartment now, but on twilit evenings I'm glad to see lights on in the living room. I never mention to Eleanor anymore—I know she knows, and I don't mind if she's forgotten—that this is where I grew up.

As I've noted earlier, my father's co-translator of the Euripides plays was John Harvey McLean, M.A., about whom I know nothing except that he came from Scotland and presumably returned there either before or after the Second World War. Nor do I know the source of my impression that at some time Jock, as my father called him, had given our family a toaster. We seemed to accumulate toasters, none ever fully functional, so I'm not sure which one was the McLean toaster. I like to think it was the most unusual and memorable one in our collection: a small, prim machine with doors on each side instead of a slot on top. You pulled the door open by a little wooden handle, inserted a slice of bread, and slammed the door shut again—or two doors, if you wanted to make two slices of toast. I think this unusual object ended up, or at least spent many years, in the Closet of Many Shelves, the name my family gave years ago to a tiny room, really a walk-in closet, in the house in Vermont. In the Closet of Many Shelves, this toaster would have been one of a crop of disused or dysfunctional toasters nobody had been willing to throw away. How durable is durable? What lasts? The strangest things lodge where, in Robert Frost's phrase about poetry, they can't be gotten rid of.

One evening, sitting in the red love seat, looking through Hadas and McLean's *The Plays of Euripides*, I finally ventured out of the rarefied realm of italics. Not in lyric poetry but in plain prose, Medea coolly addresses the Chorus: "Women of Corinth, do not criticize me." Criticize rang a querulous domestic bell: my father's voice, or my mother's, or my sister's, taking me to task—criticizing me—for being too critical. How clearly I could hear the tone of Medea's voice as she spoke this line, taking the offensive, silencing the opposition. A woman alone, distant, vulnerable, defiant, fearless, she was also, I came later to understand, multiple Medeas, one face of myth peeling back to reveal another in an endless series of versions, performances, translations, interpretations, images. But one has to start somewhere, and I think it was with the fat orange Hadas & McLean *Euripides* that I started.

How best to think about Medea: a lonely wife, an exotic enchantress, a wicked witch, a murderer, a victim? In the summer of 1974 I spent a few days in the Peloponnese. All over Greece men were being called up for a possible war with Turkey over the recent invasion of Cyprus. But in the midst of this national crisis, a local paper had banner headlines about something else, a shocking murder: *VILLAGE MEDEA DROWNS TWO OF HER CHILDREN*, the headline announced. The mother had been working in the fields; the bodies of two of her several small children were found floating in a nearby irrigation tank. Two decades later, in South Carolina, Susan Smith locks her two little boys in her car, gets out, sinks the car in a lake, lies, confesses, goes to prison. No chariot drawn by dragons whisked either of these women off; not for them the insouciance of Medea's lightning-swift, somehow sarcastic flight and escape.

What did Euripides think of Medea? This is no easier a question to answer than the question what Shakespeare thought, or intended us to think, of this or that character. Lionel Trilling died only twenty-five years ago, yet there is no consensus as to whether Jim's memoir paints an accurate portrait of its author's father. How then can there be agreement on the truth of a character who flies altogether free of fact? The crucial thing, it seems to me, is that although Medea escapes at the end of Euripides' tragedy, she isn't gone. Each time the lights go down and the curtain goes up, each time the screen lights up or someone sits in a pool of lamplight and opens a book, it all begins again.

With the living, it isn't quite like that. They are recoverable, but we have to lose them in reality before we can begin to find them again. When I say, as I sometimes do, that only after people die can we get them back in anything resembling clarity or wholeness, I'm often confronted by an uneasy silence; and no wonder. Even though I try to avoid expressing this unsettling idea to friends who are newly bereaved, it remains unsettling. People who hear it often look as uneasy as the guests at 460 Riverside must have when our spectral doorknob twisted around apparently of its own accord. Get them back—what do I mean?

Revenants, ghosts? I hadn't thought of this getting back as ghostly, but of course it is. When Diana Trilling evokes the beauty of an infant, she is summoning the sweet simple spirit of her baby before he turned into the tense and solemn little boy Jim remembers being and I myself remember knowing—the child whose terror of elevators prompted his mother, herself phobic, to write an earnest letter to Erik Erikson requesting the expert's sage counsel. Remembering her sleeping child, recovering the memory through language, she also recreates her own and her husband's awe and joy at having become parents of this miraculous creature. Not that the baby Jim had died, exactly; but babies do disappear when they grow up, and our ways of getting them back are limited.

Sometimes a fearful event will permit, even necessitate, a recurrence, a recovery of some earlier loss. Reeve Lindbergh describes how the death of her son at the age of two allowed her mother to sit with the baby's body, something Mrs. Lindbergh had never been able to do when her own son had been kidnapped decades earlier. More often the past will take us by surprise in some less harsh way. In James Merrill's memoir, *A*

Different Person, there is a wonderful moment in which he describes how the presence of a grown grandson affects a woman friend:

> ... her grandson, once a little boy crowned with water-lilies, now an architect in his thirties, entered the room announcing that he and his girlfriend would after all not stay for supper but try to beat the traffic back to Athens. As she took in his words, love changed Mina before my eyes into a crooning, headwaggling peasant granny: "Eat something first, my child! Take a warm sweater with you!"—not until he was out of sight reverting to the woman I knew.

So I need to reconsider my first formulation: only after people and things disappear, rather than die, is it possible to recover them. Nabokov writes poignantly of his losses:

> Tamara [his first girlfriend], Russia, the wildwood grading into old gardens, ... the sight of my mother getting down on her hands and knees to kiss the earth every time we came back to the country from town for the summer ... these are things that fate one day bundled up pellmell and tossed into the sea, completely severing me from my boyhood.

And yet in what he has written he has recreated all these lost people and places in loving and vivid detail.

So much from my first twelve years comes back to me as I writeback from wherever lost things disappear to. What matters is to trust in the possibility of a return, and one return seems to herald another. Alma Mater's owlet; Earl with his can of polish and his explosive sneezes and his "Don't fall down, now"; the Athena in Butler Library; Missy Roberts and me playing on Doll Rock, in Rangeley, Maine, in the summer of 1953; her deaf brother John yelling "Frog doctor! Frog doctor!" that same summer when he saw a frog that he thought looked unwell; my grandmother reading me "The Pobble Who Has No Toes" in her deep soft voice; my mother's feigned and my grandmother's genuine shock that our cat Butterscotch had gotten onto the table and had been licking the butter off the butter dish; Missy Roberts and me rehearsing our production of "Pyramus and Thisbe" in Missy's bedroom at 464 Riverside; Lydia Davis's father, in their apartment on Morningside Drive, carving a ham at Sunday dinner (some fat splashed onto my tan skirt) while explaining the origin of a proverb; my sister and me playing paper dolls on Sunday mornings while our parents slept late; Medea's bold "Women of Corinth, do not criticize me"; my first encountering a searing book like Miguel del Castillo's *Child of Our Time* or a beautiful book like *Six Poets of Modern Greece*—books which came into the house because my father was reviewing them—reading them avidly after school while eating chicken noodle soup or devil's food cookies or Chef Boyardee canned ravioli. Of all these memories the books are the most durable, the most fully recoverable: my mother and grandmother, Earl, and Robert Gorham Davis, are dead, but only open the book and out strides Medea, public and loud and gleaming, contemptuous of the whips and scorns of time.

Around the time I was in ninth grade, I fell in love with the poems of E. E. Cummings, and even wrote some poems myself that I tried to make float on the page as his did. But one of my favorite poems of Cummings didn't float; it was anchored, though I don't know if I noticed this at the time, by rhyme, and in particular by rhyme and meter: "Jehovah buried, Satan dead / do fearers worship Much and Quick," it began, and the pace and sharpness of the lines made me pay attention: "obey says toc, submit says tic / Eternity's a Five-Year Plan / if Joy and Pain shall hang in hock / who dares to call himself a man?"

In the poem's last line, that refrain was repeated, but this time a Greek word, or a word in Greek letters, appeared there: what did those three letters spell out? I knew. Which is to say both that I could sound out the letters and that I knew what the resulting sound—the sound of a four-letter word in English—meant. Nevertheless, not quite confident of my own ability to transliterate, I took the Cummings poem to my father and stood there while he read it. He and I had already, I think, read some Catullus together, and some Cicero; he had taught me the Greek alphabet; he could sight-read anything. He looked at the word for a long time, then back at me. "I can't read it," he said.

He could, of course. I could, sort of. Now I can.

TALKING TO MY FATHER

How to talk to the dead? The business bristles with obstacles. First of all, there's the difficulty of access: how to approach them or get them to approach you? In the *Odyssey*, the dead to whom Odysseus wishes to speak first have to taste sacrificial blood obtained under conditions strictly spelled out beforehand by Circe. Even Odysseus's mother licks the blood from his sword, an unsettling juxtaposition. Allegorical interpretations cluster around this high price paid for colloquy with shades.

Then there's the impossibility of touching the dead. Odysseus tries to embrace his mother:

> How I longed
> to embrace my mother's spirit, dead as she was!
> Three times I rushed toward her, desperate to hold her,
> three times she fluttered through my fingers, sifting away
> like a shadow, dissolving like a dream, and each time
> the grief cut to the heart, sharper, yes, and I,
> I cried out to her, words winging into the darkness:
> "Mother—why not wait for me?—How I long to hold you!—
> so even here, in the House of Death, we can fling
> our loving arms around each other, take some joy
> in the tears that numb the heart."
>   (*Odyssey* XI 233–45, tr. Robert Fagles)

In the *Aeneid*, Aeneas's father Anchises has been eagerly awaiting the hero in the underworld:

> And when he saw Aeneas making toward him
> Over the grass, he stretched his hands out, blissful.

The tears poured down his cheeks, and he exclaimed,
"You've come at last?—love made you take this hard road,
Just as I thought?—and can I see your face,
My child, hear your beloved voice, and answer?
Really, I counted on this, calculated
The time, and anxious hope did not deceive me . . ."
Aeneas answered, "Father, your sad image,
Which often meets me, called me to this realm. . . .
My hand—
Clasp it and don't retreat from my embrace."
The tears poured down his face. Three times he tried
To throw his arms around his father's neck,
Three times the form slid from his useless hands,
Like weightless wind or dreams that fly away.

    (*Aeneid* VI 685–91; 695–702, tr. Robert Fagles)

In a psychologically realistic paradox, the shades (one thinks of Achilles, Agamemnon, even Dido) who are less closely bound to the living visitor by ties of blood seem to be less elusive, if only because the visitor to the House of Death may not be so eager to embrace them.

A further difficulty is that the dead sometimes seem more comfortable speaking to one another than to the fleshly visitor. In the fourth Canto of the *Inferno*, Dante is allowed to join Homer, Horace, Ovid, Lucan, and Virgil in the circle of virtuous pagans, but we are not allowed to hear the poets' conversation: "So we walked onward, moving toward the light, / and the things that were said among us it is good / not to say here, as to say them there was right" (Michael Palma translation). This is another kind of barrier to access; we get to hear what Francesca or Brunetto Latini say to Dante, but not what his fellow poets have to say. I'm reminded of being a little girl venturing in her nightgown to the top of the stairs in our Vermont house, listening to the grownups talking and laughing downstairs, wanting to join in the fun. But their words were not intended for me to hear. In order to join such conversations, we need to grow up.

Or maybe we need to die. The distinction blurs. Think of the denizens of the cemetery in *Our Town*, talking quietly to each other in the background. Or the grownups, barely audible on the bus, in Elizabeth Bishop's "The Moose," reminding the listener who hears fragments of their hushed talk of hearing, as a child, grownups talking in bed in another room: "In the creakings and noises, / an old conversation / — not concerning us, / but recognizable, somewhere, / back in the bus: / Grandparents' voices // uninterruptedly / talking, in Eternity. . ." That "in Eternity" leaps to prominence in the context of conversations among, if not with, the dead, conversations we strain to overhear.

A common way to try to access the kind of partially overheard conversations harking back to childhood that Bishop describes (though her reference to eternity provides a ghostly tinge) is to compare notes with someone else who was there and might remember, say pooling information with a sibling. In this connection, maybe it's significant that both Odysseus and Aeneas are only children with no such means of comparison. Dante too feels like a distinctly solitary character; there's no one among the living with whom he can debrief, except (a big except) the reader.

Even if one does have a sibling who might serve as a reality check, it's a truism that every child grows up in a different family, which is to say with a different perspective and different memories. A few years ago, comparing notes about our mother, who had died in 1992, my sister and I each remembered vividly a piece of worldly wisdom she had passed on to us when we were of college age. We were different people, and the advice we remembered was different. Our mother, a woman of measured, thoughtful and weighty utterances, had (perhaps repeatedly) admonished me: "Remember, honey, people are funny about money." To my sister, she had said, "When you move into a new apartment, always bring light bulbs and soap." These pronouncements, both practical and somehow oracular, don't cancel each other out. But each does show a different side of their source.

Recovering the words of our dead is not only challenging but lonely. Whether the medium is a dream, a Ouija board, an archive of letters, or a meticulously researched reconstruction, the dead person who is gone and whom we seek to reconstruct, the silent person to whom we wish to restore speech, is not only fugitive, elusive, unhuggable. He or she, in whatever form we recover them, is individually tailored to us: our idiosyncratic recreation. Whether we're comparing notes about a parent with a sibling or trying to remember why we loved a certain teacher or friend, what we finally come up with is ours alone.

This loneliness is part of what the darkly luminous phrase from the sixth book of the *Aeneid*—*Quisque suos patimur manes*—means to me now. Anchises is explaining to his son on the latter's visit to the underworld what happens to souls after death. Here is how Sarah Ruden renders part of the passage:

> So souls are disciplined and pay the price
> of old wrongdoing. Some are splayed, exposed
> To hollow winds; a flood submerges some,
> Washing out wickedness; fire scorches some pure.
> Each bears his own ghosts, then a few are sent
> To live in broad Elysium's happy fields,
> Till Time's great circle is completed . . .
>
> (*Aeneid* VI 739–45)

Each bears his own ghosts. Ruden, whose translation of the *Aeneid* is virtually line for line, has managed to compress the four words of the Latin into only five English words. Here are a handful of strikingly different other ways this mysterious phrase has been rendered: "All have their Manes, and those Manes bear" (Dryden, 1697); "We all endure / Our ghostly retribution" (Christopher Pearse Cranch, 1872); "Each our own shade-correction we endure" (T. H. Delabère May, 19th c.); "Each of us finds in the next world his own level" (Cecil Day-Lewis, 1952); "First each of us must suffer his own shade" (Allen Mandelbaum, 1961); "Each of us must suffer his own demanding ghost" (Robert Fagles, 2006). In Ursula Le Guin's novel *Lavinia* (2008), which is based on the eponymous character in the *Aeneid*, the phrase is rendered "We each have to endure our own afterlife."

The ambiguities evident in this clutch of translations are pregnant and profound. There's always some sense of purgation, of punishment—Anchises is after all describing a process of judgment and purification. But there also seems to be a characteristically Vergilian introspection here, as if each of us has to live with his or her own individual legacy—not as a punishment but as a kind of lingering flavor of personality. What interests me is at least as much the *quisque* as the *Manes*. We each have to bear (or suffer, experience, endure) our own dead, including, after our deaths, ourselves. I may be straying from the Latin's meaning, but the phrase seems to encompass in its four words not only the sense that after our deaths we each undergo an individually tailored process of purification, but also that we experience the death of anyone we care about differently from the way anyone else will experience that death.

It seems fitting that I've scooped these words from their context in a lecture Anchises is delivering. Aeneas has asked him, "Father, do some souls really soar back skyward / From here, returning into sluggish bodies? / What dreadful longing sends them toward the light?" The entire answer is magnificent, but somehow the four words *Quisque suos patimur manes* went straight to my heart, as they evidently went straight to Le Guin's. And if I'd been Aeneas, listening to his father's expatiation, I think these would have been the words that stayed with me.

For the paradoxical fact is that less can often mean more. Light bulbs and soap; people are funny about money—easy to remember. The more of a record (especially a written record) our dead leave, the more we must have recourse to cherry picking a significant word, a remembered remark—what Homer calls a *kledon* (according to Cunliffe's *Lexicon of the Homeric Dialect*, "an omen or presage, something said which bears a significance of which the speaker is unconscious, a speech that serves as an omen"). James Merrill, writing about Cavafy, mentions "those moments familiar to us all when the stranger's idle word or the friend's sudden presence happens to strike deeply into our spirits." The stranger or the friend, though, are not our beloved dead, and theirs are words we don't have to dig for. If the deceased person with whom we long to converse has left an abundant written record, maybe a semi-aleatory method works best, a lazy kind of *sortes virgilianae*: let chance determine which phrase jumps out.

What I'm circling here is the most recent of my periodic impulses to commune with the *manes* of my father, Moses Hadas (1900–1966). The obstacles to any such colloquy turn out to be more numerous than the heads of Cerberus. I was seventeen when Moses died. A self-absorbed adolescent, therefore, I missed one opportunity after another in his last years to ask him, while it was still possible for us to talk, about his past: family, education, career, war, even such adventures as a trip to Israel with Eric Sevareid to tape a TV feature on the Shrine of the Book. Nor was my father particularly forthcoming as a personality. He had a reticence I think I recognize in myself—a reticence complicated by a quality of adaptability I fumblingly touched upon in "The Many Lives of Moses Hadas," a piece I wrote for *Columbia Magazine* in 2000:

His work as teacher and scholar was a constant, but this work was performed by, at different times, an Orthodox Jew and—as he once described himself to some proselytizing Jehovah's Witnesses—a godless person. . . . He was a Southerner by upbringing and accent, then a

New Yorker. He was a rabbi, then a professor, then, like many academics of his generation, an O.S.S. operative who, more unusually, took an active interest in Greek politics after the war, and then a professor again, not to mention a talking head on TV and a tele-lecturer. He was a scholar at home in three ancient languages who was also a Groucho Marx fan. He was a husband and father to two very different families in succession. . . . It's as if it were possible, just barely, to live all these lives, but only if no time was wasted talking about them. Or writing about them—for much of Hadas's personality, let alone his experience, remains outside the scope of his written work.

My half-brother David Hadas hints at both the reticence and the adaptability when he writes in his Foreword to a reprint of Moses' last book, *Fables of a Jewish Aesop*, "Many people found him very Southern. When he wanted to, Moses could also seem very Jewish." David's own reticence here has a sidelong, charged eloquence I missed when I first read this little piece, which so far as I know was the only tribute to his father David, a reluctant writer, ever put on paper. I wish that David were still available to talk to about (among other things) Moses—how many questions I'd ask him! But David too has now joined the ranks of complicated shades accessible only through individual efforts. Ask David's colleagues, students, and children about him and you get (what else?) a mosaic. So what kind of *manes* of my long departed father am I experiencing or bearing or suffering now? There are scattered snapshots of physical memories, freeze-frame glimpses. We used to lie side by side, on his and my mother's bed, reading Cicero's *De Senectute* when I was a junior in high school and he was too tired after a day's teaching to sit up. There are a few letters he wrote to me over the years, or rather my memories of those letters, which have themselves been swallowed up by time. There are a few things he said, or I think he said, to me. There's a late conversation sitting on a bench near Grant's Tomb. A final phone call. Increasingly, it seems to me, our exchanges were burdened or stretched thin by the gap of forty-eight years between our ages and a weight of weariness and preoccupation that he never talked about but that seems palpable to me now. But this cloud of mortality (for that is what it was) also pressed triviality out of our conversations. Much went unsaid—there were things that he knew I knew, and I think I knew he knew this—but nothing that I remember of what was said strikes me as trivial or evasive. Without naming either of them, he and I shared love and reticence.

Now that I am rapidly approaching the age at which my father died, it is to his writings I have to turn if I want to be addressed as an adult. Not that his books are addressed to me—but then poetry, which has always been my tutelary genre, isn't addressed to anyone in particular either. Written or spoken, an utterance—Homer's winged words—flies free of its occasion. I recently revisited my father's 1962 book *Old Wine, New Bottles: A Humanist Teacher at Work*. As any significant book does, it had changed for me over time. Now myself a veteran of more than thirty years in the classroom, I was most interested in the passages about teaching. Sharon Olds used to remind her students to worry less about who they were speaking to than who they were speaking for—a useful piece of advice to bear in mind.

> I am a teacher (*Old Wine, New Bottles* begins) . . . I have written books and given public lectures, but these I have regarded as part of my teaching . . . what goes on in my own and a thousand other classrooms is more important than the large affairs carried on in the shining palaces of aluminum and glass downtown. For I believe that education is mankind's most important enterprise.

Yes! I thought. Nor is this just a rah-rah promotional statement. What underlies it is among other things a wistful acknowledgment of limits:

> The greatest advantage education can offer is that it enables a short-lived and time-bound individual to move in several cultural climates simultaneously . . .

Short-lived: my father wrote these words a few years before his death at sixty-six. Time-bound: a condition of our brief human lifespan. Several cultural climates simultaneously: as I wrote in "The Many Lives of Moses Hadas," my father was a multi-culturalist *avant la lettre*. He seldom writes directly about being Jewish, but his 1959 book *Hellenistic Culture: Fusion and Diffusion* is devoted to the fertile merging of different cultural traditions, a theme which is a subtext as well of *Fables of a Jewish Aesop*. This posthumously published volume is doubly eloquent not only in its juxtaposition of "fables" and "Jewish," but in that the fables were translated by my father. In more than one way, his last book was a cross-over.

For, of course, one way to effect cultural transmission, to "enable a short-lived and time-bound individual" who is probably also linguistically challenged "to move in several cultural climates simultaneously" is translation. Moses' own lingering unease with even the notion of the kind of unscholarly popularization implied by the existence of classics in translation comes through clearly in more than one passage of *Old Wine, New Bottles*. Whenever he mentions this issue, he comes closer than usual to unveiling his own mixed feelings. Characteristically, he also leaves something out.

> . . . [I]t has taken me many years to shed the feeling of guilt in working with translations, which many others could do as well, to the possible neglect of the things I had been trained to do. I did not finally shake the feeling off until all of my own teachers were retired, but I have continued with teaching translations and have gloried in it.

Omitted here is the fact that Moses proceeded (presumably once he had shed his burden of guilt), to do a great many translations himself; *Fables of a Jewish Aesop* was the last in a long series of translations from German, Greek, and Latin. Was this work accomplished "to the possible neglect of the things I had been trained to do?" The topic, plainly a troublesome one, arises again elsewhere in *Old Wine, New Bottles*:

> Professional exclusiveness has happily been relaxed, but vestiges of it persist, as I can testify from personal experience. When I was invited, two or three years ago [that is, about 1959] to address a meeting of teachers on problems of teaching classics in translation, the distinguished scholar who introduced me informed the audience that I was a man who made translations, wrote popularizing interpretations, and even reviewed books in my field for newspapers; he plainly meant no unkindness, but just as plainly found it remarkable that the professor of Greek in a reputable university should stray so far from the traditional boundaries. About 1940, I published a study of the religion of Plutarch in a scholarly but nonclassical periodical, and was told by a senior colleague, who was also a warm friend, that I had done very wrong not to publish it in a classical periodical. When I realized that he was in earnest, I said, "But the classicists already know; this will inter-

est other people and should be made available to them." "Your responsibility is to your own profession," my colleague said.

This issue of professional responsibility is one of many I wish I had raised with my father; one of many open questions to which I have to find answers in what he wrote. I also wonder whether he felt that his trip to Israel with Eric Sevareid, or his telephone lectures to Black colleges, meant he was neglecting the things he had been trained to do. I imagine that as the years went by, Moses got used to this versatility. After all, as he wrote, "I have written books and given public lectures, but these I have regarded as part of my teaching." Still, there remains the sense of a busy, accomplished, and rather short life with no breathing space for a rest—a sense I feel more keenly (as I get older and more tired) that he himself felt—not that he ever mentioned it.

Another question I never thought to ask during my father's lifetime: was there any lingering feeling of guilt, not at working on translations, but at a more personal kind of transformation: leaving the Jewish community in which he had been raised, leaving his early career as a rabbi, leaving his first wife and their teenaged children? Religion is an issue Moses skirts in his more—his relatively—autobiographical work. When he uses the word "spiritual" in *Old Wine, New Bottles*, it's generally in the context of his overt and abiding concern, education. For education and spirituality turn out to overlap. I enjoyed this tart sentence, which I'd missed on earlier readings: "For most of the centuries of European history qualifying education as spiritual would be as tautological as calling water wet."

Finally, I had also missed this remarkable passage, which begins in the context of classical pedagogy but moves to deeper waters:

> To say that the classics were abolished from the curriculum by men who had studied them and then restored by men who had not is exaggeration, but it comes near enough truth to make the official guardians of the classical tradition uncomfortable. The sequence of ossification, revitalization, ossification, revitalization, is a phenomenon common to all spiritual concerns [among which, as we've seen, Moses includes education], and particularly noticeable in religion. Zeal tends to calcify into a rote ritualism, and is then revivified, to the chagrin and often against the opposition of the official priesthood, by a man from the desert who is not a member of the prophets' guild. The renewal, if it is

effective, is then incorporated into the body of the tradition in charge of the priesthood, again hardens into spiritless routine, and again invites revivification at the hands of people who have no vested interests in the subject, to the discomfort of those who have.

Wasn't Moses himself, in his daring career as a classicist, "a man from the desert"? If so, then the members of the prophets' guild, those with a vested interest in the subject, the "clerkly teachers," as he calls them elsewhere, were surely his elders, his own teachers, the resisters of change, who had to retire before he could shed the feeling of guilt at being a translator and popularizer. Also implied, more subtly, is that this outlier from the desert also failed to join the prophets' guild because his allegiance, at least by birth and upbringing, was to another tribe.

This, then, is the demanding ghost to whom these days I find myself reaching out; the ghostly retribution I am enduring; the shade I am suffering. I open my arms to embrace Moses, and he slips away. But the words are there.

LESSONS OF POETRY

On a recent drizzly Sunday afternoon, I walked six blocks to the UPS store and sent off a box of papers to my archive. Housed in Rutgers's Alexander Library in New Brunswick, New Jersey, the Rachel Hadas Papers now consists of some forty boxes of my correspondence, drafts, and so on, dating back to 1992. This particular box contained printouts from my visits, usually one each semester, to the freshman English composition classes taught by my Rutgers-Newark colleague John Straus during the years 2006 to 2017.

It works like this: a week or two beforehand, John gives the students a few of my poems and solicits written questions about them—questions he then passes to me. My responses, when we all get together in the classroom, including the inevitable digressions, form the contents of the visits to John's class. Intellectual panhandling, John calls this long-standing practice. I've thought of writing about these visits, or perhaps collaborating with John on a piece about them, but haven't yet done so. Should I feel a pang, then, to be shipping off this carton full of folders stuffed with student questions? If I ever want to write about my time spent in John's classes, won't I need to consult all this paper?

Writing in detail about what transpires in the classroom is like catching a butterfly by one fragile wing and then pinning the hapless creature to a board, the better to examine it. The butterfly dies in the process. Even if I'd kept the papers I just shipped off to New Brunswick, I would lack the patience to write an account. I'd have to reinvent so much! The paper trail is a one-sided correspondence: it records the students' questions, but not my answers.

This paperwork is true to the dynamic of teaching. Henry Adams said: "A teacher affects eternity; he can never tell where his influence stops." I'd go a step further: the teacher may not even know where, if anywhere, his influence starts. Yes, we're all in the classroom together;

but who is listening, and what are they hearing, and who will retain what? It's not only that I have no way of knowing where or whether my words will find a foothold; it's that once those words have, in the Homeric formulation, escaped the fence of my teeth—once they've flown out into the air—I'm inclined to forget them. Those winged words certainly don't need to be packed in a box and sent off to an archive. They take up no space at all.

Teaching literature is an elusive business. There is a text; there are students; there's a teacher. This assembly leaves plenty of room for idiosyncrasy and improvisation. Teaching a course on myth in literature last spring, I thought to bring three different hats (baseball caps, actually) to the classroom, labeled respectively "Myth", "Literature," and "Writing." My original intention was to don whichever hat seemed relevant to what the class was doing at the time. But of course the subjects don't divide up that neatly; I'd have been changing hats all the time.

Looking back over the steady trickle of poems I've written about teaching in the thirty-odd years I've spent in and out of classrooms, I find a lot of references to the classrooms themselves. More specifically, I find references to classroom doors. My poem "Conklin 455, 3:55 PM, Wednesday, March 3, 2004" captures the moment I stood, hand on the doorknob, before walking into the classroom to teach poetry. Earlier that day, I'd learned of my brother David's death. In "Pomegranate Variations" (1994), a poem about teaching the myth of Persephone and actually bringing a pomegranate to class, I quote myself as saying "Behind shut doors we're safe. / Now out with it." At the end of the poem, "The hour is over. Tentatively someone / from outside tries the door."

My classroom poems from ten or twenty years ago seem to be speaking about a much less alarming world than the one students and teachers live in now. I was recently reminded in another way of how the profession of teaching has changed. In a book entitled *Awake at Work* (2006), Michael Carroll stresses the importance of paying attention on the job, of being mindfully alert to conditions that may change at any moment. Carroll lists professions "where letting go of preconceptions and being fully present to circumstances as they unfold are absolutely vital: air traffic controller, fire fighter, emergency medical responder, teacher." Somehow I doubt that Carroll thought of saving lives as one of the things a teacher has to be "fully present to." I imagine he was thinking of the way emotional and cognitive weather can quickly change in the classroom.

But now teachers are being asked to be prepared for the same kind of situations that are the daily experience of firefighters and other emergency responders. Ashley Nicolas, who served in Afghanistan before becoming a high school teacher in the US, recently wrote a detailed account of the routine process of drilling to prepare her classroom for an attack. "My classroom would be one of the first an attacker coming through the front entrance would see. So I set out to make it a 'hard target'. . . . The classroom was big, with doors at opposite ends. . . . I pondered how to construct impromptu barricades to delay or confuse an attacker."

Six months ago, as my Mythology in Literature class at Rutgers-Newark was reaching the end of its leisurely reading of the Odyssey, the shootings at Douglas High School in Parkland, Florida, once again changed the sense of what a school means, what a classroom is. We had been talking about Homeric similes, which are adept at, among other things, evoking human violence by referring to the natural world. I found myself thinking of the slaughtered Suitors near the end of the poem:

> Odysseus scanned his house to see if any man
> still skulked alive, still hoped to avoid black death.
> But he found them one and all in blood and dust . . .
> great hauls of them down and out like fish that fishermen
> drag from the churning grey surf in looped and coiling nets
> and fling ashore on a sweeping hook of beach—some noble catch
> heaped on the sand, twitching, lusting for fresh salt sea
> but the Sungod hammers down and burns their lives out . . .
> so the suitors lay in heaps, corpse covering corpse.
>
>   (*Odyssey* XXII, tr. Fagles)

Just before this simile, Odysseus spares the lives of two men, who "scurried out of the house at once / and crouched at the altar-stone of mighty Zeus— / glancing left and right, / fearing death would strike at any moment." At the scene of the Parkland shootings, *The New York Times* reported that Deputy Scot Peterson, who remained outside the high school for several minutes after the shooting began, was seen "seeking cover behind a concrete column leading to a stairwell."

When I wrote "Conklin 455" in 2004, my threshold moment was balanced between my beloved brother's not unexpected death on the one hand and poetry on the other—poetry my brother and I had shared, poetry I was about to go in and teach. Fourteen years later, in the same Conklin Hall, but in what feels like a different country, my threshold moment might be about death ready to burst in and hunt down my students and me. Poetry doesn't work all that differently. Who the recipient is, what will happen to his or her words, isn't in the poet's control. As to where those words come from, questions like, "What were you trying to say?" and "Where do you get your ideas?"—the kind of questions students ask me year after year—are doomed not to be answered, or not answered satisfactorily. For they are the wrong questions.

When my father, Moses Hadas, died in 1966, I was seventeen. Now that I'm older than he ever lived to be, and have myself spent decades in the classroom, his occasional writings about teaching speak to me directly. In a late unpublished talk "On Teaching the Classics in Translation" he drew a useful distinction:

> It is easier to lecture about the time and place of a book, the culture that produced it, the special historical or linguistic problems involved in it. It is harder . . . to face the book as a masterpiece and to help the student understand why it is a masterpiece. . . . If you dodge the book and conceal your fecklessness by loud noises in the outworks, the whole enterprise becomes fraudulent. There are crambooks from which your students can get all the knowledge you purvey with their bare feet on the table . . .

And Moses also wrote, in *Old Wine, New Bottles: A Humanist Teacher at Work*: "what goes on in my own and a thousand other classrooms is more important than the large affairs carried on in the shining palaces of aluminum and glass downtown"—the business "palaces" of midtown Manhattan. But my father never spelled out exactly what he said in the classroom.

THIS IS WHAT I WAS MEANT TO DO

Iᴛ's ᴍᴜᴄʜ ᴇᴀsɪᴇʀ to recapture the experience of a class when you're not the one teaching it. In recent years, it's become my practice to invite guest lecturers to all the courses I teach. The students get to hear another voice, and so do I; we all enjoy a change of timbre and style, pace and approach. And I'm not too old, I hope, to learn something. So if the guest speaker gives a little writing assignment, I'm happy to scribble along for as long as the students do. One never knows what a random prompt might yield. In this case, it was the unexpected harvest of a recovered dream.

The visiting lecturer gives the class in literature and medicine a choice of four prompts. Think of a time, he says, when you didn't know what to do. Or: think of a time when you were doing something for the very first time. Or: think of a time when you felt you were your best self; when you were doing what you were meant to do. Or: if you feel stuck and don't know what to write about, then write about what it feels like to feel stuck.

What do I want to write about? When Dr. Paul Gross gave my under-graduates the choice of these four prompts this morning, I'd taken a bathroom break. But now, toward the end of the afternoon graduate seminar in literature and medicine, when he asks the students to write, I think I'll write too. After all, Paul, an openfaced, engaging man, is also writing along with the students.

I find myself braiding together images in a recent dream (a dream that had, however cloudily, stayed with me) with the satisfaction of seeing the students, heads bent, busily writing, writing, writing. The satisfaction of teaching; the sense, at the end of the semester, that some difference had been made, something imparted. These two things—writing poems that trawled through dream imagery and landed unexpected images and insights and made sense of them; and teaching—the inner room and the outer room—these elicited my best self. These are the things I'm meant to be doing. So I choose, somewhat to my own surprise, the most positive prompt of the four.

I was meant to walk into a room and look around and listen. But first: in the morning, before I go to work, to recover, uncover, recreate, name the steps descending to the water. To capture, before it dissolves, the staircase leading down to a stretch of sand where the surf is roiling. Down there on the beach, something is being turned over and over, something hard to see, swathed or rinsed clean by grey and white foam. The waves are booming and silent, somehow both at once.

The stairs leading down to the water are made of stone. They have been somewhat hollowed out by the tread of many feet, and rain fills these little hollows. Or maybe it is not rain but salt water that has sloshed up the steps as the waves broke on the beach. Or maybe the water is a mix: fresh and salt, rain and tears.

The stone the stairs are made of is light-colored, porous, like limestone or travertine. In the hollow of one of them, I now see, the water has pooled a bit deeper; and in this little puddle something is moving. A turtle is paddling, moving its four feet, trying to swim. I think the turtle is alive, but I can't be certain; maybe it's dead and its feet are only swaying in the current.

I was meant to trace the stairs down to the water's edge. Someone has walked here before I have—indeed, many someones. Others will follow me. You are not obliged to finish the work, neither are you free to abandon it. A process, rather. A ritual; even a celebration. To go down the stairs toward some elemental edge; to sense oneself as one person in a long line. And not a chorus line, dancers kicking their shapely legs in unison; a more sober line, a frieze across the sky. A line moving across and through time.

"Where can we live but days?" asks Philip Larkin. The work of waking and bearing witness to dreams; the work of teaching: these are my day jobs. Morning work, says Thoreau. The line of past and future walking down these stairs may be composed of days and nothing else. Of people who wake up in the morning and struggle out of bed and, in a line of other people, face the day.

There's no one else on the staircase, in the sandscape, on the beach, except that turtle, if it is alive. I myself am both there and not there, like the dreamer in a dream or the teacher in a classroom standing back and letting the process happen. A teacher is one person in a long ghostly line: present but also absent.

To trace that staircase, to take dictation from the unheard, to make room for the invisible—all of this, I scribble in the silence as Paul and the students also scribble, is what I was meant to do. The mild splashings on the stairs take on a shape; a silent voiceover carves the air. Here one could supply any number of questions and answers—things I say, things my students say, things the texts we are reading say. And yet in the solitude and silence of this staircase down to the water, not one word has been spoken—not out loud.

I look around at my eleven graduate students—no, ten today, Brian (he'll email me the next day) is at the hospital with his dog, which needs emergency surgery. Heads bent, gazes inward, small private smiles: their reference points are interior, probing backward toward an encounter at the end of a remembered vista, distant even in their young life histories. It feels almost like a violation even to look around at the circle of people writing, writing, writing, such are the webs of privacy they are separately spinning. Does Angela's intersect with Todd's across the room? Maggie's with Sara's? Leslie's with Eliza's? Silently, the loss, or wound, or conversation, or gift, or joy, or parting—memories snatched back and set down here—float out into the air. Paul has summoned them all, conjured them with these simple-sounding prompts, the same Open Sesame with which he has conjured my staircase down to the water. This is what he was meant to do—one of many things.

Ten minutes! Put away your pen and paper.

We can only go down the water steps one by one. Those who came before, those who come after: they're invisible, it takes an act of imagination to envision them. We ourselves are only temporarily visible. But since, temporarily, here we are, then this is what I was meant to do.

II

Storage and Retrieval

A LETTER TO J. D. SALINGER

April 22, 2000

Dear Mr. Salinger,

When I think of you, I think first of *The Catcher in the Rye*. Proust tells us that the books we love always remain (or is it always should remain?) in our minds, if not actually in our possession, in the copies in which we first read them. I first read a paperback edition of *Catcher*. I forget the publisher (Avon? Pocket books?) and the price (25 cents?), but I clearly remember the shiny cover, which depicts a realistic, almost photographed looking Holden Caulfield, tall and stern-looking in profile, wearing his hunting hat. He's standing on a city street and looks a bit too much like a movie poster of the period, just as the haggard but sexy Winston Smith on the cover of *1984* around the same time looks more heroic than Orwell probably intended.

This paperback lived in my older sister's room, a tiny oblong, halfway down the long, dark, winding hall of our ground-floor apartment, a room that had originally been intended to be a maid's room. In her glassed-in bookcase were many enticing books. What come to mind now are paperbacks: *Cat on a Hot Tin Roof, Measure for Measure*, and Henry Miller's *Sexus*. Why these three? Because the kinds of words I was learning from *The Catcher in the Rye* turned up in them as well: "lech" or "whore," for example, though probably only *Catcher* was a source of "fart."

These other books I flipped around in by the age of nine or ten, enjoying, for example, the photographs of Elizabeth Taylor in a slip and Paul Newman in pajamas in *Cat*. But *The Catcher in the Rye* I inhaled. ("I read it right straight through. / I was too shy to stop," writes Elizabeth Bishop in "The Waiting Room" of the almost seven-year-old's experience with *National Geographic*.)

In those days, it came naturally to me to memorize, more or less, books I liked, since the books I liked I read over and over. My many early readings of *Catcher* blur and merge in my mind, but they or their composite remain vivid when I open the book today and realize I know it nearly by heart, italics and all. And the same is true of the *Nine Stories*. "Olives and wax—I never go anywhere without 'em." "You take a really sleepy man, Esmé . . ."

The summer I was ten or so, I had a tiny part in William Saroyan's play *The Time of Your Life* when the play was performed at Bread Loaf. I played the bartender's daughter (my line was a proud "That's my father"), and I must have spent a lot of time listening to rehearsals or, on stage, hanging around the bar, because some of the lines spoken by other characters remain so vivid to me. Kitty, a prostitute, says to some man who's annoying her, "I'm a whore, you son of a bitch. You know what I do. And I know what you do." It's hard to believe in 2000, but that line was raunchy fare for an innocent little girl around 1958. I did and didn't understand what it meant.

And something like the same doubleness clings to my memory of these early encounters with your work. I learned new words, and understood, more or less, what they meant. But what the books had to say to me was not merely a matter of whores and farts. There was a very different message, if that's the word, intertwined with the bravado, the scenes of New York at night, the loneliness and disillusionment. Peel back Holden's unease and indignation, his desire to expose the phony world of grownups, peel back the bellhop, the prostitute, Ackley; and the atmosphere that rises from *The Catcher in the Rye* turns out, for me at least, to be one of kindness, comfort, patience, and safety. These qualities reside not so much in the world of the book (though they can be found there if you look), but in its language; in the voice of the narrator. Of course this voice takes the form, in *Catcher*, of Holden's voice; but a similar if not identical wryness, sense of detail, and overall alertness to the gamut of human behavior can be heard in the voice of "A Perfect Day for Bananafish," "Down at the Dinghy," "For Esmé with Love and Squalor"—the list goes on. The squalor, in other words, is always being balanced by love.

Last summer, teaching at the Sewanee Writers Conference, I and my family spent twelve days in a borrowed faculty house on campus. It was a nice little house, its upstairs still undergoing renovation, and I love Sewanee, where I had taught several other summers. But these nearly two weeks were an uncomfortable period. Many people at the conference, including me, came down with vicious colds which weren't improved by the contrast between the unremitting heat outside and the refrigerated temperatures of the air-conditioning inside. My husband came down with the cold and was quite sick. Our fifteen-year-old son and the friend he had brought along for solidarity slept till noon every day and prowled, or slunk, around the campus the rest of the time, spending hours at the local coffee shop and disappearing into the dorm rooms of new, glamorously older friends, both undergraduates and townies, from whom they picked up anti-gown attitudes. Superimpose on this a strenuous schedule of workshops, conferences, readings, more readings, endless literary conversations. I could hardly wait for this hot and cold interlude to end.

But the time was significantly improved when I came upon a copy of *Raise High the Roof Beam, Carpenters* on our hosts' bookshelves. There it all was: the heat, the sense of time stretching out endlessly, the being jammed together in space and time with other equally uncomfortable people. Not having first read *Carpenters* as a nine-year-old (perhaps I'd been fifteen), I'd forgotten how hilarious the story of Seymour's abortive wedding and that endless traffic jam was. More squalor than love this time around, perhaps. But again, peel back the Matron of Honor and the taxi driver and the tiny deaf mute uncle and the words BooBoo has scrawled in lipstick on the mirror, and there is an enormous and consoling patience in the telling. Reading about that boiling hot non-wedding made the shivery, sweaty, sneezy, achy, teenage-ridden time in that little house into something I could begin to assimilate. It reminded me of my love of reading. It was an escape and a refuge. It even made me homesick for Manhattan.

I could go on, but this is probably more than enough. Thank you, Mr. Salinger. It's easy to say that I will never forget your books; I have forgotten scarcely a word you've written.

Your fan,
Rachel Hadas

WAITING WITH KIPLING

Rereading *Kim* recently, I encountered words I hadn't known the first or even the second time I read Rudyard Kipling's novel. For example, *kichree*: dal with vegetables. My son had introduced me to this dish around 2009, when he returned from a year in Nepal. And *madrissah*: a Muslim school. *Kim* was published in 1901, exactly a century before 9/11, yet like many Westerners, I imagine, I learned the latter term only after the Twin Towers fell. It goes without saying that *kichree* and *madrissahs*—let alone more familiar words such as *tsunami*—preceded by many centuries, even by millennia, our provincial Western knowledge of them. These words, and the things they signified, were waiting, until they finally came to life for me.

I was waiting, too. I read—reread—*Kim* in a big waiting room at 111 Centre Street, in Lower Manhattan. Most of the hundred or so potential jurors waiting in the room were reading, or at least staring at their smartphones. The room was like a shabbier but calmer airport lounge, without the TV screens and the announcements. There were no flights to catch—perhaps the jury pool would catch us. Under the bemused gaze of the clerk, we could do nothing but wait—and read. Where now do we read but in waiting rooms? Where but in waiting rooms do we live? A cheerful lady named Gert, who seated herself next to me the first morning, was trying to finish *The Boys in the Boat* in time for her book group's next meeting. Another imminent event in Gert's life was her husband's cancer surgery.

After lunch on a sunny bench in Foley Square, my eyes got heavy. I put aside my hardcover copy of *Kim* and switched to *Stoicism Today: Selected Writings* on my Kindle. And here, a pleasant surprise—my father's name, Moses Hadas, twinkled from time to time on the device's glassy surface. Not so surprising, maybe; he had edited *The Stoic Philosophy of Seneca* in 1958. Still, unexpected—and good to know that a younger generation is drinking at that well. The patience and perspective that Stoicism offers are useful in many situations, especially when one is waiting around for jury duty.

It was in the note concluding Laura Inman's essay "Happiness for Sale: What Would Seneca Say?" that my father's name first leaped out at me. Now that I am roughly the same age as my parents were when they died, there's no need to address or think of them as Mommy and Daddy. Moses, I say inwardly, come back. Can't we talk about Seneca and Plutarch? Elizabeth, come back. Tell me about the first time you ever read *Kim*, or the first time it was read to you. How old were you? I know *Kim* was one of your favorite books, but I don't know how I know that. Did you tell me, or did someone else?

When we think back to our parents in their youth, we rarely imagine them as bored or lonely. After all, they had no time to be lonely once we arrived. It's easier for me to envision my parents reading. I have no idea just when my father inhaled the Stoic writers, probably fairly early in his life. And my mother and her mother (whom I remember reading "The Pobble Who Has No Toes" and "The Owl and the Pussycat" to me) knew and loved Edward Lear's nonsense poems, the Alice books, *The Jungle Books*, and, certainly, *Kim*. People used to ask me, on some kind of Lamarckian principle, whether, having grown up as the daughter of a classicist, I knew ancient Greek from an early age. Alas, the answer was no; I had to acquire Greek, which I did laboriously and incompletely. But when it comes to books absorbed very early in life, the idea of acquired characteristics being inherited is a lot more convincing.

That night, before I fell asleep, a sentence that sounded as if it came from *Kim* reverberated in my head. It featured the old lama, the Tibetan holy man whose disciple Kim becomes early in the story. Although central to the novel, the frail, unworldly lama is peripheral to life itself. He moves across the crowded stage of India in quest of his River, but he never ceases to pine for the clear, cold air of his northern monastery. The lama needs Kim's protection because he is a stranger in the world.

The sentence that kept playing in my head was, *The lama nestled by the gate.*

I tried to make sense of this. The monastery gate? The gate of the museum in Lahore where the lama first encounters Kim? The Grand Trunk Road, which threads through the heart of *Kim*, perceived as some kind of mystic portal through which we all must pass? My parents passed through the portal ahead of me, of course, leaving a few clues behind, twinkling like my father's name on the smudgy screen of my Kindle. Sometimes the clues are as inscrutable as the Red Bull of Kim's father's regiment, morphed into a myth for the orphaned child, yet also an emblem that turns out to play a crucial part in Kim's life.

The sentence chanted itself into a sort of Pooh hum, which is how many of my poems (and not only mine, I suspect) get started:

> It was early. It got late.
> The lama nestled by the gate.
>
> What do you see when you meditate?
> Someone leaning on a gate.

At this point, my improvised jingle about the lama sounded a lot like the opening stanza of the White Knight's song in *Through the Looking-Glass*: "I'll tell thee everything I can; / There's little to relate. / I saw an aged aged man, / A-sitting on a gate."

That quatrain, in turn, could take me back to the Wordsworth poem "Resolution and Independence," which Lewis Carroll parodies in the White Knight's poem. Did Kipling know the Wordsworth poem? He must have. Did he know the Alice books? I'd be surprised if not. Kipling was born in 1865, the year *Alice's Adventures in Wonderland* was published. Intersections of books and people: an endless web.

My jury room neighbor Gert was, it turned out, also an English professor. Neither of us was called to a pool of potential jurors; we got to sit and read in the waiting room for two lavish days, after which I was free to go to the country and Gert could attend to her husband. When, at the end of the second day, the clerk—now revealed as genial—distributed our proofs of service, I told him that we two professors of English had clustered together. With a *namaste* bow, the clerk saluted us both in parting.

THE HONORS STUDENT,
THE PLAGIARIST, AND THE FAN

CHRISTINE, an honors student, having written a poem in admiring imitation of someone else's poem, and having then been sternly reprimanded for this close resemblance, naturally therefore wants to know what the deal is. So, as gingerly I dip a foot into this murky pond, here goes.

Ownership first: though crucial, never clear. Whose are the words, to start with? The words are yours, Christine, and they are not. Charmed and seduced, you succumb, you reinvent, you pay homage. Are you at once an artist and an heiress? "I am a man of fortune greeting heirs," wrote Stevens in "*Le Monocle de Mon Oncle*," and something like this formulation of Pass-It-On always occurs to me when I think of literary inheritance.

Imitation, pastiche: such terms, however imprecise, assume the existence of a prior world whose language nobody can claim to own, only to inherit. Think of recipes, those yellowed, gravy-spotted index cards: who first concocted that delicious stew subtly re-seasoned and set forth for a fresh tableful of hungry guests? Not you, Christine. Not you. Next, origin. But this turns out to be indistinguishable from possession.

Squatter's rights? Whose is your life, your body, your inheritance, your genome, your (quaint word) fortune, your portion? *Moira*, the Greek word often translated "fate," means portion or share, your slice of the pie. Who owns your past? Who made you—and does making equal ownership? Whose is the fresh green spring so many poems praise, including yours, also including the poem your poem is imitating? "Hath the rain a father, or who hath begotten the drops of dew?" "The force that through the green fuse drives the flower"—what makes the blossoms burst along the boughs? Poems have copyright; seasons, the weather, the world do not.

Nevertheless, Christine, you are, for the time being, mistress and guardian of what, articulated into syllables, your mother, father, grandparents, tracing back and back, passed on down to you: syllables they themselves inherited, lips, tongue, teeth, breath, and blood all reaching too far back to imagine, let alone to say or see.

For where does the power of language come from if not from this strong sense of being simultaneously interior (inside the head, inside the mouth, what kind of word has escaped the fence of your teeth) and anterior, traced back through the labyrinth, an inheritance, a hardy heirloom somehow still in use? Is this sense the source of our blithe confidence, Christine, that words are both private and public, both venerable and freshly minted? And where can such confidence come from, such an ability to let the words bubble uncontrollably up, up, up through the medium of your youth, attention, and awe? Precisely this confidence allowed you to write the new ode celebrating and imitating the old beauty of what you had just read.

The honors student and the plagiarist have this in common: they ardently fetishize the word. They understand perhaps better than other people do that a magic power inheres in language and that this power, unevenly dealt out as it is, is precious. Naturally, they want this power. *Wants it, my preciousss!* Questions of mere ownership are trumped by the contagion of the spell, the gorgeous incantation—theirs for the admiring? For the taking. For the talking.

Dreamily you drift down the hall, Christine, rolling lines and phrases around inside your mouth and playing them in your head. The plagiarist skips off giggling, pockets abulge with riches. Both fan and plagiarist, though, are drawn infallibly toward what both with a sure instinct recognize and thirst and hunger for. They feel no need to second-guess their hunger and thirst; they want to gulp down the juicy whole.

Such hearty, prompt, confident appetites are a far cry from the email queries that trickle in to me from time to time, from readers for whom my poems, though pleasure-giving or even powerful, nonetheless seem to be encoded messages, the secret idiom of some lofty sphere far from the daily, prosaic realm in which (or so they imagine) one talks and writes and lives. For these correspondents (should I call them fans?), both denotation and connotation are at once upstaged and fertilized by secrets. What does it all mean? they want to know. What are you trying to say?

For these readers, evidently, a poem's language must always obey crucial if hidden guidelines, and it is these (the guidelines, not the language) that require analysis. Thus each image corresponds to some fact a cunning poet (me) has concealed by tucking the thematic kernel away, deep in the pulpy texture of mere verse. Lucretius said he couched his Epicurean philosophy in poetry as doctors rub honey around the rim of a cup in order to mask the bitter taste of the medicine inside.

Is this poem autobiographical? they ask. *Is your personal psychology being explored in this work?* These are the questions that send me reeling, giddy but grateful, back toward you, Christine, who understand that words have legs and stretch them, that they are faithless, mobile, elusive, that they stroll, stride, or sprint far from their point of origin.

How do I envision that point? Neither as syllables in a baby's mouth nor as the starting gate for some tense race, the crowd cheering as the horses, hoofs drumming, approach the finish line. No, the starting point might be a sleepy country town, a village the aspiring provincial inevitably leaves for the big city, maybe to return and maybe not, but carrying its image in her heart, and speaking, at least a little bit, in its accent forever after. Or it might just be a single printed page. A right-hand page in the book. A paragraph in the middle of that page. A single sentence in that paragraph.

USE A BRAND-NEW WORD THREE TIMES

"Use a brand-new word three times; then it's yours." This is a piece of advice I trustingly pass on to trusting students even though I have no idea where it came from or whether it's really true. True: what would that mean? For the aphorism, if that's what it is, raises more questions than it answers.

First off the bat, what is meant by *use*? To speak a word and to write it aren't the same thing. Take some noun scooped from a venerable word-hoard, glistening like dragon gold, bright as if freshly minted: has it existed before being spoken, has it been forgotten in the mists of time, is it waiting like buried treasure to be rediscovered?

"Every time I read the word *world* I wonder is it a typo and should I delete the 'l,'" writes the poet Greg Delanty. His father was a printer, so Delanty is no doubt extra alert to scrambled, added, or missing letters. But the world in the word and the word in the world are in fact dizzying. There was a time this word you now (having used it three times) presumably possess was still inchoate—was mere raw syllables rolling around inside not just your but the race's infant mouth. Not yet having, as Homer says, escaped the fence of the teeth, the word was ineffable, unsayable.

But before words leave the nest to try their wings in, as Auden says, the neutral air, do the concepts they frame exist? *Fibromyalgia, dingbat, factitious, kerfuffle, maidenhair, Marfan*—the list could go on indefinitely, with words newly learned or rediscovered or just fortuitously (not fortunately) found—*sortes vergilianae*—with a finger in the dictionary. A huge ripe grape, a juicy glossary: Keats's melancholic's strenuous tongue crushed the fruit and set the whole world free. The whole word free.

Use your new word, write or say it; what happens then? Well, willy-nilly you become part of what's been called a linguistic community, a group which, it is assumed, will, by and large, agree on matters included in but not limited to a glossary. On the margins of the community, questions arise. An individual inquiry about a single word may prove, under scrutiny, to be a tentative questioning, a timid probe, of something more than a noun, adjective, or verb.

In *The Thin Man*, teenaged Gilbert Wynant asks Nick Charles, "Is there much incest?" Again, querying a word for something indicates the boy is circling much bigger game. The answer comes slowly, carefully, precisely as my mother would reply when pressed to deconstruct a social fib. For asked to explain the world—the word?—grownups maddeningly can't or won't.

"There's some," says Nick.

"How much?" Gilbert persists.

"There's just no way to know. But there's some—that's why they've got a name for it."

The truth is out there—might a later generation have offered this as a (non) answer? Whether, at any rate, Gilbert is satisfied by Nick's non-answer is a point on which my own curiosity has to go hungry. Nick, or Hammett, has other fish to fry. Words, like thrillers, flash tantalizing secrets at us and then whisk them away.

Words can be reviled as empty promises—in a word, lies. They can be scoffed at as labels one applies at one's own risk, realizing they're flat, affectless, inexact, incomplete. But it's not all that bad. Words are rich beyond our feeble fathoming. The hardest ones, in a way, are those which, having always thought we knew them, we don't think we have to use in order to make them our own. Take such transparencies as *love* or *mother* or *democracy* or *happy* or *family* or *home*. These words are tough and renewable, recyclable, however worn with use. They are words we need—or they need us. The mutual need springs from the way the world behaves, a constant change and sameness, a slow seasonal sifting Wallace Stevens saw as a deciduous process, the words falling like—but let him have the last word:

These leaves are the poem, the icon and the man.
These are a cure of the ground and of ourselves

In the predicate that there is nothing else.

THROUGH THE SMOKE OF THIS ONE

Somewhere between words on a page and reported or recalled speech, the genre of aphorism or proverb both arises from and seems to invite anonymity. No one who quotes a proverb can be other than vague about its provenance. Yet scooped out of context, what sounds like a proverb may be an excerpt. Reviewing Rudolf Flesch's *The Book of Unusual Quotations* in the *Times Literary Supplement* in 1959, D. B. Wyndham Lewis touches upon questions of attribution which straddle the literary and proverbial. "A footnote or two," writes Lewis, "would resolve a few queries concerning attribution. 'I am still learning,' for example—is this originally Michelangelo's or Goya's? And surely 'Fish and visitors smell in three days,' attributed to Benjamin Franklin, is an old Spanish joke?"

Spanish? David Crystal's compendious *As They Say in Zanzibar: Proverbial Wisdom from Around the World* classifies the geographical source of "A guest and a fish after three days are poison" as France. But not so fast. In his introduction, Crystal lists "a few variations on the guest theme taken from Selwyn Gurney Champion's huge collection of translated cultural proverbs":

A fish and a guest go bad on the third day and must be thrown out (BASQUE)
Fish and guests smell at three days old (DANISH)
A guest, like a fish, stinks the third day (DUTCH)
A fish and a guest after three days are poison (ENGLISH)
Guests and fish will get old on the third day (ESTONIAN)

Crystal confesses to "grasping the nettle and selecting one country to represent us all."

The murkiness around attributions which nagged at Wyndham Lewis in 1959 (even as he complained that Flesch suffered from attributional vagueness) has only thickened in the succeeding half century. In a recent "Shouts and Murmurs" piece in *The New Yorker*, George Saunders (no doubt with tongue in cheek, but still) writes, "As someone once said, T. S. Eliot perhaps, 'We are the world.'" Last week I received a card adorned with a photo of two sulky Persian cats and a quote: "When my cats aren't happy, I'm not happy, not because I care about their mood but because I know they're just sitting there thinking up ways to get even." The quote was attributed to Shelley. Really? The card turned out to have been published by a series called QuoteUnQuote. "As someone once said, Shelley perhaps."

Much more precise than proverbs or quotations on greeting cards are epigraphs. Or so I used to think. My blithe assumption was that any epigraph was a careful and reliable word-for-word excerpt from a named source and that its presence signaled, if not the author's familiarity with the entire oeuvre from which he or she was quoting, then at least familiarity with a single sentence and its provenance. How wrong I was. T. S. Eliot may not have said "We are the world," but it does seem germane that he famously (and presciently) wrote in 1932:

> Immature poets imitate; mature poets steal. . . . The good poet welds his theft into a whole of feeling which is unique, utterly different from that from which it was torn. . . . A good poet will usually borrow from authors remote in time, or alien in language, or diverse in interest.

Robert Frost, writing in 1925, expresses a similar thought more organically, even meteorologically: ". . . the manner of a poet's germination is less like that of a bean in the ground than a waterspout at sea. He has to begin as a cloud of all the other poets he ever read. That can't be helped . . ." And George Seferis, a great deployer of echoes and a translator of Eliot into modern Greek, puts it simply in a luminous late poem (1966): "Our words are the children of many people."

Granted, Eliot, Frost, and Seferis presumably didn't have deployers of epigraphs in mind; they were thinking of poets (Eliot and Frost) or just anyone who uses language, which is to say everyone (Seferis). But wrench their words only a little bit out of context ("tear" is the verb Eliot uses) and the sense of something new made of old ingredients, or something old but renewable and renewed, emerges. If I try to think about epigraphs in the same way Eliot and Frost thought about poets, in the same way Seferis thought about anyone who uses language at all, I feel less captious and uncomfortable, though still a bit dazed (and I still find it impossible to believe that Shelley uttered that line about cats—at least not in those precise words).

A sentence I've long found evocative turns out to be almost as hard to trace as the line about fish and guests: "There is another world, and it is in this one." It doesn't sound like a proverb, though the more you scrutinize it the more it begins to blur around the edges: I have a strong sense of general familiarity here, together with an absence of any specific recollection. But I do have the general impression that I encountered this line many years ago in the work of a famous writer. Was it Proust? Rilke?

I'm certainly not alone in liking this idea, or sentence, or image, however one defines it. Plenty of writers have also responded to the line by referring to it. I most recently ran across it, together with an attribution, in a passage in the poet, psychologist, and Zen author John Tarrant's 1998 book *The Light Inside the Dark*: "Beneath or inside the life we lead every day is another life. This unseen life runs like a river beneath the city, beneath work, family, ambition, beneath our pleasures and griefs. 'There is another world,' says Paul Éluard, 'and it is in this one.'"

But was it Paul Éluard? Yeats is also frequently cited as the source of this sentiment, though it seems hard to pin down the line to any particular passage. Sherman Alexie and Patrick White both use the "another world" line as an epigraph to their respective novels *The Absolutely True Diary of a Part-Time Indian* and *The Solid Mandala*. An art exhibit was entitled "There is another world, but it is in this one—but does it float?" And the list of echoes, borrowings, and parallels could go on and on.

That single word *another* has a strong resonance and casts a long shadow. "Thou hast committed / Fornication; but that was in another country, / And besides, the wench is dead" (*The Jew of Malta*, 1594). Is that other country the source of James Baldwin's 1962 novel *Another Country*? Can the use of a single word as common as "another" constitute an allusion or echo all by itself?

The preposition "in" might well give us pause, too. Where exactly is that other world again? Gary Snyder, in "Through the Smoke Hole," writes: "There is another world above this one; or outside of this one; the way to it is thru the smoke of this one, & the hole that smoke goes through. The ladder is the way through the smoke hole; the ladder holds up, some say, the world above; it might have been a tree or pole; I think it is merely a way."

Through the smoke of this one: I can think of worse ways of evoking allusion.`

FABRIC IN GHANA

MARCH 6, 2016 is the fifty-ninth anniversary of Ghanaian independence. At the new Kempinski Hotel in downtown Accra, the even newer 1957 Art Gallery opens with a two-pronged show of work by the artist Serge Attukwei Clottey. Inside the gallery, the works on show are large panels composed of many small squares cut out of yellow plastic water cans and wired together. Many of these pieces drip off the gallery walls and onto the floor. These are somewhat reminiscent of the art of Ghanaian artist El Anatsui. Outside the hotel, just before the gallery proper opens, Clottey presents a very different project: a parade-like piece of performance art. In the soft light of twilight, a long double line of young people of both sexes, all in white-face, all carrying heavy bags, some wearing women's bright dresses, files up the driveway, through the lobby, and onto the central lawn of the hotel's atrium, where the trees are hung with more empty plastic water cans. The silent marchers, those not already fully dressed, take clothes from their bags and put them on. They mime the neighborly give and take of village women, as they sink in small groups into seated positions on the grass. Clottey, wearing a gas mask, leads the marchers. The handout accompanying the performance tells us that this work, entitled "My Mother's Wardrobe," was inspired by the artist's mother's death.

In Ghana, a country of twenty-five million people where between forty and fifty languages are spoken ("it depends on whom you ask," says Professor Helen Yitah of the University of Ghana at Legon in Accra), cloth might be said to speak louder than words. "Consciousness," wrote Merleau-Ponty, "is like a fold in the fabric." Whether in Clottey's performance piece or in the traditional kente which isn't ubiquitous but is common enough to form a kind of visual leitmotif, or in the bright and elegantly patterned garments worn by both women and men—some women, some men—on the city street, in the villages, or on a college campus, many of the fabrics on display seem to speak different dialects of a single tongue.

At the Nubuke Foundation near Legon, the young artist Fatric Bewong makes varied use of cloth in a show which opens the day before the 1957 Gallery's launch of Clottey. Bewong paints small, bright square panels which could hang singly but form compelling clusters of four or six or eight. She incorporates both fabric and plastic into her canvas compositions. Other works of hers make heavier and more ironic use of recycling: a bridal figurine wears ingeniously tailored plastic bags. Bewong also drapes heavy swags of intricately patterned cloth onto walls or across corners; like Clottey's, these works seem to drip from wall onto floor. Both Clottey's performance piece and Bewong's fabric installations convey a sense of nostalgic celebration ruefully inflected by a consideration of the practical problems of recycling. What to do with traditional costumes? Cram them into big plastic carriers, tote them through a hotel lobby, put them on. Alternatively, drape them across the wall. The folds of the fabric, like consciousness, are complicated, a word which means "pleated." "Shall I uncrumple this much-crumpled thing?" asks Wallace Stevens in *"Le Monocle de Mon Oncle."* Again, the mind as fabric. But the fabric itself is ambiguous and challenging.

An all but overwhelming practical problem in Ghana, and not only in Ghana, is pollution. At Accra's trendy Trashy Bags store, where you can buy cleverly constructed shopping bags which fold small and zip into bright purses, all crafted from discarded plastic bags, the hopeful slogan is "Cleaning up Ghana one bag at a time." If only! Step from immaculate store or hotel or art gallery onto the street or the beach, and the smell of burning garbage, the sight of waves of plastic bags, empty cans, old tires, old shoes, you name it, isn't far away.

The young artists of Ghana, or some of them, haven't turned their backs on the disaster of the environment. Not that they have the solution; how could they? But their work neither ignores the problems of living in this place at this time nor engages in self-righteous finger-pointing. It's thoughtful, at once somewhat practical and mystical. Practical? Beautiful traditional fabrics—wear them and walk up a hotel driveway, to be captured on hundreds of smart phones. Drape them on a wall in a configuration so lush and dramatic and painterly that a visitor is tempted to buy it. But then how to get it home? How to drape it there? How to keep it clean? Curatorial challenges abound. Easier as well as cheaper to buy a small and probably mass-produced wooden mask or string of beads as a keepsake. Maybe not so practical after all.

A more mystical approach is illustrated by the work of Ibrahim Mahama, a young artist who, like Clottey and Bewong, trained in the distinguished art department of KNUST (Kwame Nkrumah University of Science and Technology), the big university in Kumasi. A fabric work of Mahama's hangs in the lobby of the Kempinski; but a more ambitious project, a series of his installations, is the subject of an artist's talk delivered early on the same day the 1957 gallery opens. As the soft-spoken Mahama answers questions, an air of puzzlement, possibility, and poetic associations lingers in the room. Even reduced to slides, the work he's presenting invites pondering.

Mahama's use of traditional fabric involves not colorful cloth but old jute gunny sacks (he trades new sacks for old) which he employs women to stitch together, many at a time, to form a long sort of carpet, curtain, or train, depending on how you think of it. An image of the bearers of this heavy bundle unrolling the rough textile suggests a red carpet. (Where are the movie stars—or is this more the kind of drapery Agamemnon paced along to his doom?) These sacks, though, aren't red; they're soft brown or grey, with bluish tints. Some sacks are marked with initials or other inscriptions, whether printed logos of a cocoa company or names of the women who did the stitching. Sewn together, they look a bit like delicately faded madras. They also, of course, suggest a vast quilt. And this quilt, or drape, or whatever one wants to call it, Mahama suspends from a building's roof or a bridge. Aerial drone shots show startlingly dreamlike scenes: a dormitory at KNUST suddenly wavering in a soft veil, or a Kumasi bridge mysteriously clothed. The roof of the National Theater, near the Kempinski Hotel, is currently covered with one of these drapes. They're generally taken down after only a few days; but the uncanniness remains.

The AIDS quilt is garish by comparison, as is Christo's orange plastic installation, "The Gates," which adorned Central Park in 2005. Whether it's the softly textured look of Mahama's drapes (repurposed from sacks which from close up, we're told, are still redolent of their former contents) or the fact that the often raw and graceless or dilapidated structures they drape are in need of some sort of mediation, these installations, which blur outlines, also make us look twice at what we'd never looked at before.

"When the building was covered," says Mahama, "suddenly it was visible. You install, you remove—but the space is changed by what you've done. Consciously or unconsciously, something happens there."

No one disagrees. Rather, questions evolve into attempts to evoke the uncanniness of these installations. "The building becomes an altar draped in sackcloth," says my husband, a video artist. "It becomes fluid; it starts to breathe." Robin Riskin, an American working on her MFA in curatorial studies at KNUST, adds that the installation can look concave or convex depending on which way the wind is blowing. "The buildings become actors in a theater," she says. And the numinous note struck by the image of the altar recurs when Bonaventure Soh Bejeng Ndikung, an urbane gallerist originally from Cameroon and now based in Germany, observes: "One doesn't have to force it, but at the point when you cover something, it becomes a mystery. These three main religions we fool around with—they all involve the absent body."

ONE APRIL DAY

THE CATALOG of the exhibit "Vestiges and Verse: Notes from the New-fangled Epic," at the American Folk Art Museum in New York, fails to note that the complex and ambitious architectural drawings of Achilles G. Rizzoli (1896–1981) incorporate numerous sonnets. True, we're told that in "the late 1920s until 1934, [Rizzoli's] attention was primarily centered on writing literature and poetry." (Literature and poetry? Two separate species?) Then, when Rizzoli's literary efforts found no publishers, he focused on drawing and worked as an architectural draftsman. But a close look at Rizzoli's large and meticulous black-and-white drawings—they look more like blueprints—reveals sonnets lettered in almost every one: poetic form unobtrusively deployed, rhyme and meter flawless, the boxy sonnet shape punctuating the pages like a window letting light into a wall, into the box of a room, organizing space. Not that Rizzoli's art accommodates many empty spaces. All its surfaces are embellished in crisp black and white: images, prayers, aphorisms, words collaborating with images. Not an inch of paper is wasted. Still, there's a sense throughout Rizzoli's work of a spaciousness notably absent from some of the work of the other self-taught artists in this remarkable show, with its collages and constructs and schemata, eloquent, idiosyncratic, and private.

An unremittingly cold spring is beginning, in this second week of April in New York, to relent and soften into sunshine. Snowdrops, daffodils, forsythia, a promise of magnolia blossoms. In Richard Tucker Park by Lincoln Center, balloons festoon a statue. In Straus Park in Morningside Heights, the annual commemoration of the sinking of the *Titanic* is about to be observed. The lavishness and tenderness and cruelty and absurdity of the world are especially on display every spring, a contrast captured precisely by Robert Lowell's phrase "our magnolia ignite . . . their murderous five days' white." The sky opens to warmth and light even as it closes for someone, even as it constantly closes and opens. "Right behind / my limousine is someone else's hearse / unnoticed," writes Deborah Warren in her poem "About Suffering." A year ahead of me at Radcliffe, Deborah was one of the English majors in Whitman Hall who used to wear rubber gloves when they were reading novels in Signet Classics editions, since the ink tended to come off on their hands. I was a classics major who bit my fingernails; no rubber gloves for me. For the past twenty years, Deborah has taken the gloves off, or repurposed them; she has been writing—sculpting?—exquisitely chiseled poems.

Not every hearse, of course, is unnoticed. Today's hearse has attracted plenty of notice in many circles: the death of J. D. McClatchy, word of which reached me earlier this morning. This particular someone was a poet, editor, librettist, critic, teacher, a man of great generosity and seemingly inexhaustible energy, a man many people knew. Indefatigable; mortal. Sandy McClatchy's illness didn't prevent him from working on poems and a libretto right up until the end.

Every spring, the world shrinks and expands, seeming smaller because someone we know left it, larger because the good news, the very generously good news, of this particular life flings brightly colored streamers back over the years, over the trail of memories, the encounters and conversations. Death always gives something back to the living.

Is it possible to braid them together: the spring, slow to arrive but now advancing fast; the terrifying state of our country and the world; our granddaughter, fifteen months old, toddling with her bottle in one fist, her new teeth, her smiles of discovery and trust; this death? To honor the poetry, the blossoms, and the blight? The unlikely lavishness and extravagance of the season, of the art in the American Folk Art Museum, its manic mimicry, artists busy at their work of organizing loneliness in space, of representing some version of the world—it all feels like cause for celebration.

The gift of art keeps giving. Later in the day that began with news of Sandy's death and moved on to the sunny stroll to Lincoln Square, the flowering parks, and the art exhibit, a book arrives: Stephen Yenser's annotated edition of James Merrill's *The Book of Ephraim*. The endpapers reproduce a few of Merrill's notes and doodles, which at first glance look like smaller, sketchier versions of some of the art on display in "Vestiges and Verse." But they turn out to be reproductions of Merrill's jottings toward, rough blueprints for, the astonishing poetic edifice that *Ephraim* became. In the book I find a card: "Compliments of the Author." I'm reminded that in March of 1995, a month after Merrill's death, his last book of poems, *A Scattering of Salts*, arrived one afternoon in the mail. The book contained a card: "Compliments of the Author." Who says that poets die?

Rizzoli's "symbolization" drawings, the catalog tells us, "represent metamorphoses of friends, neighbors, and family members . . . personalized depictions function as memorials and vestiges." "Well," as Merrill almost wrote at the end of his poem "An Urban Convalescence," "that is what art does." (What he actually wrote is "that is what life does.")

A poet dead, streams of memories, an exhibit that exhumes and elegantly displays obscure private art, the spring advancing, an unexpected and welcome book arriving out of the blue. Blossoms and balloons. Hearses and strollers. Embedded sonnets everywhere you look.

VANISHING IN PLAIN SIGHT

Faced with the wealth of images in Olivia Parker's exhibit "Vanishing in Plain Sight" (Peabody Essex Museum, Salem, MA, Fall 2019), a record of her husband John's disappearance as he was progressively consumed by Alzheimer's Disease, it's hard to know where to begin. The photographic sequences are eloquent and unforgettable, packing a range of emotion and reflection into each frame. As if it weren't enough to be an extraordinary photographer, Parker is also a pithy and perceptive writer. One way of approaching "Vanishing in Plain Sight," then, is to consider Parker's writings about her own work at various stages of her career.

Long before her husband's diagnosis, Parker's various accounts of her artistic preoccupations, her obsessions and omissions, have a proleptic quality, as if she's somehow anticipating the turn her husband's life, and therefore her art, would take. For example, of her 2008 exhibit "The Eye's Mind," Parker comments that "Most of my books, tablets, and pages have more pictures than words. A few are tribal books that have left their culture because no one can read them anymore; they are visual now."

No one can read them anymore is an apt description of the relation to language of people with advanced Alzheimer's. Such patients have more and more trouble reading, writing, and, eventually, speaking. And what they do write, or what they say, is increasingly illegible or incomprehensible. Eventually, their efforts to communicate almost always stop.

Of the 2015 "Office Supplies" sequence in "Vanishing," Parker notes, "John wanted to be sure he had enough office supplies, but since he forgot what he had bought he was always buying more." The office supplies—paper clips, rubber bands—pertained to the career that had become a thing of the past. "As his illness progressed John would not pick up a pen to write or even scribble."

"Last Writing"—an attempt to recall all the places the Parkers had visited on their honeymoon—seems to show scribbles. One can make out a few words: "the," "reported."

Tribal books that have left their culture because no one can read them anymore; they are visual now. Whether or not Parker was aware of this at the time, the contextual shift from art to dementia and back again is both uncanny and poignant. John, formerly a professional in the field of finance, has left that culture behind—or it has left him. But transformed—could one say "rescued"?—by Parker's photographs, his progression, his succession of new selves, becomes visual, rich with meanings that inhere partly in the gaze of the beholder.

Parker's precise title and notes to each sequence in "Vanishing" don't exactly describe what the images depict. Rather, her words offer a concise guide to the transformative flux occurring—quickly, slowly, subtly, blatantly—in John's condition; and therefore also in Parker's life and art. In her introduction to her 1978 book *Signs of Life*, Parker notes "the protean quality of time and light, the way we perceive the continual flux of reality." Perhaps this alertness to the flux, decades before her husband's diagnosis, helped prepare Parker for the intimate flux visited upon her world by Alzheimer's. "I wonder," she wrote in 1987, "at the vast changes in the human world in an instant of geologic time." Other changes, smaller in scope but equally confounding, awaited Parker.

Parker had long been fascinated by transitions: from ripeness toward decay, from life toward death. Also in *Signs of Life*, she writes: "Objects that are, or have been living things, those at the edge of change, interest me . . . a rose fully formed, but at the edge of decay." Themes of transformation are crucial in mythology and literature as well as art and nature. And turning to Stoic philosophy, a beautiful passage on the changes wrought by decay occurs in the *Meditations* of Marcus Aurelius. Marcus ponders the transformations wrought by time. The entire section applies remarkably well to "Vanishing":

> . . . even the incidental effects of the processes of Nature have their own charm and attraction. Take the baking of bread. The loaf splits open here and there, and those very cracks, in one way a failure of the baker's profession, somehow catch the eye and give particular stimulus to our appetite. Figs likewise burst open at full maturity: and in olives ripened on the tree the very proximity of decay lends a special beauty to the fruit. Similarly the ears of corn nodding down to the ground, the lion's puckered brow, the foam gushing from the boar's mouth, and

much besides—looked at in isolation these things are far from lovely, but their consequence on the processes of Nature enhances them and gives them attraction. So any man with a feeling and deeper insight for the workings of the Whole will find some pleasure in almost every aspect of their disposition . . . he will see a kind of bloom or fresh beauty in an old woman or an old man . . . (*Meditations* 3.2, tr. Martin Hammond).

Marcus's "proximity of decay" anticipates Parker's notion of "edge," a word which occurs twice in the passage from *Signs of Life* quoted above. Of course photographs have edges; the form contains the flux. Living close to dementia, the caregiver is on the edge, or just on edge. Can we say that the person with Alzheimer's is going over the edge? Parker's work in "Vanishing" continually interrogates and revisits such liminalities, such transitions from one state of being to another. John is gradually but visibly transformed by the progress of the disease, but Parker and her art are not immune to the effects of time either. In a way, her work records the changes in the husband, the wife, and the wife's art.

In her 2009 essay "Bugs," Parker writes, "For the last five years, during the renovation of our house, I have been photographing ordinary things that I had never looked at closely." *The last five years* . . . Parker tells us that her husband's diagnosis occurred "five years ago," presumably five years before John's death late in 2016, though the five-year figure might also mean five years before the 2018 completion of "Vanishing." (In fact the diagnosis occurred in 2013, fairly late in the progress of the disease.) Whatever the date, that coupling of "the renovation of our house" with "ordinary things I had never looked at closely" could easily apply to the process of habituation imposed by living next to (or on the edge of) Alzheimer's. "Ordinary things," objects that were always there, take on a life of their own. The binder clips in "Clips" are scattered across the page like stars thickly clustered in a constellation—or like a swarm of insects. But that's only the first image in the office sequence. In the succeeding images, the little black binders, increasingly blurry and unrecognizable, are relegated to the edge of the frame; they're on their way out. The paper tags in the following sequence undergo a more detailed process of deliquescence, ending in a blur of cloudy greyish white. No more labels.

In her introduction to *Weighing the Planets*, Parker writes, "The objects become a new language for me. My intention is not to document objects but to see them in a new context where they take on a presence dependent on the world within each photograph."

Weighing the Planets is dated 1987, many years before John's diagnosis. Again, though, there's that uncannily proleptic resonance: transformed by a new context, objects take on a new meaning. Parker herself might be unable to tell us whether she's aware of these ghostly correspondences across the arc of her career. Art; dementia. New contexts; new worlds. Familiar things transformed.

I'm a writer, not a photographer. When my late husband George Edwards, a composer and professor of music, became ill with early-onset dementia at about the age of sixty, I used words, not images, to make sense of what was happening to him and to me. George died in 2011, aged sixty-eight. *Strange Relation*, my 2011 memoir (published a few months before George's death), turns to poetry, to other literature, and to my experience teaching, as its vehicles. But my book enacts the same struggle to make meaning that's omnipresent in "Vanishing." My memoir's title borrows from Wallace Stevens's line in "Notes Toward a Supreme Fiction": "Life's nonsense pierces us with strange relation." Faced with the nonsense Alzheimer's inexorably imposes, I did precisely what Parker did; I used the means at my disposal, the tools of my art, the tools I'd been using for many decades, tools that felt familiar and comfortable to me—to make sense.

Finding herself in the extreme situation of living alongside someone who is, as Parker aptly puts it, vanishing in plain sight, the caregiver, the wife, the witness needs to bring all her resources to bear. If she's a writer, she'll write. If she's a carpenter, she'll build. If she's a musician, she'll make music. And if she's an artist, she'll make art.

If one is an artist, then the tools are already there. Although they may now be put to new and unexpected uses, the very familiarity of these tools is reassuring. I wrote in the Prologue to *Strange Relation*: "In the case of a situation as elusive and amorphous, but also as powerful and all-consuming, as George's illness, poetry's gift of trope often sheds crucial light on the prevailing gloom." Everything is necessary and nothing is sufficient in such cases. But art is a powerful resource.

Even if one isn't an artist already, the extreme experience of bearing witness to progressive decline may well push one in the direction of creating art. The urge is multiply determined: one wants to document the changes. One wants to take time for oneself doing something pleasurable and interesting. Surely, out of what has depressingly been called a thirty-six-hour day, one hour can be spent *making* something that will survive the bewildering flux of duties, details, and deterioration that are each day's fare. Again, Wallace Stevens supplied me with an invaluable trope: the imagination, he said repeatedly, presses back against the pressure of reality. When the reality you live with or alongside is Alzheimer's, you need to exert a strong counter-pressure.

And there's another motivation as well that spurs us to make art out of this experience. Poems or photographs or paintings or memoirs constitute responses, however incomplete, to the well-meaning and unanswerable questions that come at caregivers. How did you do it? How are you? How is he? When did it begin? How did it begin? Does he recognize you? To such questions, my memoir and Parker's "Vanishing," and many other books and works of art, are, in their respective ways, answers.

It goes without saying that such questions cannot be simply or definitively answered. They can only be answered in moments, in snatches, with tropes, with images. With an elegance that sometimes belies how mournful and disturbing they are, Parker's photographs in "Vanishing" capture in flight the ineluctable nature of change. For "it"—her whole experience in all its parts—was never "like" this or that. It was always in the process of transition, of becoming. The white poodle's soulful face ("Rosie 2016") is gradually overtaken by a blur, and ends in darkness, with the shadowed shape still possible to make out. Parker's own face ("Self Portrait"), blurred to begin with, torques like a Francis Bacon painting until in the last image of the sequence we see only one black-clad shoulder and a smear where the face might be.

Might an abrupt decapitation be kinder? The process of dissolution seems almost more cruel for being so insidious. All the photographs in "Vanishing" both recapitulate and freshly imagine the progressive dismantling effected by Alzheimer's. Each sequence is dated, but we never know how much time elapses between the clearly delineated head of the poodle and the blizzard-y blur that ends the "Rosie" sequence, or, in "Self-Portrait," between the wife's features—already quite obscured—and the final anonymity.

In the note accompanying "Quake," a sequence dated 2017, the year following John's death, Parker asks one of her unanswerable questions, although it's easy to think we know the answer: "Did John feel as though his world was spinning away from the center of his being?" Spinning; torque; blur. The sequence preceding "Quake" is entitled "The Center Cannot Hold." Parker is here quoting W. B. Yeats's poem "The Second

Coming": "Things fall apart, the center cannot hold, / Mere anarchy is loosed upon the world . . ." Yeats's language here slots perfectly into what the experience of Alzheimer's feels like, or rather what the onlooker imagines it may feel like. Parker's notes to "Rage I" have a detached, meteorological tone, until the clinical aspect comes into view: "When rage built rapidly, it focused momentarily, turned inward and then slowly spun and twisted to a conclusion. Occasionally it spun out of control resulting in restraint and a trip to a medical facility." Focused, turned, spun, twisted—one thinks of a tornado.

The way Parker uses this line from Yeats's poem in a rich, if dire, new context, thereby both enhancing her own vision and giving Yeats's line fresh life, is a technique I recognize. As I entered the world of caregiving, I constantly had recourse to texts that hadn't, presumably, been occasioned by observing dementia, any more than "The Second Coming" had been. Cavafy's "Walls," Philip Larkin's "As Bad as a Mile," Hans Christian Andersen's "The Snow Queen"—all sprang into a new focus. I'd known these texts before, often for years, but they came to mean something more and different. Parker was surely familiar with the Yeats poem before John became ill; she was used to paper clips and rubber bands and bugs, doors and windows and lights. But in a way I profoundly recognize, familiar passages or everyday things became freighted with new meaning, illumined by a tragic new light.

In the murk of dementia, Parker's photographs generate just such a light. "Vanishing in Plain Sight" is courageous, meticulous, utterly unsentimental. The emotions of fear, grief, anger, impatience, confusion, frustration, and exhaustion which are the daily fare of caregivers are here relegated to a space beyond the edge (that word again) of the frame.

In one sense, this work isn't about Parker at all. As photographers do, she tactfully remains (except in "Self-Portrait") behind her camera. And yet in another sense, of course this work is about her. Again, there's a correspondence between "Vanishing" and my memoir. In the Introduction to *Strange Relation*, I wrote:

This story . . . lacks both a clear beginning and a final resolution. Within the cloudy confines of those years . . . I tried to keep track; I tried to tell the truth. Nevertheless, it is largely a one-sided truth. Even long before his diagnosis, George had become increasingly uncommunicative. As he lost more and more language and agency, he naturally said and did less and less. . . . Much as I might like to, then, I cannot . . . record his thoughts . . . I don't know what they were; and I think that there were fewer and fewer of them as time went on. So . . . I can't claim to be telling the story from his point of view. For better or worse, this is my story.

And "Vanishing in Plain Sight" is Parker's story. We've seen that this story isn't coterminous with John's diagnosis, institutionalization, or death. Occasionally her notes take us to a time long before the diagnosis, as when she writes of "Disorientation" (dated 2017, after John's death), "For years he devoured novels. I should have suspected something was wrong twelve years ago, when he stopped reading novels." Parker only discovered the notes John began keeping early in his illness after he was no longer living at home. Diagnosis typically happens many years after the onset of the disease. This "20-20 hindsight effect," as I think of it, was true of Parker and John; it was true of me and George.

And her work continues. Parker writes in the front matter of "Vanishing":

> Although I have now included pictures that move through John's death, I am in the process of going back to finish images I had not completed. Also, I am still having ideas for more photographs. I cannot know exactly what he saw in his mind. All I can do is imagine what I think could have been going on and leave it as a starting point to talk about a dreadful disease.

But Parker doesn't do herself justice; she can do much more than imagine. She can and she does present images that imprint themselves indelibly on other people's minds, images that speak eloquently of the ineffable.

Like the project that became "Vanishing" and in a sense remains unfinished, Parker's gifts didn't end with John's illness or death. Mine didn't end with George's illness or death. We continued to do what we were best at doing; and countless other caregivers could say the same. In a situation that defied logic, we tried to use our minds.

I conclude this meditation on Parker's beautiful and painful work with another passage from Marcus Aurelius—a very somber passage at that. Not long before setting forth his thoughts, which have already been cited, on ripeness and decay, Marcus warns us that we may lose our mental faculties long before our physical selves wear out.

... if we live longer, there is no guarantee that our mind will likewise retain that power to comprehend and study the world which contributes to our experience of things divine and human. If dementia sets in, there will be no failure of faculties such as breathing, feeding, imagination, desire: before these go, the earlier extinction is of one's proper use of oneself, one's accurate assessment of the gradations of duty, one's ability to analyze impressions, one's understanding of whether the time has come to leave this life . . . So we must have a sense of urgency, not only for the ever closer approach of death, but also because our comprehension of the world and our ability to pay proper attention will fade before we do.

This passage may seem disheartening. And yet the sense of urgency Marcus mentions is simply a realistic notation of the impulse we all feel as we age, to make use of our faculties while we can. Alzheimer's accelerates the process of mental decay, but no one is exempt from time. And since in general, as Marcus calmly notes, "our comprehension of the world and our ability to pay proper attention will fade before we do," we need to pay attention now. To make art, to tell the truth, as best we can, now. This is what Olivia Parker has done.

THE TREMBLING WEB
AND THE STORAGE FACILITY

THE SUMMER 2016 issue of *Raritan*, Volume XXXVI Number 1, arrived not long ago; and (with a nod to the first sentence of *Howards End*) one may as well begin there. I only irregularly subscribe to *Raritan*, but I'm always happy to read the issues which make their way to me because I have work in them. About my two small poems in this particular issue, more later. When I opened the quarterly, the second thing I turned to was an essay with an arresting title: "All Poems End with the Word Paradise." The author of the essay was Kenneth Gross.

Though I doubt if I'd now recognize him on the street, I knew Kenneth Gross slightly a decade ago and more. Most likely we'd originally crossed paths at a meeting (when I still attended such meetings) of the Association of Literary Scholars and Critics. The last time I saw Kenneth was when we had a drink together at the MLA convention in Philadelphia in late December 2006. I was at the convention only because I'd agreed to be on a panel devoted to sound effects in the poetry of Wallace Stevens.

It had been a strange, crowded afternoon. Fresh off the train from New York, I'd had lunch near the University of Pennsylvania Medical School with Dr. John Trojanowski, an expert in fronto-temporal dementia whom I'd encountered back in September at a conference in San Francisco devoted to that murky non-Alzheimer's dementia. As a reluctant recruit to the world of FTD in my capacity as a caregiver, I'd been happy to talk to anyone from whom I thought I might learn something. And indeed, in January 2007, I was to take the train to Philly again, this time with my husband, in order to consult Trojanowski's colleague Murray Grossman, whom I had also met at the FTD conference and who was an expert in the disease.

Today—December 30, 2006—en route from lunch to the hotel where the panel would take place, I took off one figurative hat and put on another: I emerged from the taxi no longer a harried spousal caregiver but rather a poet and an academic. After the Stevens panel, I went out to dinner with a fellow panelist, Tom Cable, a scholar from Texas whom I'd known for years. With Tom, I headed back to the neighborhood of the University of Pennsylvania, where we ate at the White Dog Café, a beloved haunt of my son's when he was a student at Swarthmore. After dinner, it was back to the MLA hotel, where Tom had some academic function to attend and where I was to meet Kenneth Gross for a drink. I remember almost nothing of my conversation with Ken. It had been a long day. What I do remember is going back to my hotel room after our drink, turning on the TV, and learning that Saddam Hussein had been hanged.

What a concatenation of memories, then, strung itself together when I read Ken's name in *Raritan*! The individual links in the chain are surprisingly vivid, but put them together and the result is as jumbled as a dream. As one gets older, dreams and memories become increasingly indistinguishable anyway. The occasions mashed together or juxtaposed; the different roles I was playing; the varied fields of knowledge, each with its distinct vocabulary and bibliography, each impinging on my life from a different direction, each with its own kind of urgency: had this congeries been in abeyance for the decade that had elapsed from 2006 to 2016? I do remember that beneath the patchy surface of the events of that December day was the constant pulse of anxiety, also dreamlike but all too real: who was looking after my husband at home? No doubt one of the aides I'd recently begun hiring from an agency called Home Instead. "Instead" of what? That was never specified—it didn't need to be. A year later, in January 2008, at the end of my rope, I'd opt for that instead.

December 2006 marked the end of a year spent busily acquiring knowledge, or at least names. As if words could make a difference, I'd been wanting since early 2005 to learn a precise name for my husband's diagnosis. That search was what had taken me to San Francisco in September 2006. For the first time in twenty-five years, I'd skipped the first week of classes at Rutgers and gotten on a plane. I remember sitting in a bar on the top floor of the hotel where the dementia conference was being held. Watching the fog roll in from the bay, I chatted with two California men whose wives suffered from the same murky malady as my husband. I learned a lot at that conference, but even there, the focus gradually and inexorably shifted from the elusive condition or conditions called FTD to the more mundane challenges of how to cope from day to day. Indeed, only when George's brain was autopsied, in the fall of 2011, was it possible to ascertain that he had after all been suffering not from FTD but from Alzheimer's, albeit an "abnormal presentation." And it no longer mattered. In the absence of anything resembling a cure, it had never mattered.

As if words could make a difference. But for me they always have made all the difference in the world—that is, in one of the worlds that brought me to Philadelphia on the next to last day of 2006. That realm is the place where the practical problems of day to day living, the flurry and babble of scientific nomenclature and the euphemisms of the caregiving world, fall away, and where what prevails is a strangely tranquil landscape which both is and is not personal and timely. It is the realm which Gross's *Raritan* essay so eloquently evokes and celebrates. It is the realm of poetry.

The ostensible subject of Gross's essay is Coleridge's *Kubla Khan,* a poem that does indeed end with the word "paradise." But as Gross hyperbolically suggests midway through his essay (and the hyperbole is echoed in his title), there is a sense in which all poems are one, so that all poems end with this word. He writes:

> I have a bad habit of finding in any poem that really absorbs me, if only for a moment, the archetype of all other poems, a kind of insistent double or shadow of them. It is as if that one poem were simultaneously the only poem and all poems.

Before settling down to discuss *Kubla Khan,* Gross describes reading a plethora of poems during what sounds like a sabbatical leave, when he is "free for a season to wander . . . taking up books by impulse and whim rather than a fixed plan." He's in search of "something very basic . . . call it poetry's way of knowing." But he finds himself becalmed in the midst of "too many poems, and too many books about poems," until his partner Liza challenges him to name the one poem he can't do without—the "poem of many, one," as Coleridge's friend Wordsworth in his *Immortality Ode* memorably refers to a tree which is, in Gross's words, simultaneously the only tree and all trees. That poem turns out to be *Kubla Khan.*

Given the bad habit Gross confesses to of finding in any absorbing poem the archetype of other poems, his essay inevitably opens out from

Kubla Khan to talk about how all poems behave, so that, as he puts it, "a single lyric seems to offer an idiosyncratic diagram of a larger, still unknown landscape." Thus for Gross in this mood, all poems are composed after having fallen asleep over a book; all poems are pleasure domes under threat; somewhere in all poems there is an "oh"; all poems fix their design in water; and so on.

And though my own tendency, especially when I'm teaching, is not to equate all poems to all other poems but on the contrary to distinguish how differently different poems set about expressing what they have to express, doing the work they do, nevertheless I found Gross's "bad habit" intriguing and contagious. I especially liked the notion that all poems are written after falling asleep over a book. (One thinks, for example, of the "mysterious dream" in *Il Penseroso*, waving "at his wings in airy stream . . .") A lot of prose gets written that way too—not quite literally after falling asleep, but after opening a book and letting it lead you where you seem to want or need to go. After all, I chanced to see Gross's essay only because it happened to be in the same issue of *Raritan* as my poems. Fortuitous, contingent—but then such contingency is of the essence of intertextuality, to give a cumbersome and needlessly abstract name to the being or the dynamic also known as the Library Angel. I encountered this term in Robert Moss's book *The Three 'Only' Things: Tapping the Power of Dreams, Coincidence and Imagination*. When we approach books with enough fervor, Moss writes, "the benign entity that Arthur Koestler called the Library Angel becomes more and more active, ensuring that the book we need appears, or falls open at the right page, just when we need it." Just where Koestler says this Moss doesn't reveal. No doubt some Library Angel knows.

As I paged through *Raritan*, what next caught my eye was a long, ambitious poem by Gabriel Levin, a name that sounded familiar. Levin (my exact contemporary, born in 1948) turned out to be the son of the novelist Meyer Levin, whose 1956 novel *Compulsion*, about the Leopold and Loeb case, I suddenly remembered having gulped down a few years after it first appeared. I also remembered that my late husband's father had gone to the same Chicago high school that Leopold and/or Loeb had attended—a connection as random as the fact that I'd last seen Ken Gross on the same day that Saddam Hussein was executed. In the spider web of contingency, literature and life nudge up against one another, the web trembles, and we use one kind of experience to anchor another one.

"Experience," writes Henry James in *The Art of Fiction*, "is never limited, and it is never complete; it is an immense sensibility, a kind of huge spider-web of the finest silken threads suspended in the chamber of consciousness, and catching every air-borne particle in its tissue."

I understood right away that Levin's poem, appropriately entitled "What Drew Me On," was complex and accomplished, but I couldn't easily or quickly wrap my mind around the four very different sections of the poem, some themselves subdivided.

What I did absorb—what drew me on—was Levin's "By Way of a Preface," a prose paragraph which explains that his inspiration for the poem was the work of Tel Aviv artist Tamara Rikman. At its very inception, then, Levin's poem could be described as the result of a collaboration—a meeting of artistic minds as unexpected as it was fruitful. Here, perhaps, the Library Angel was at work in the realm of visual art as well.

Levin was inspired by Rikman's art; but as he recounts how he conceived his poem, its chief sources seem to have been literary. He writes:

> The skeleton of a poem appeared to be taking shape: a twelfth-century Hebrew poem had come to mind in which the poet contemplates the stars through the tattered holes of his overcoat, which in turn led me to Plato's magnificent "Vision of Er" at the end of the *Republic*.

The antecedent of that second "which" could be either the overcoat or the Hebrew poem—no matter. All poems, Gross reminds us even if he calls the perception a bad habit, are types of other poems. Follow the web of texts (both words that refer to weaving), and you'll stumble onto unexpected turnings and connections. A thread can guide you deeper into the labyrinth, or through it. "I just follow the thread," says Curdie's mother in *The Princess and the Goblin*. Wife and mother of miners, Mrs. Peterson is adept at untangling the balls of thread (the clues, in the original sense of the word) her husband and son use to guide them through the darkness of the mine.

I put down *Raritan*, got out of bed, padded down the long hall to the living room, and pulled Edith Hamilton and Huntington Cairns's edition of the *Collected Dialogues of Plato* off the shelf. Back in bed, I found the Vision of Er.

Had I really never read this astonishing—what to call it? Passage is an inadequate word. Interlude? Fantasia? Better just settle on myth.

Texts are and are not as easy to forget as the person with whom one shared a drink at a conference a decade ago. They go in and out of focus;

but texts are more permanent than people are, and much more patient. They wait until the Library Angel taps you on the shoulder.

Reading along in Er, I was stopped by a word:

And a man must take with him to the house of death an adamantine faith in this, that even there he may be undazzled by riches and similar trumpery . . .

(*Republic* 619a, tr. Paul Shorey)

I'd always liked "trump" as a verb, as in my oft-repeated dictum to students that in poetry the how trumps the what. But I'd recently begun to feel that I could no longer use this bumptiously vigorous monosyllable with impunity. It grated, it thumped, it echoed. And now here was another splendid word that had come to smell fishy: trumpery. Isn't this a word that Caliban uses, disgusted that Stephano and Trinculo are so attracted, near the end of *The Tempest*, by the sparkly clothes hanging on the line? I had to check, and I padded down the hall again. It turned out to be Prospero who uses the word "trumpery" when he's giving instructions to Ariel: "The trumpery in my house, go bring it hither / For stale to catch these thieves" (IV.i.186–7). Later in the same scene, though, Caliban calls the gaudy clothing "trash" and "luggage." So my memory hadn't been too far off.

I checked to see what other translators of *The Republic* had made of what Shorey calls trumpery. Cornford has "wealth and such-like evils"; Grube has "wealth and similar evils"; Bloom has "wealth and such evils"; Reeve has "wealth and other such evils." "Trumpery" was, I had to admit, more vigorous and memorable than any of these other versions.

By way of his reference to the Vision of Er, Gabriel Levin had taken me on a circuitous route and, via the vagaries of translation, to an unexpected if temporary dead end. Here was a word I was very tired of hearing and reading staring me in the face. Not Levin's fault; certainly not Plato's; not even Paul Shorey's. Blame the Library Angel.

But as that angel and every reader knows, words always lead on to other words. If the word "trumpery" presented a nasty little cul de sac, the Vision of Er as a whole opened a vast territory of imagination. Kenneth Gross writes, as I've already quoted, that "A single lyric seems to offer an idiosyncratic diagram of a larger, still unknown landscape"— and what is Er's vision if not an expansive and transcendent unknown landscape? If the proper name of a dreadful man brings one up short, then all the more reason to remember that there is a world elsewhere, and that that world is enormous.

Earlier in the Vision of Er, we are told that

> the souls clean and pure . . . appeared to have come as it were from a long journey and gladly departed to the meadow and encamped there as at a festival, and acquaintances greeted one another, and those which came from the earth questioned the others about conditions up yonder, and those from heaven asked how it fared with those others (614e).

Reading this, I realized that Robert Frost's magnificent (and almost never anthologized) early poem "The Trial by Existence" is rich with Platonic echoes, with its "light forever . . . morning light" and its hills "verdured pasture-wise" and its "slant spirits trooping by / In streams and cross- and counter-streams." A more obvious echo of the Er passage in "The Trial by Existence" can be found in the beautiful couplet "The light of heaven falls whole and white / And is not shattered into dyes," where we can, in turn, surely hear Shelley's *Adonais*. Frost had probably read Plato; he had certainly read Shelley, who had certainly read Plato.

> The One remains, the many change and pass;
> Heaven's light forever shines, Earth's shadows fly;
> Life, like a dome of many-coloured glass,
> Stains the white radiance of eternity . . .

And Shelley's dome takes us back to *Kubla Khan*, written in 1797, when Shelley was five years old. The light (white in Shelley and Frost); the dome (shared by Coleridge and Shelley); the paradisiacal sense shared by all these poems—all such elements probably ultimately derive from Plato. But since poems comprise an infinitely spacious realm, the derivation allows for some unexpected twists and turns in the mind and memory of each reader. Here is Gross on the single word "dome" in *Kubla Khan*:

> The word "dome" . . . seemed to name not just a high, spherical roof but a whole realm, a home of sorts (though I didn't know the word's source in the Latin *domus*). And how could you decree a "dome"? The august warrior-emperor Kubla decreeing that place of pleasure reminded me a little of the sick child who shapes a world with toys and blankets in Robert Louis Stevenson's "The Land of Counterpane," a poem I also

read early, though I didn't really know what a counterpane was, and imagined that it had something to do with pain.

Allusion, intertextuality, echo; the gently meandering or crazily zigzagging path (or the patchwork counterpane) from one passage to another: in this realm, a single word (and not only "trumpery") can do a remarkable amount of work. As one of my students wrote in a line I later appropriated for a cento, "It's an impossibility to map the mind." Still, from large motions of the mind ("large-mannered motions of [Jove's] mythy mind," as Wallace Stevens puts it in *Notes Toward a Supreme Fiction*), there's a trail for us to follow, as if we were Hansel and Gretel following breadcrumbs. Kenneth Gross, in the same issue of *Raritan* as my poems, took me to Levin. Levin took me to Er, which led me through heavenly spaces back to *Kubla Khan* and hence back to Gross.

The breadcrumb Gross ends with is the word "milk," as in "drunk the milk of Paradise," the magical final line of *Kubla Khan*. Perhaps it is that mention of milk, Gross writes, that puts him in mind of James Merrill's "Lost in Translation," a poem that as Gross notes "ends with a reverie on missing puzzle pieces, lost notes, lost words and books, lost names, buried truths, things lost in translation, and also things revived, built in air"—and isn't that pleasure dome also built in air? Merrill's poem ends with waste miraculously turning "to shade and fiber, milk and memory."

That milk, Gross doesn't mention, is coconut milk, for surely the palm in question is a coconut palm. But the lost poem he (Gross) does mention is Rilke's translation into German of Valéry's poem *Palme*. Merrill writes in "Lost in Translation" that he has been unable to locate a copy of the Rilke translation in Athens (those were the days before the internet). Merrill's epigraph, though, is taken from his memory (memories having been stronger in the pre-internet era) of Rilke's translation of four superb lines from *Palme*. In Valéry's French, they read:

> Ces jours qui te semblent vides
> Et perdus pour l'univers
> Ont des racines avides
> Qui travaillent les déserts.

Or in Merrill's own translation, since he was himself to translate *Palme*:

> These days which, like yourself,
> Seem empty and effaced,

Have avid roots which delve
To work deep in the waste.

I was pleased to notice recently that the rich phrase "to work deep in the waste" was used by a reviewer writing in the *Bellevue Literary Review* on two books of poetry about trauma. In recycling their suffering into art, the reviewer said, referencing Merrill but probably not thinking about Valéry or a palm in the desert, the poets had, she observed, worked deep in the waste. The reviewer had herself repurposed Merrill's transformation of Valéry's line.

"Milk and memory" at the end of "Lost in Translation": does that phrase (in addition to summoning Valéry's coconut palm) echo Coleridge's "milk of paradise"? Very possibly. Or it could be an unconscious echo—they happen all the time.

What about the two poems of mine that had brought *Raritan* into the house in the first place? One, "Embarkation," was wholly occasioned—really, wholly inspired—by my having seen Jodorowsky's film *The Dance of Reality*. Why didn't I say as much in an epigraph? Was I trying to make my poem either more accessible or more mysterious than it would have been with a helpful note? Why, in other words, didn't I write a little version of something like Gabriel Levin's "By Way of a Preface"? Why indeed? My other *Raritan* poem, "Route 2B," has more local roots than "Embarkation"; there really is a Route 2B near the house in Vermont where we spend summers. Yet "Route 2B" also draws upon dream material—and besides, isn't 2B inevitably a reference, however involuntary, to *Hamlet*? Almost any given word in *Hamlet* has been used as a rich source of allusion. Ian McEwan's new novel, a spinoff of *Hamlet*, is entitled *Nutshell*, a pithy one-word allusion. "Oh god," says the Prince to Rosencrantz and Guildenstern, "I could be bounded in a nutshell and count myself a king of infinite space, were it not that I have bad dreams." A single word or a pair of words—"nutshell," "2B"—opens the door to a literary realm, a kingdom of the imagination, one more tendril of the immense web.

In addition to literary echoes, and on what might seem a more practical plane, "Route 2B" evinces a not-so-veiled preoccupation with what Marie Kondo, in her recent global best-seller about de-cluttering, rather euphemistically (or is that just her translator?) calls "tidying up": I write "Clear out / the attic, shed, storage facility." The infinite space, the avid roots, the pleasure dome, the paradise—they are hard to find, they're invisible, they're interior. They lie in wait in allusions, memories, and

PIECE BY PIECE

echoes—echoes both intentional and inadvertent. The best storage facility for these unexpected riches, these patient dividends of reading and dreaming, is the same realm, or part of the same realm, as James's huge spider-web—a place where things may be captured but nothing is necessarily lost. That place is poetry.

III

Remembering the Future

AN INTERVIEW WITH RACHEL HADAS *by* JESSICA GREENBAUM

JG Rachel, I want to let readers know we first met in 1986 when you chose me for *The Nation*'s Discovery Prize. So I was pretty well disposed towards you from the start! In the three-plus decades since then you have modeled—aside from friendship—scholarship and teaching, good citizenship in the literary community, and a determined focus for your own work (sometimes with personal tragedy roaring in your ear). Your borderless range, from poetry to classicism, to translation, to drama, to memoir, to the non-fiction of your last collection, *Talking to the Dead*, describes a woman of letters. As the author of twenty-one books, can you describe where you began? At this turn in life can you speak a bit about your personal vision of your path as a writer? What encouragements from whom, what books you read, what responses sparked a full-on fire?

RH My childhood was lucky, and the bookworm doesn't fall far from the tree. I was a poet pretty much from the start; my sister, who was alphabetizing our parents' books on the shelves as a tot, became an editor. We were both read to from a very early age; and my mother, who always knew what book to give to which child (and not only to her own two children) and when, gave me some wonderful poetry anthologies when I was ten or so: John Hollander and Harold Bloom's *The Wind and the Rain* and Louis Untermeyer's *The Magic Circle*. I inhaled those books, but the poems I imitated were all lyric—not the narrative poems Untermeyer generously provides. I never had the impulse to write a story, though I loved reading stories. I was drawn to the way poetry connects the outer and the inner world, how it's almost always about feelings but rarely *only* about feelings; how excellent poems can be, and often are, very short; how poetry almost begs to be, is engineered to be, memorized. The sound of the words, the patterns they make! The *how* more than the *what*.

My father died when I was seventeen, and poetry became for me then, and has remained, a friend, a companion, an outlet, a guide. James Merrill refers to the life raft of language; Toni Bernhard, a wise and practical Buddhist writer, calls the breath in meditation a kind of support, a banister, which one can hold on or let go of or return to. This has always been true for me of poetry—as a kind of dependable support, a guiding presence or principle—even if I didn't always understand at a given time just how true. When I was living in Greece and pretty much in Greek in my early twenties; and later, when my son was born, when my mother died, when my late husband was ill and incommunicado for years, and most recently when I fell head over heels in love at the age of sixty-four: poetry was reliably there, to read and remember and, sooner or later, to write.

And poetry has been for me a reliable presence in the classroom, too, whether or not it's been on the syllabus, and whether that classroom has been on the Rutgers-Newark campus or in a basement room on West 20th Street in the Gay Men's Health Crisis building, or at a summer institute for Advanced Placement English teachers in St. Johnsbury, Vermont, or in a big hot lecture hall, fan blowing papers off the table, at Kwame Nkrumah University of Science and Technology in Kumasi, Ghana. Poetry is part of my tool kit as a teacher.

JG Your poem in *The Golden Road*, "First Persons," ends: "I am leaning toward transparency. / I hope to end as echo of a word," but I also see that volume as the one that leaned toward an emotional transparency, a greater candor about your personal journey. And by the time we read *Questions in the Vestibule*, the poems invite us into the speaker's present more wholly still. Were you aware of this evolution? Has the lyric poem itself evolved for you as well?

RH I guess evolution isn't all that intentional a process, is it? My use of language has (I hope) gotten leaner and meaner. I want to be understood; I don't want to bore or confuse. And yet what occasions poems for me, what I want them to do for me or for others, probably hasn't changed all that much. James Merrill, as I said a minute ago, beautifully refers in *The Changing Light at Sandover* to "the life-raft of language." So yes, poems come out of my life—probably more clearly now than before, as you've suggested. They spring from my losses and loves, my reading and teaching, my travel and dreams, and they lift and float me, raft-like, through all these experiences of living. Poems are remarkably flexible instruments or artifacts or processes, whether we conceive of them as nouns or verbs. And they accommodate, they flourish in, conditions of change, sometimes radical change, sometimes gradual, sometimes sudden.

JG Can you describe what you are asking of your poems? What do you want them to do for you on the page?

RH I'd rephrase this, with your permission: what did my poems used to do? What do they do now?

My poems were elegiac from the start. Or rather, they were imitative before that (Cummings, Keats, Eliot, Shakespeare, Housman . . .), but jump-started into elegy by my father's death. "Death is the mother of beauty," Stevens reminds us. My muse was elegiac and self-involved—maybe she was just adolescent. In college, I wrote love poems, of course, and poems about seasons. The Latin love elegies I was studying showed me that one doesn't need to reinvent the wheel of poetry; that other love poems were always already there. Catullus translates Sappho. And so on.

And then, when I lived in Greece in my early twenties: the beauty of Samos gave rise to landscape poems, too many adjectives, trying to reflect that beauty but also full of sadness and longing. I'd say these early poems were trying to capture or recapture, in addition to the landscape and culture, something fleeting—both to mourn/celebrate it and just to record it, to get it down on paper. My father's death, coming into adulthood—I was trying to process all that somehow. Poems have always functioned for me both as notations for memory and as a space to test out feelings.

Many decades passed, but I'd say my poems now acknowledge transience rather than push against it. They still take pictures of moments, capture fleeting images from dreams, but (I dearly hope) less heavily, portentously. Earlier you quoted from my poem "First Persons": "I am leaning toward transparency." I think I was groping toward the notion that my poems had had too much about me me me me. My favorite lines from that poem come earlier in it: "Even as the shadows of experience lengthen, / one's core seems less substantial." I wrote that poem nearly a decade ago, and it seems truer to me now than I understood at the time. Poems have that magical ability to remember the future.

So looking at old poems now can bring back a landscape, a conversation, a dream, a walk, a class I was teaching, a book I was reading. Someone called me (it was probably a left-handed compliment if it was a compliment at all) a wet-paint poet. I don't seem to think very hard about my best work; when it's going well, it goes pretty fast, even if fast means half a dozen drafts or more. I don't hunt for material or obsess about form. These decisions make themselves at some subliminal level. Sometimes a phrase someone uses in conversation, or a sentence I've read, gets stirred into the mix.

JG "Poems have the magic ability to remember the future"! What a terrific truth. Speaking of a different future, your path in your work and publishing your work, when have you felt you had to chart your own course—whether with the publishing world, or the expectations of those around you, or the status quo in any way?

RH A merciful oblivion seems to cloud and soften my varied and not always easy experiences of getting my work published. I've never had one faithful publisher, but I've been fairly fortunate: Wesleyan, Princeton, now Northwestern University Press; Paul Dry . . . My books do not particularly sell, and my poetry is pretty personal, so I sometimes remember to be surprised and delighted that it's as well published as it is. Like many poets I know, perhaps especially those of, ahem, a certain age, I'm not gifted at PR, not immersed in social media. I don't want to go on book tours. So—again—I feel fortunate when someone knocks at the door. That said, it's easier to publish poems in magazines than to publish a book.

As my trail of past books gets longer, I do feel more confident making my own decisions about the next book. At present, I'm happy to be working with the folks at Measure Press on my next book or two or three. When I thought about it a year ago, it seemed clear to me that slim or slimmish volumes were the way to go, not a door-stopper of a Collected or even Selected, though possibly that's in my future. So *Poems for Camilla* will be published in Fall 2018, and, probably, a collection called *Love and Dread* perhaps a year after that. The Camilla poems I wrote between February and July 2017. I was on sabbatical that spring; our granddaughter Camilla was born that January, a few days before Trump was inaugurated. And (being on sabbatical and having the time), I was going through the *Aeneid*, and seeing the darkness and dread of the second half of the epic in a way that had escaped me before and that was reflected in the political—the national—the global arena.

JG I'm so glad you brought up the political epidemic our country is enduring right now, because I wanted to ask you to talk a bit about how the goings on in the world press some poems into being, and shape response for you as a poet and teacher. I'm thinking specifically of *Unending Dialogue*, the anthology you edited from a workshop you ran at the Gay Men's Health Crisis during the peak of the AIDS plague.

RH Well, thinking back, the project of the anthology arose very naturally, intuitively, maybe organically, from the amazing poems that were coming into the workshop at GMHC every week. I can't remember quite how or when I thought of combining the best of them into an anthology. I do remember one wintry Sunday afternoon lying on my stomach on the living room floor of my mother's apartment (she was in the hospital; I was there to feed her cats) shuffling through poems. I love that process of sifting and arranging, whether it's an anthology, a book of one's own, whatever. Editing a much more recent anthology for CavanKerry Press, *The Waiting Room Reader II*, was also a lot of fun.

I can't remember much about the process of finding a publisher. It was a long time ago. But I'm so glad *Unending Dialogue* is out in the world. David Groff used some poems from *Unending Dialogue* in his fine collection of work by poets who had died of AIDS, *Persistent Voices*, which came out in 2009. For years after *Unending Dialogue* was published, I used to hear from composers wanting to set some of those poems; I had become a de facto literary executor for Charles and Tony and James and the rest.

To confront a fear makes you feel less afraid. Trump has been, god help us, a boon to poetry; at least one anthology *Resistance, Rebellion, Life*, edited by Amit Majmudar, appeared last year, and there will be others. My students, reading Euripides's *Iphigenia in Aulis* at the time of the 2016 election, pounced on some of the imagery and ideas; I hardly had to move a muscle.

JG Let's go back a step, to your mention of *The Waiting Room Reader* (2013). The anthology holds a rich chorus of voices that can accompany us in that freighted area, the medical waiting room. Can you describe what lets you know a manuscript is a whole book?

RH The process of making an executive (or arbitrary?) decision, whether about an individual poem or an entire manuscript, gets simpler as the time for waffling gets shorter. Less is more. Not that books or poems have to be vanishingly short—but I seem to have less patience for filler, for wordiness. I want my individual poems to be better, and for the collections to consist of strong poems. I'm getting better at, or seem to have developed more of a feeling for, titles and the order of poems too, but I don't believe books of poems have to be read in order. Young poets obsess about the placement of each poem in their first book, and I understand that, but I'm not sure how much it matters in the end.

I like to advise students to wring the extra moisture, squeeze the flab, out of poems as if they're wringing out a wet washcloth. A surprising amount of fluid emerges if you press hard. You mention, Jess, "emotional transparency" and "greater candor" in my recent book *Questions in the Vestibule* (2016), and I am grateful for those words and do hope they are true. But possibly the clarity or candor or transparency also derive from a greater verbal economy. This principle of economy should work for an entire book as well as the individual poem. Frost said somewhere "I'd like to lodge a few poems where they're hard to get rid of." In very few collections, finally, does every poem feel necessary, crucial; but that kind of urgency is nevertheless what one should go for. My earlier books often contain too many poems that are too long. One tries to learn.

JG Does teaching have a part to play in your synthesis of literature within your own work?

RH In a word, YES! And it's interesting you should ask, Jess, because I've been thinking and writing a lot about teaching in the past few years— often, admittedly, in prose—for example, the "curated"—as you nicely put it to me once—faux round table discussion "Reading, Writing, Teaching, Time" in *Talking to the Dead*. "Talking to My Father," also in *Talking to the Dead*, dips into some of my father's published and unpublished writings on the subject of teaching.

Right now I'm working on a brief essay about teaching, inspired by having recently sent off to my archive a bulging box of paperwork from ten years' worth of visits to a Rutgers colleague's freshman English classes. One of my ideas in this little piece is that it's very hard to capture on paper what transpires in the classroom. In fact I do have a number of poems about teaching written since 1981, when I began my very happy teaching career at Rutgers-Newark—not a huge number, but it's a steady trickle. And very often these poems triangulate: the students/me/a text. So yes, some kind of synthesis takes place. I'd point to (in no particular order) "Pomegranate Variations" in *Indelible* (2001); "Conklin 455" and "Simile, Analogy, Mimesis," from *The River of Forgetfulness* (2006); and a little burst of such poems from early on in my teaching life, "Teaching Emily Dickinson," "Teaching the Iliad," "Philoctetes," and "Teacher Between Terms," all from *Pass It On* (1989). There are also the poems from my time running the poetry workshop you mentioned at GMHC between 1989 and 1993, which tend to be named (as is "Conklin 455") after the room where the teaching took place: "Lower Level EE," for example. But then I realize that "Coleman 1443" was not a classroom but a hospital room where I was visiting a dying student. Text, student, teacher, and death: beyond triangulation. I feel that classrooms are sacred spaces, and it's strange and dreadful to be thinking, in the context of the latest school shooting, about locked doors, added exits, and so on. I wonder what my father (1900–1966) would have said.

There's more to say on this subject, clearly. I'll just add for now that though many poets teach and many English teachers are poets, not too much about teaching seems to make its way into many poems, which is too bad. But I may well be wrong, or out of date, on this. Anyway, the answer to your question is, again, you bet! I may put together a slim volume of poems about teaching.

JG Can you talk about the video projects you are working on with your husband, the artist Shalom Gorewitz? What dimensions does it add to those you know so well? Are there other experiments in form and/or content you are engaged with right now in your work?

RH My husband Shalom and I started collaborating almost as soon as we became a couple in the spring of 2013—I was sick, we consulted a diviner, did a ceremony involving the ocean, he videoed it with the intention of working on the video while I was in the hospital for surgery, which all happened as planned. Seeing an early version of the video inspired a poem which I then revised and which went into a later version—two overlapping sensibilities, merging, not interrupting each other but sometimes taking turns, sometimes layered over each other. It's been an amazing artistic ride the past few years as we each go on separately doing the work we have each been doing for many decades, but also working together in sometimes unexpected and experimental and delicious ways. You can go to www.rachelandshalomshow.com to see more.

Shalom has brought color into my life in many different ways, and has also, in ways that are hard to specify, but have been clear to me from the start, encouraged me to let silence speak more—in my poems, in daily living.

An Interview with Rachel Hadas

Beyond my work with Shalom, collaboration has been an important strand in what I do poetically, and it's always fun. Translating is, of course, a form of talking with the dead, a form of allowing the living and the dead to converse. I've enjoyed translating since I was an undergraduate tackling Tibullus. My 1994 book *Other Worlds Than This* (Rutgers University Press) includes translations from Latin, French, and Modern Greek. My translation of Euripides' romance *Helen* (University of Pennsylvania Press, 1997) and of his two Iphigenia plays (published in 2018 by Northwestern University Press) were a lot of fun to do (Shalom calls translation my Sudoku) and would, I hope, have tickled my father Moses Hadas, a classicist who also loved and translated Euripides.

Only a few weeks ago, I learned that John Ashbery, when he was first living in New York, took and loved a course in Greek drama with Moses at Columbia in 1950. Who knew? Neither of them ever mentioned this coincidence to me—but then why should they? It's not as if Moses knew who Ashbery was going to become.

Another form of collaboration, if that's what it is, transpires when I snatch a phrase out of the air on the wing, scoop it out of a conversation and plant it in a poem. The other day over coffee a friend uttered the wonderful (and perfectly iambic) clause "However cool he may have thought he was . . ." and I spun two poems from that unfinished thought, one a villanelle. Too new to know if it's any good.

Also, it's become my practice, when I teach a poetry workshop, to write a cento using lines lifted from my students' work—there's one of those, entitled simply "Cento," in *Questions in the Vestibule*. The older I get, the more I feel that poetry is both a very private expression and a shared project. Like language—you couldn't do it without help; someone was there before you. But also, no one else can write what you write.

JG Private and shared—it's so helpful to remember this, how the solo endeavor has our worlds outside our door, and the door is ajar. Rachel, what poets might you note as being guides, inspirations, companions over the years?

RH This is surprisingly hard for me to answer, and the answer has to be that poets might not have been the most crucial guides. The simplest answer is, my parents, whose profound literacy and work ethics I internalized or inherited. I'll loop back to that in a moment. In college, I enjoyed studying poetry with Robert Fitzgerald, whose light quicksilver touch was graceful and on point and never wounding—the idea of studying with Lowell scared me. My mentor in graduate school, Edmund Keeley, who has just turned ninety, is a cherished friend now, but I didn't know him terribly well when I was his student. My friendship with James Merrill, whom I met in Athens in 1969 and knew well until his death in 1995, perhaps spoiled me for the poets I met later—they tended to be much more self-important than Jimmy, much less funny, and less talented. When Jimmy and I were neighbors in Athens around 1974, he actually did give me a few lessons, which I'll never forget. Since then, I have been fortunate to know so many wonderful writers over the years. You! Molly Peacock! Phillis Levin! Marilyn Hacker! Lydia Davis (not principally a poet but a terrific writer and a very old friend)! Alicia Stallings! Judith Baumel! Gardner McFall! The list could go on. Not that all the writers I know and admire are women. But I do have special and increasing admiration for the women who teach, write, cook dinner, stay in touch with friends, sometimes raise a child or two or more . . . how we do it, or have done it, we don't know, but we do. As I get older, I am warmed by the friendship of younger poets . . . examples abound, but I think of Rowan Ricardo Phillips, for example, or Keith O'Shaughnessy, or Moira Egan, or Adrianne Kalfopoulou, or Jennifer Franklin. Some of these people were my students, but not all. All are diligent, scrupulous, and talented artists who stick at their work through all kinds of challenges and discouragements, with energy and zest and gallantry. But I haven't been in the habit (with few and awkward exceptions) of showing my poems to people to get critiques. The muse is, to quote a title of Stevens's, an interior paramour. I learn best from what I've read, even if over the years I probably also forget a great deal of it. And to return to my father and mother: my little memoir of my mother that was recently published in *Writers and Their Mothers*, edited by Dale Salwak (Palgrave MacMillan), ends by quoting a passage from the Roman historian Tacitus that my mother sent me after my father's death. Yes, she was a Latin teacher; but how many mothers would think to console their teenage daughters this way? This excerpt isn't from Tacitus's history but from a eulogy for his father-in-law, and although it isn't precisely about poetry, reading, or writing, it goes to the heart of your question about guides, inspirations, companions. . . . "The human face," writes Tacitus, "like that face itself, is feeble and perishable, whereas the essence of the soul is eternal, never to be caught and expressed by the material and skill of a stranger, but only by you in your own living."

IV

Translations and Transitions

TAKES ON ARCADIA

Stephen Minta, *On a Voiceless Shore: Byron in Greece* (Henry Holt, 1998)
David Solway, *The Anatomy of Arcadia* (Véhicule Press, 1992)
Patricia Storace, *Dinner with Persephone* (Pantheon, 1996)

ALL THE BOOKS I consider here were published in the 1990s. Hence they were written well before the refugee crisis of the twenty-first century put Greece on the front pages. They were also written before the work of A. E. Stallings and Mary Norris, to name only two writers, put Greek language and culture in the spotlight. On the other hand, countless earlier writers, from Greece as well as many other countries, have also been enchanted and obsessed by both the idea and the particularities of Greece—Byron, Cavafy, Seferis, Patrick Leigh Fermor, Henry Miller, and James Merrill, to name only a few. Accordingly, to engage with the language and landscape, the culture and history of Greece is also to be in touch with other writers who have been there. In a recent interview, A. E. Stallings, a poet who has lived in Greece since 1999 and who has translated Hesiod's *Works and Days*, the mock-epic *The Battle Between the Frogs and the Mice*, and portions of the Cretan Renaissance epic *Erotokritos*, observes that living in Greece, she experiences "a feeling of living diachronically, with various pasts and presents and futures rubbing shoulders."

Stephen Minta's, David Solway's, and Patricia Storace's books are each now more than twenty years old. They're not obsolete, far from it; rather, one can think of them as having joined the swelling chorus of voices talking about what it is too simple to call a place and too abstract to call an idea. Each of these canny and elegantly written books adds a layer to the endlessly palimpsestic text that is Greece.

"The ancient remains and the contemporary sorrow," wrote George Seferis, one of the greatest of modern Greek poets, capturing the poignant contrasts that await the traveler to Greece. Freud compared the psychoanalyst's excavations to those of the archaeologist: layer after layer must be uncovered until the core, the mystery of the self, is laid bare. Once illuminated, that hidden treasure could be "returned to the possession of the ego." The celebrated treasures of Greece are stratified for the traveler: Neolithic remains, Classical ruins, Hellenistic, Roman, Byzantine . . . and that's only the architecture. Moreover, superimposed on the ancient remains in this palimpsest are the changing meanings of Greece for successive waves of travelers, many of whom thirst not to unearth what Seferis elsewhere calls "old stones that cannot be deciphered," but to follow the path of pleasure-seeking blazed by their predecessors.

In *On a Voiceless Shore: Byron in Greece*, Stephen Minta summarizes the phenomenon:

> The love affair with the Mediterranean goes on and on and few are completely immune. Byron, it is true, would have hated the crowds, but the tourists who arrive each day by thousands all through the long Greek summer are the natural heirs of his own youthful Greece. The nude beaches and smoke-filled tavernas would now be his hunting grounds. . . .
>
> This is the Greece of sun, sea, and the body, a world Byron discovered, made his own. Curiously, despite all the invasions, it is a Greece that still invites a fantasy of intimacy and belonging:
>
> > *Place me on Sunium's marbled steep,*
> > *Where nothing, save the waves and I,*
> > *May hear our mutual murmurs sweep . . .*
>
> It is the country of eternal youth, framed by the eternally old. The holiday brochures are filled with ancient columns, plodding donkeys, and old women in black. These images live on, side by side with the glittering sea and the ripening flesh, proof that the serenity of age follows naturally on the frenzy of youth.

I would substitute "longing" for "belonging" (and I seriously question that last sentence) but Minta does ably capture the contrasts.

Greece is not only a palimpsest or an archaeological site, something to be burrowed into layer by layer; it's also a Rorschach test. Even if what drew and continues to draw successive generations of tourists is the "Greece of sun, sea, and the body," that Greece—if only because plenty of the visitors have been writers—has been recorded and interpreted in strikingly various ways. Among the Anglophone poets and novelists who have tackled the topic of Greece since Byron (Durrell, Miller, and Merrill, to name only a few), different temperaments are at play on the same inscrutable reality that the books under review reflect.

An academic, or at least a sometime academic, Stephen Minta teaches Comparative Literature at the University of York; perhaps that explains why his *On the Voiceless Shore* is the only one of these books to come equipped with such useful accouterments as an index and a brief bibliographical note (Minta and Solway both provide maps; Storace lacks and needs one). Minta follows in the footsteps of Byron and his friend Hobhouse on their 1809 trip to Greece and Albania. Into his account of their journey, he deftly dovetails his own experiences along more or less the same route, which leaves him room for laconic commentary on travel in general as well as a few reticent asides about his own life. This reticence, sometimes bordering on obscurity where the author's own past is concerned, turns out to be a shared feature of all three books.

My problem with Minta is not that he has so little to say about himself, but that his book seems to lose bite and focus as it proceeds. Perhaps this slackening off is meant to be a subtle way of following in Byron's footsteps, since Byron's return trip to Greece, culminating in the poet's death in Missolonghi in 1824, Minta of course cannot follow to the end. Whatever the reason, *On a Voiceless Shore* turns from a kind of personal travel-cum-history into something much closer to plain history. Even Minta's comments (quoted above) on the perennial appeal of Greece seem oddly uninflected. Since Minta, though shrewd and observant, is too quiet a writer to supply much Byronic brio, it is to be found in this book only when Byron's actual words are quoted.

Despite also being stingy with autobiography, David Solway, in *The Anatomy of Arcadia*, and Patricia Storace, in *Dinner with Persephone*, play more distinctive roles in their own books. Both write with style and wit; touched by the "fantasy of intimacy and (be)longing" Minta mentions, both grow acerbic about this sweet dream. Storace is dry and understated in her notation of ironies and incongruities; Solway, as his title suggests, is ready to grapple with the myth of Arcadia.

Indeed, Solway's book, which was published a few years ago in Canada and is too little known here, can be read as a deliberate demolition of this myth, combining the modes of literary criticism, travel writing, and memoir into an elaborate cautionary tale. Solway's year with his family on Paxos is now the foreground and now the background of his book; throughout his accounts of weather, money, domestic and medical mishaps, and beautiful vistas, the writer's preoccupation with the human hunger for paradise throbs like a stubborn headache. In this land of sea and sun where Solway has chosen to spend a year,

> What is it I am learning? How to light wet matches, how to make do without electricity and water (when the pump knocks off), how to stay dry when the rain prises through the roof tiles, how to huddle in front of a small, box-like, inadequate heater, how to deal with the wily, cunning and likeable inhabitants of this historical backwater. . . .
>
> Karin [his wife] is learning how to tend artichokes and boil *chorta* (dandelion stems), how to plug leaks, refasten shutters, glue Afrolex strips, cook in a half-squatting posture, and identify the myriad herbs and flowers that spring out of every rock and clump of earth, like an affirmation of Pan's survival. What we are really learning, I think, is how to live without the romantic delusion of a golden age, a golden clime, the chryso-alternate, that sustains us in our common, everyday existence.
>
> It seems we all need to believe in the Utopian fantasy of an innocent world we are convinced must exist somewhere, whether on the littoral of the Mediterranean or in the obscure recesses of History. There is of course no such world and there never was.

Seesawing between jeremiad and urbane irony, the above passage typifies both the local discontinuities and the larger balance of Solway's book, the prevailing mood of which is an alert, self-conscious uneasiness. Sometimes Solway indulges this fantasy of Arcadia; at other times (notably when he fusses and fumes about the late British actor Peter Bull's book about Paxos), the fantasy strikes him as contemptible and dangerous, escapism in the radical sense of trying to flee oneself. Foolish, then, and also ultimately futile:

> If one capitulates to this denial of the self and its constituent rigors, and blunders away its constantly diminishing reserves of awareness and austerity, then one's entire life assumes the proportions of a dedicated flight from reality . . . And where do these exiles and fugitives go? At the other end of the round earth's imagined corners awaits the blissful land of Arcadia to receive its Boeing-loads of visitors and tourists. But it should be remembered that Arcadia is also portable and, like

Cavafy's Alexandria, always comes along as a natal part of one's own interior climate and geography. All that Paxos [does] is to objectify . . . that internal, utopian topography. "All travel," said Saul Bellow in *Henderson the Rain King*, "is mental travel."

This astringent tone is what I miss in Minta's account of the eternal pull of Greece—that, and the essential paradox that we carry our own utopias around with us, whether they're construed as *eutopia* (the good place) or *outopia* (no place).

This paradox begs the question why, if heaven and hell are already inside us, we still go chasing around the globe in search of them. "We carry the ruins of the self to the ruins of Palmyra," said Emerson. In "Questions of Travel" Elizabeth Bishop asks:

> Is it lack of imagination that makes us come
> to imagined places, not just stay at home?
> Or could Pascal have been not entirely right
> about just sitting quietly in one's room?

Even if the flight from reality turns out to be only one more flight back into the self, the difference between one self and another still means that the student of Arcadia gains the pleasure of comparing notes. (What is Henry Miller's take on Greece, for example, compared to that of James Merrill?) Books are a great invention in part because they exempt us from the necessity of literally treading, like Good King Wenceslas' page, in our master's footsteps. No doubt I can appreciate travelers' accounts of Greece all the better because I myself used to inhabit that particular Arcadia; but I don't need to trudge around on the trail of Solway or Storace, Miller or Merrill. Isn't part of the pleasure of reading about other people's travels this option of remaining "quietly in one's room"? As I read about Solway's wife plugging leaks or cooking in a squatting posture, I vividly remembered my years on Samos and envied neither my young self nor my contemporary Solway's middle-aged Arcadian venture.

Reading Solway, I sometimes felt lucky to be in the presence of such a perspicuous, unsentimental, and elegant writer. Here are two wonderful paragraphs:

> But what fascinates me in particular is the concrete, vivid, and unforgettable lesson the island teaches in the paradoxical duality—duplicity might be a better word—of life. Paxos is one of the most

beautiful islands in the entire Greek archipelago: green, testered with olive groves, puckered with valleys and webbed with pathways leading from the hills to the beach-indented coastline. Everywhere there are flowers, hibiscus, bougainvillaea, dog rose, oleander, jasmine; the air is thick with the scent of heather, oregano, basil and sage. The sunsets rival their Caribbean competitors, the whole sky turning a smoky pink alternating with patches of pewter grey and dusty blue as the sun, swollen and fulvid, seems with its almost tactile weight, like a huge blood-pomegranate, to heave the sea upward as it sinks. The sensation of displacement is palpable. And on halcyon afternoons the topmost olive-leaves are tipped silver-green with a kind of glancing scintillation (I think of Pound's 'glaucous') so the sky seems almost sequined or scaled with light.

Yet one goes for a walk through these light-checkered groves and the skeletons of innumerable birds crunch underfoot. For hours every morning, in the gaps between the distant incendiary crackle of gunshots and the close-range detonations, the air has the eerie stillness of a sarcophagus and reeks of cordite. Nothing moves. Nothing sings. It is almost like a bodying forth of Sophocles' half-mythical Lemnos where the birds never sang and the air was always acrid. One sits at the garden cable and suddenly a singed feather drifts past one's face, from out of nowhere. Blood speckles the cream bowl. It is all pure Poussin, *Et in Arcadia Ego*. For this island with its fragrance and colour is about as close to Arcadia as you can get today, and yet everywhere the perpetual reminder of gunshots; of birds trussed up in the market place, swarming with wasps that plunge their insect snouts into the eyeholes and guzzle; of little heaps of charred feathers and thin, fluted bones at the corners of the paths; and everywhere the cartridge shells, millions of them, on the road, littering every mound and tussock, in rich chromatic circles beneath the trees as if they were some tropical species of leaf, more colourful even than the burgeoning and various flora of the island, gradually replacing the island's powdery topsoil.

For the writer as well as the reader, then, literature is a more comfortable paradise than the most ravishing landscape. As Auden wisely asks in Merrill's *Sandover* trilogy, "is not Arcadia to dwell among / Greenwood perspectives of the mother tongue?" Accordingly, when Solway isn't lamenting the Paxiot climate or detailing the complexities of daily life there (the bottled gas runs out at the worst possible time)—in other words, when he is free to roam the more spacious groves of litera-ture—he writes incisively not only about the folly of hunting for Arcadia but about the whole matter of travel books:

> There is a sense in which all literature, or at least fiction, is travel lit-erature. The country to which and in which the author is traveling, which he is describing and probing, is not a nation or a people or a landscape in the ordinary sense, but a *concept*. That is, he is traveling in the realm of ideas, and the territory which he marks out for study may be in its essence something abstract and impalpable, at any rate, non-geographical. . . .
>
> Is this equation reversible? Is travel literature an inverse form of fic-tion-writing? Are all travel books really novels?

Since he's writing a travel book, not a dissertation, Solway provides no definitive answers to these questions. Still, his persistent speculations amount to a memorable anatomy not so much of Arcadia as of the vari-ous elements of both travel writing and fiction. Solway's pastoral realm, like those of other writers who find themselves in Greece, may be inhab-ited by shepherds, but students of literature make the maps and serve as tour guides.

Solway claims that ". . . all literature, *at least fiction*, is travel litera-ture." What has happened to poetry? Is it a coincidence that some of the best known English-speaking writers on the subject of Greece have been chiefly celebrated as poets? Surely Solway, who is a poet, would agree that the realm of ideas to which Arcadian pilgrims venture is not the exclusive preserve of the novelist.

Let's take a brief detour back in time. If we look at Greece through the eyes of Henry Miller and James Merrill respectively, theme and style are inextricably intertwined in each writer's sensibility—or, more to the point, in his prose. Thus the Rorschach effect holds: What Miller and Merrill perceive may be externally the same but seems subjectively worlds apart.

In what may be an early sketch for *The Colossus of Maroussi*, Miller holds forth on nothing less than the mystical essence of Greece:

> There is no old or new here, only Greece, which is perpetual and per-petuating. Greece continues to make Greece and will go on making Greece until the Fifth Race of man is extinguished. And what makes

Greece primordially Greek is contradiction. One can never grasp Greece: Greece seizes one by the hair, by the throat, the eyes, the nose and mouth. Greece invades you like a woman's breath, like a sweet poison, like an intoxicated river, like a tapeworm hollowing out your guts. Greece has no real history: Greece is timeless, ageless—and androgynous. It is here that the occult "builders" stopped a while to rest and in doing so became men again, became mortal and died, passed away, and their secrets with them, Thus Greece sank below the known level of the world to become the navel of another brighter world, the hidden seat of wisdom, the hallowed nothingness wherein the mystery sleeps, endures and perpetuates itself.

(Unpublished 1939 excerpt courtesy of Avi Sharon)

This passage reads less like fiction than myth—and with its ranting, hectic, hyperbolic diction, like a kind of poetry. In its expansive unself-consciousness, its aggressive monologuing, Miller's prose could hardly be more different from the feline, deceptively tentative gestures of Merrill's 1965 *nouveau roman, The (Diblos) Notebook*. Where Miller's reiterated "one" seems to include anyone and everyone in its grand sweep, Merrill discriminates. Not only do his various characters respond individually to the landscape and language of Greece, but since the narrator is a young man working at his first novel, artistic asides abound. Such marginalia can be read as a writer's notes to himself about genre, one of the lenses through which we perceive the world:

In form & tone the book must derive from the conventional International Novel of the last century—full of scenery and scenes illustrating the at times comic failure of American and European manners to adjust to one another. Nothing of *Phèdre* here.

Which is to say, nothing tragic, heroic, grand, remote.

The same aspects of Greece that presumably enthralled Miller are also present in Merrill. But in *The (Diblos) Notebook*, language and landscape are subjected to delicately ironic probings and emerge looking both more refined and more self-conscious. The crossings-out and restartings in the passage below are Merrill's way of showing that this "novel" is still a work in progress, in the notebook stage. We can see how the writer grapples with the problem of avoiding cliché; also how he wavers between third and first person:

From the moment of my arrival, I

the world was transfigured for me. The language, the landscape, alike overwhelmed

both of which I had pondered, as it were, in reproduction, now over-whelmed me with their (truth) and (beauty). I was more at home than I could ever have dreamed. Like a statue

As if in a museum some figure streaked & pocked, a "Roman copy of a lost Greek original," and looked at for decades by none but anatomy students, had suddenly been discovered to *be* the original, ~~Orestes~~   I

thanks, say, to little more than a ray of sun entering the honey-cells of marble, I felt my whole person cleansed and restored. My skin turned olive brown. The Latinate vocabulary to which I leaned when speaking or thinking in English gave way to authentic, simple forms: rock, sea, sun, wine, goat, sky.

That The land was poor & stony, that the modern language had been, like the wine, thinned and impregnated with resin, made no dif-ference. I myself felt poor & pungent enough to take my place among the marble rubble, the lizards, spiny plants, clouds of dust and sparkle of salt water—all those things on which the Greek sun dotes & which are intolerable without it.

I wouldn't want to do without either Miller or Merrill. But as Orwell says of Tolstoy and Dickens, they're as different as a sausage and a rose; their purposes barely intersect.

If, to return to *The Anatomy of Arcadia*, Solway had spent less time complaining about a book by the non-writer Peter Bull, he might have left himself more room to consider the work of travelers to Greece who are indubitably writers. (In fairness, Miller makes it onto what appears to be a short list of books Solway considers genuine travel writing. I should also confess that I enjoy Solway's propensity for complaint; it feels sincere; besides, he's often funny in his misery.) But since Bull, like Solway, spent time on Paxos, Bull's book, however inadequate, exerts on Solway a horrible, irresistible pull. I know the feeling: We can't help wanting to see what other people have written about places we ourselves are not only living in but writing about. This lust is a vice for which the cure is to go home and sit quietly in one's room.

I have saved the lushest and most elusive of these books for last. Patri-cia Storace's *Dinner with Persephone* is a demanding book—the reader must pay close attention, and ideally should know something about

Greece already, to get even an inkling of how much knowledge and care have gone into the construction of every paragraph, every sentence. The book rewards absorption by absorbing you in turn. *Dinner with Persephone* is not only chockful of information about Greece as a whole and in its parts—landscape, language, culture, religion, history, overall temperament—but casts a spell: it's a beautiful book. Minta writes well and Solway better, but next to Storace's weighty poise, unerring eye, and sense of construction and pace, *On a Voiceless Shore* can feel flat and humdrum, *The Anatomy of Arcadia* disheveled and repetitious.

Dinner with Persephone resists summary. It is an account of a year Storace recently spent in Greece; based in a small flat in Athens, she traveled a good deal, talked to all sorts of people, and paid close, indeed mesmerized attention to everything from architecture to Easter rituals, from nightclubs to the sound of a sigh. Often Storace wears her learning lightly, but she can and does call upon solid reserves of information when the occasion demands it. Since many occasions do just that, the resulting excurses on history, language, religion, geography, mythology, and so on make this a hard book simply to skim. Like the notorious, stubbornly mysterious meal her title refers to, the feast Storace offers in this book pulls you inward, downward, backward.

Where Minta describes Greece as "the country of eternal youth, framed by the eternally old," Storace strokes only a thin, confusing veneer of newness over its ancient depths. In addition to stores of information, Storace is equipped with unlimited curiosity and a keen eye, as well as with a poet's confidence that (appearances sometimes to the contrary) everything she sees or hears has a deeper significance, secret or counter-intuitive but never wholly inaccessible. Given buried meanings, Storace is determined to ferret them out: If learning Greek requires a teacher and a dictionary, then interpreting the language of dreams calls for a dream book, or rather two dream books. The old one (Artemidoros, writing in the second century) Storace has brought with her; the new one she buys, early in her stay, from a street vendor.

The dream book is one of the leitmotifs which endow *Dinner with Persephone* with resonance and rhythm; another is the passage of the year, each season bringing its own festival observances. Storace tries to visit various parts of Greece for the various holidays, so her account layers geography over ritual or vice versa. Far from a guidebook or travelogue, her book nevertheless covers a good deal of territory, from Corfu to Thasos, from Naxos to Mystras, from Agrapha to Thessaloniki, Mytilene, and finally the Turkish coast. Each place (ferry, hotel, café, church, mountain) gives off a distinctive aroma, distilled of landscape, weather, the time of year, or Storace's mood, and of the temperament or behavior of the people she happens to meet. One of the joys of this book is Storace's economical accounts of various random encounters, often unremarkable and startling, which frequently segue into meditations on larger matters; a few are sufficient unto themselves.

Early in her stay in Athens, still jet-lagged and disoriented, Storace finds herself on a trolley:

> I have a copy of *The Adventures of Huckleberry Finn* on my lap, which I brought with me, along with Artemidorus's *Oneirokritika* [the old dream book], Boswell's *Life of Samuel Johnson*, a cookbook of Claudia Roden's, and a few others. But the barrage of new sights from the window makes it hard for me to concentrate on anything else. *Huckleberry Finn* is suddenly lifted out of my hands and examined by a stout middle-aged lady wearing brown support hose and an arsenal of jewelry. She puts it back into my hands with neither prelude nor farewell, and communicates her finding to her seat partner. "*Galliki glossa*," she says firmly, "French," gesturing toward me. "A French girl."

On another occasion, Storace, traveling on Naxos, passes a villager on the street:

> "Succulent, very tasty, *akhh*, my little mother," one man says as I walk by, confident that I hear things only in my own language, whatever that might be; he uses an adjective that descends from the ancient Greek word for homecoming, *nostos*, used of Odysseus's return to his motherland; someone fancifully told me that the meaning of the modern word evolved because homecoming was for Odysseus as sweet as the savor of home-cooked food.

From the sequence tasty (*nostime*), home cooking, homecoming (*nostos*), and Odysseus, Storace is led to ponder the role of women in the Greek imagination and in Greek history. Thus an overheard sentence which could be dismissed as no more than a verbalized wolf whistle draws her into a reverie (or a digression, if you want to see it in that light) that circles around an inscrutable and, for her, an endlessly fascinating topic: language:

> Words are like the facets of diamonds, showing only the shades of meaning in a language that history and experience, prejudice, ideology, politics, myth, desire, have cut out of them. It seems there is something poignantly and fruitfully incomplete in each language; each has its partial brilliances and inadequacies, each is a dream of the truth.

With its succinct catalog ("history . . . desire") and its mention of "a dream of the truth," this passage reads like an index of Storace's preoccupations. It may be that the controlled surface of her prose and the relaxed pace of her meanderings mask a set of stern obsessions, but if so, they are successful disguises, for *Dinner with Persephone* feels more poetic than it does programmatic.

Storace is happy to retail information and to tell us what she sees and hears; but her underlying reticence is rarely breached. For a book so deliciously rich in detail, *Dinner with Persephone* is not only understated, but downright laconic, and not just on personal matters. This is one place Storace recalls Minta, who sagely comments midway through *On a Voiceless Shore*:

> When traveling, it is always better to listen than to talk. This is something I learned a long time ago and it is a rule I have seldom broken without regret. The approach favors observation over engagement, of course, and it has its limitations. You no doubt miss some interesting moments; but then you escape some of the worst moments too.

It's not that Storace never had conversations with people in Greece. Rather, she favored observation over engagement and measured very carefully how many of her own words (or for that matter, anyone else's) to pass on to the reader. Rationing words is rare in travel writers. Even the most torrential monologuers she encounters are not allowed to overwhelm us; she may have had to sit through hours of their outpourings, but she knows just when the reader will have had enough. We are never nudged toward conclusions or told how to feel—or treated to more than the tiniest slivers of autobiography. For readers less incurious than I am, or more attracted to narrative, this withheld quality may become frustrating; for me, it savors of mystery, authority, and a kind of controlled munificence. I am happy to learn what Storace saw, entranced to be privy to the conversations she reports; and I rarely want to know more than she wants to tell me.

The few grains of autobiography that make their way through Storace's fine-meshed sieve are tantalizing; parts of her personality adhere to her strange surroundings. Such remnants of one's past can be disconcerting; thus, hanging lingerie out to dry on her balcony the day after arriving in Athens, Storace suffers from vertigo:

> I have never lost a freezing childhood fear of heights, and to lean out over a fatal drop to dry my laundry gives me a sudden image of the characters in *North by Northwest* as they scramble over Mount Rushmore with a gunman in pursuit. I have to close my eyes for each garment.

Another quality she turns out never to have lost proves much more useful: a way of coping with importunate passes. There are several entertaining examples, of which I quote the following because of its rare, sidelong reference to Storace's upbringing. Toward the end of her stay in Greece, Storace, visiting Thessaloniki, calls on a publisher to whom she has a letter of introduction:

> The publisher turns out to be a small wiry man from Kefallonia, with a book-crammed office. I walk around the shelves to get an idea of what he has published, when suddenly there is a helping hand on my hair, then one on my shoulder, then one on my breast. I dodge away, having been trained in Anglo-Saxon style martial arts, of which the basic underlying principle is to deny that anything has happened. So I crowd the room with remarks . . . I keep leaping out of his reach into intellectual frontiers . . .

Such basic training is certainly useful.

Though certain characteristics seem constant, Storace also finds that in this new place she is a new person. Early in her stay, a passerby on an Athens street accosts her:

> "Hurry," he says, "hurry up. I want to have coffee with you." A struggle ensues over my packages, which I win, thanks to my new height . . . I am no longer small as I was in the United States, but have become magically taller than average.

At lunch with friends later that day, Storace notes another sea change in herself:

> The table starts an obscenity party, teaching me these phrases with mischievous delight, as if they were teaching them to a talking parrot. And oddly, I, who blush easily in English, can reel off the worst phrases in Greek with phlegmatic indifference. The blush seems to depend on some encounter between a child self and an adult self which can't be reproduced in a language you learn as an adult.

Part of the dream of Arcadia is transformation. This quest is what Solway has in mind when he sternly warns against "the denial of the self and its constituent rigors"; it's what Merrill is describing when he writes "I felt my whole person cleansed and restored." That the dream of change and renewal cannot ever be wholly fulfilled doesn't make it any less natural a desire, particularly for the traveler midway through life's journey. Who, no longer young, wouldn't be seduced by what Miller calls the ahistorical, "timeless, ageless" Greece?

Tough-minded without being cynical, Storace not only understands this longing for renewal; implicitly, "having stepped through the mirror to this country," she shares it. She is the only one of these authors to connect the visions and vagaries of travel explicitly with the passage from childhood to adulthood. There is much in life, she seems to be suggesting, "which can't be reproduced in a language you learn as an adult." Perhaps it is Storace's unapologetic grown-upness which allows her to see so clearly. But who ever said that accurate perception means that what you notice is simple? What she observes—and even more what she hears—tends to be symbolic, mythological, above all ambiguous:

> So now you know, Patricia, that in Greece when you hear a story, you must expect to hear its shadow, the simultaneous counterstory. Because . . . we have eaten the six pomegranate seeds here, and all our stories come in two versions, and the story that is told in hell will sound different from the same story as they tell it in heaven. And you know that in Greece you must never use the past tense when you are speaking of Alexander the Great, although you also know that he is dead.

One remembers Solway's sense of the "paradoxical duality—duplicity might be a better word—of life." The truth, as Oscar Wilde remarked, is rarely pure and never simple; in Greece, at least, it's dependably complex and double—and especially so, as Storace suggests, in a language that speaks with forked tongue.

I mentioned earlier that Storace's reticence about her early life isn't unique among these books. Minta has a couple of evocative if vague paragraphs about his English country boyhood ("I grew up on a farm, surrounded by the rusting carcasses of old cars, the smell of mimosa, and the noise of the sea . . ."). Solway is happy to tell us about his stays in Greece in the sixties but says nothing of his (Canadian?) childhood. Other than the sidelong glances already noted (childhood dizziness, training during girlhood in how to cope with a lech), Storace drops a single autobiographical fact, which I had noted and then all but forgotten. But in a surprising, almost oracular way, I was reminded of it by a stranger.

One evening late last fall I was on my way home from work, standing on the uptown IRT express, swaying with fatigue and absent-mindedness. My canvas bag with its cargo of books on Greek myth was gaping, evidently, at my feet. Maybe something in my face was also open, inviting. For whatever reason, the woman I was looming over suddenly looked up at me and smiled. Then, with so friendly a gesture that I wondered if we hadn't met somewhere, she held up for my inspection the book she was reading. Or was it my book, fallen out of my bag, she was holding up to show she'd retrieved it? The book was *Dinner with Persephone*. But for the fact that hers was a paperback and mine a hardcover, I would have thought that the woman was showing me my own copy (which in fact was safe in my bag). It was strange to see the contents of my own head mirroring me, as simultaneously occult and public as the slit of scarlet pomegranate innards flirting forth like a petticoat ruffle on the cover of the book. My fellow *Dinner with Persephone* lover and I agreed, as we trudged up the stairs to Ninety-Sixth Street, that it was a wonderful book. I volunteered that I was going to review it. "So why did she go to Greece, do you know?" the woman asked me. "That must be important, I think, don't you? Because it says on page nine that she never knew her parents, and that might be a clue that going to Greece was a sort of searching for her roots." "If so," I said, "it's a clue that's never followed up on." I added that the book's reticence was one of the things I liked about it. Then we parted amicably at the corner of Ninety-Sixth and Broadway.

I checked the reference when I got home. The passage, which is indeed on page nine, is perhaps the first place in *Dinner with Persephone* where the uncanniness of the new world of Greece is connected with the strange transition (especially strange in Storace's case) from childhood to adulthood. She has been learning about the national heroes Kolokotronis, Solomos, and Makriyannis, a context my fellow subway rider had unsurprisingly ignored or forgotten:

> Most non-Greeks, in my experience, had never heard of any of these men. I never had myself until the first time I came here, and felt the eerie sensation of disorientation I recognized from my childhood; I had grown up without knowing my parents, although intensely aware of their existence in my own body, made out of elements of theirs. So I knew something about beings who are powerfully present without being visible to others, and I knew something about lost worlds, even though my lost world was the past, and the lost world of Greece was the present. . . . In Greece I saw a nation both tormented and exalted by imagination.

I'm grateful for being sent back to this passage, not so much for the clue it provides (or fails to provide) to Storace's orphaned status as for its thematic importance. In both the writer and the country she temporarily adopts, there is a charged duality between past and present, absent and present, imagined and real. Somewhere among these oppositions, Arcadia, for Storace, is located.

What is it about Storace and subways—something about Persephone's journey to the underworld? Back underground a few weeks later, rereading *Dinner with Persephone* on the downtown local, noting down favorite passages, I was hooked all over again:

> There are only six passengers on the bus after we board, and a woman climbs on after us, wishing the bus driver and the passengers a general *kalimera*. Hanging over the windshield dangle a gold evil-eye charm, a madonna, a pomegranate, and a decal of the Playboy bunny.

On a neighboring page, Storace takes a taxi. The passage is too long to quote in full, but here's the flavor of part of it:

> As we drive, Pericles' radio plays a song of unrequited love, the Greek no, *okhi*, with its round absolute *o* sound . . . the *okhi* punctuated by the *aaaakh vaaakh* sounds that transcribe Greek sighs, very different from

the quality of our gentle resigned sighs . . . Greek *aaakhs* bleed and flood and empty the body, and I am reminded that Greek sounds of laughter, refusal, and desire are very different from ours. . . .

Unrequited love gives way to domestic bliss as Pericles tells Storace, in novelistic detail, the story of his marriage to an older woman, ending, "I hope you don't mind my telling you about all this, but I am so happy with her, and I need to tell someone about my secret, and it looked to me like you would understand." (Note how precisely this balances the earlier episode of the villager who incorrectly assumes Storace won't understand his comments on her succulence.)

It's hard to convey precisely why I found, and still find, much of Storace's book so enchanting. My own years in Samos are only part of the answer, only one seed of the pomegranate. Storace's own tart sweetness, and her tactful blend of reticence and detail, are also attractive, as is her ability to fall silent and simply *listen*. (Or not so simply—for all I know she may have been taping Pericles.) Always drawn onward by her account, always wanting more, I also felt confident she would never give me too much.

Whatever the reason for my absorption, reading Storace's account of Pericles' story made me miss my stop—the first time in a lifetime of subway riding that this had happened to me. I'd meant to get off at Lincoln Center; I barely managed to scramble out at Fifty-Ninth Street. Apparently unwilling to extricate myself from this sharp-edged, lyrical rendering of Arcadia, I dragged myself back to the surface; back to a particular city and century, place and time; back to the thin layer one experiences as the present.

A CLASSROOM IN CORFU

ON A MUGGY MORNING in Corfu, at Ionian University, some of whose departments are housed in what, if I understand correctly, was once a lunatic asylum, I find myself in a classroom drawing an arc from left to right across a whiteboard. The marker's running out of ink—a familiar dilemma that brings back One Washington Park, the Business School building at Rutgers-Newark where I taught only last week and will teach again next week. I enjoy smuggling a literature course into this building under the radar of finance. My literature students are the outliers at the Business School; the black-suited business majors rarely make eye contact in the elevators. An aging poet like me is invisible. But here on a Greek island, in this long, narrow classroom, all eyes seem to be fixed on what I'm scribbling.

Paschalis, our host, has scurried out to fetch a fresh marker, so I can finish what I'm putting on the board. The marker he now hands me is black, but a rainbow would have been more appropriate than this monochrome line to convey the blurry gradations, the endless degrees and compromises and subtypes, that translation entails. On the far left of the arc I write LITERAL/WORD FOR WORD. "The letter killeth, but the spirit giveth life," is how some versions translate Paul's words in the third chapter of 2 Corinthians. I'm tempted to write this sentence on the whiteboard; if the Greek were at my fingertips, I'd write it out as well. But I dismiss that idea (no time for it) while my hand is still busily writing.

Is a word-for-word translation ever even possible? The better we know the source language, the more choices and possibilities we see, and the more obstacles and ambiguities crop up. The rising arc as I sketch it takes us toward a middle ground—a kingdom of compromise between literal and what Paschalis at dinner last night called licentiousness.

This middle realm—isn't it where most of us live? If we're conversing in another language, we fumble along some invisible line of demarcation near the middle of the range of possible renderings. If we're translating a text, how close to the literal do we want to stick, even if we could? The separate words, the connotations of the original: how close can we approach to these, even supposing we know what they are?

With ancient texts, we don't know and we can't know. Quoting a boastful translator of Homer only to dispute him, Matthew Arnold declares in "On Translating Homer" that "we cannot possibly tell how the *Iliad* 'affected its natural hearers' . . . It is our translator's business," Arnold continues,

> to reproduce the effect of Homer, and the most powerful emotion of the unlearned English reader can never assure him whether he has reproduced this, or whether he has produced something else. . . . No one can tell him how Homer affected the Greeks; but there are those who can tell him how Homer affects *them*.

Arnold is right. It's pointless to claim, as Arnold's confident contemporary did, that each new translation brings back the flavor or effect of the original. What flavor? What effect?

Further along the right-hand, downward slope of the arc as I sketch it, the strictures of translation loosen up. Toward this edge of the territory, translators begin to feel more able to stray, to follow their noses, to take liberties. Liberties: the word suggests freedom to stretch their wings, the wings of the target language, and flutter or even fly some distance from the source language—a distinct relief after the cramped constraints at the literal end. But (and this thought comes to me in the stuffy oblong room at Ionian University, where I'm still scribbling on the whiteboard) such freedom can also, paradoxically, mean the very opposite of airy fluttering. That is, such freedom provides a sense of being grounded—of feeling the confidence of connection with one's own world.

For as a translator approaches his or her own idiom and era, they have no choice but to gain confidence in their own language. If they don't, their translation will be dead in the water. Wallace Stevens writes in "Of Modern Poetry" that modern poetry (or what he calls "The poem of the mind in the act of finding / What will suffice") "has to be living, to learn the speech of the place. / It has to face the men of the time and to meet / The women of the time." George Seferis writes in his *Three Secret*

Poems that "our words are the children of many people. / They are sown, are born like infants, / take root, are nourished with blood." Auden writes of the dead poet in his "In Memory of W. B. Yeats" that "Now he is scattered among a hundred cities / And wholly given over to unfamiliar affections . . . The words of a dead man / Are modified in the guts of the living." None of these powerful passages has translation specifically in mind; but all of them concern language, communication, and change. All of them eloquently evoke an energy and authority that transcend the poet alone in his or her study. There is a past, an almost biological past, that the poet draws on; and there's a potential audience out there who must be able to understand. Between the past and the future, what is required is change—"to learn the speech of the time," as Stevens puts it. Auden's verb is "modify," but not just any modification—this one takes place in the gut. Seferis too hews close to biological process: [words] "are sown, are born like infants, / take root [like trees or plants], are nourished [like animals] with blood."

Blood. And at this juncture, I find myself talking about Konstantine Karyotakis (1896–1928). My translations of two of Karyotakis's poems are on the handout Paschalis has distributed; and since there's not enough time to read both, I decide to read my rendering of "*Spirochaetea Pallida*," a poem about syphilis and love, about imagination and risk and madness. Is it a coincidence that on the same handout is my translation of Baudelaire's sonnet "*La Fontaine de Sang*"? Blood again—and again, a poem about love and illness, infection and desire.

The resulting vortex of associations makes a mess in the middle of the whiteboard. I have to erase the arc I drew earlier to fit this new idea in, for what I'm now scribbling is a tangle of intersecting lines, a traffic jam or bird's nest of associations. Karyotakis, who may or may not have suffered from syphilis, died too early to know about AIDS; Baudelaire (1821–67), who knew more about syphilis than Karyotakis did, knew nothing of AIDS either. And yet while I was translating their two poems, sometime around 1990, I was thinking about blood and infection. My student and friend Charles Barber (1956–1992) was dying of AIDS. Charlie's daily infusion of meds through his Hickman catheter certainly influenced my solution to the problem of how to render Baudelaire's description of love as a *matelas d'aiguilles*, a mattress of needles. A mattress stuffed with pins? Nah. The solution I came up with was "Love led me to a thicket of IV's / Where bristling needles thirsted for each vein." Aha! The tingle of having solved a puzzle, that little spritz of triumph as one prepares for the next challenge, is what has led my husband to call translating my Sudoku.

Such successes, small and local, can make a difference. With luck, each fresh rendering may take its place in the crowded field of translations of Baudelaire, or the less crowded fields of translations of Karyotakis or of another poet whose name came up this morning—Solomos, whose statue we were admiring yesterday. At best, one has managed to substitute one trope for another, and—as I always try to do—one has also managed to maintain some poetic verve in the process.

But it's not only a matter of verbal acrobatics, crucial though deftness in the target language is. Only now, in this airless room in Corfu, am I belatedly beginning to understand some of Walter Benjamin's thoughts in his essay "The Task of the Translator"—an essay I've read on and off over the years and even tried to teach last spring. Until today, some of what Benjamin says in this essay seemed to me too obvious to need pointing out: ". . . a translation comes later than the original, and since the important works of world literature never find their chosen translators at the time of their origin, their translation marks their stage of continued life." Well, of course, I always thought; the original would indeed come before any translation of it. Less self-evident to me was Benjamin's further declaration that "in its afterlife—which could not be called that if it were not a transformation and a renewal of something living—the original undergoes a change. Even words with fixed meanings can undergo a maturing process."

But the images I'm considering this morning, and the attendant mess on the whiteboard, somehow make Benjamin's words clearer. Indeed, they illustrate his words. To move Baudelaire's images of blood and havoc into the world of AIDS, as I did almost intuitively in 1990, was indeed to transform and renew the French poet's constellation of meanings and feelings—not to violate or distort it, but to extend it, or as Ryan Wilson phrases it in his recent essay "The Polyvocal Poet: Tradition, Translation, and the True Original," to carry these meanings forward. Terry Eagleton says in his little book on Shakespeare that Shakespeare had clearly read Marx, Freud, Derrida, and so on. Baudelaire just as clearly knew all about the world of desire and infection I was exploring with the poets in the workshop I was running at Gay Men's Health Crisis between 1988 and 1993—a world that my students, through their poetry and conversation, were helping me to venture toward. Since Karyotakis had read Baudelaire, his vision of desire and infection was also affected (inflected?

infected?) by the contagion of the French poet's imagery. In translating Karyotakis, wasn't I rendering homage in two directions at once, back toward Baudelaire and forward towards the world of GMHC?

Examples accrued. When Charles Barber wrote a poem about his Hickman catheter entitled "Thirteen Things about a Catheter," he was—precisely as Benjamin puts it—transforming and renewing something living, so that the original, Wallace Stevens's poem "Thirteen Ways of Looking at a Blackbird," underwent a change. Yet of course the Stevens original is still there for us to read.

At the end of the day, we strolled—bats wheeling through the Old Fortress—past a building which had been the British officers' barracks sometime in the early nineteenth century. Now it was the music school of Ionian University—the same university I'd visited that morning, in the literature department on the grounds of a former lunatic asylum. To repurpose, to retrofit, to keep to the original beautiful structure without tearing it down; to then fill that structure with something new, something perhaps wholly different in nature and purpose—this, I saw, is as true of translation as it is of architecture. The new stuff in the old container will inevitably be reshaped and changed by the constraints of its new surroundings.

Does the new wine inevitably burst the old bottles into which I poured it, as Matthew and Mark would have it? My father Moses Hadas, a classicist, called one of his last books *Old Wine, New Bottles: A Humanist Teacher at Work*. That way of looking at the passing on and transforming of tradition—venerable contents, new contexts—makes sense too. Container, contained, durable, flexible—translation encompasses all these ideas. "New thresholds, new anatomies!" wrote Hart Crane. The other day I learned from the *Times Literary Supplement* that in 1893 William Morris predicted the end of the book, saying "within fifty years printing books would be an extinct art—we should all be carrying our books about in bottles with patent stoppers"—another variation on the theme of that old wine.

PHILOTIMO IN THE BEAUTY PARLOR

IN ILISSIA, a pleasant neighborhood of Athens near the Hilton, late one sunny morning in the middle of June, from my perch in the beauty parlor and from behind the veil of another language, I'm suddenly privy to what sounds like a proverb. Only seven words in Greek, it loses some of its punch in translation: *If you are an honorable person, they will trample you.*

Less aphorism, maybe, than a gnomic truth—a truth emphatically declared, with crystal diction, by a client waiting for her dye job. Who is she addressing? Everyone and no one. The manicurist (blond, petite) and pedicurist (willowy, brunette), their four hands working busily on me, nod in acknowledgment, and say a word or two. I steal a glance at the speaker, who seems uncertain whether or not I silently understand her. And this floating ambiguity, the air in the place rich with both the said and the unsaid, heightens the sense of a performance in progress—neither fake nor planned; spontaneous, improvised, but still somehow intentional.

Tomorrow we fly home. At the end of three weeks, my suitcase of impressions full to bursting—Jerusalem, Tel Aviv, Nes Tsiona. Bnai Broch, Athens, Ilissia, Votaniko, Exarchia, Aigina, Gazi, Mets, Ilissia again; dancing with the women at the wedding; sampling pistachios along the quay; floating with silent crowds at Yad Vashem; pacing around the Temple of Aphaia; always one more episode than I can quite stuff into or pull out of the bag of memory (how much weight allotted? how much space?)—the fullness and variety, the squashed layers (sit on that suitcase! fit in one more scene!) militate against an undertow, against some force as strong as gravity but hard to name. Call it lateness or recovery, call it even "lastness." The dreamlike crowds and clamor; people scurrying along the narrow alleys of the Old City; an impromptu brunch with a sudden group of seven, eight, nine people popping up in a packed restaurant in Machane Yehudah; doing my best to follow my sister-in-law through the crush at Carmel Market as she keeps vanishing into the throng, walking quickly, never looking back—these make it hard to distinguish ivory from horn. I have gone, am still going, through both gates.

For more peaceful moments, these last weeks have offered the leitmotif of the balcony. I've perched on several verandas and looked out— from Malal Street in the German Colony, from the Hotel Rachel in Aghia Marina, from Semelis Street further up the hill in Ilissia. But the beauty parlor today presents another kind of balcony. From behind the latticed screen of partial comprehension, I find myself eavesdropping on a world of distilled experience. *If you are a person who loves virtue, they'll walk all over you.*

About to go and have her dye job retouched in the next room, the aphorist gets up from the chair where she's been holding forth. Unexpectedly, she approaches me and pats my shoulder. "Now," she says, "you know the whole story." No I don't. Part of what she's been saying has escaped me, and other parts (apples and pears; a diet; a table setting; something about Cephalonia) haven't been all that interesting. But part will certainly stay with me. "Well," I say (apologetic? defensive? reassuring?), "I only understood some of it."

Now she knows beyond a doubt that I'm a foreigner. No, of course she always knew it. We both laugh a little as she leaves.

If you're a good person, they'll take advantage of you. Traveling presses the question (never far away in any case), brings it closer, holds it up to the light: who are *they?* From behind the mesh of language; from all the sheltered balconies on which I have been sitting peering out at several worlds, there resonates—it comes to me today—this underlying question. The *they* embedded in her plural verb could be two, a thousand, everyone. A group, a threat, invisible, faceless—a law like gravity: If A, then B. They'll crush you. This is the way it works.

My fingernails and toenails are bright red. I rise and smile at the kind blond and brunette and say goodbye, about to leave this place and fly away from the vantage point that features the unforgettable instruction:

If you are virtuous, then they will crush you. Who is the chorus here? And just who are *they?*

THE TRUTH OF TWO

RIGHTLY OBSERVING that translators usually pay more attention to the how of their translation practice than to the why, Harry Thomas devotes some space to the latter as well. In the preface to his radiant *The Truth of Two: Selected Translations* (2017), Thomas lists five reasons why he translated the poems in the book. Money, for one—a small reason, "for the money was small," news which will not come as a surprise to other translators of poetry. Secondly, friendship: "the pleasure of sitting at tables with friends, colleagues, and one student who either knew a language I didn't know . . . or knew one much better than I did." Thomas's third motive was "to bring over into English a kind of poem that English lacks; this was especially the case with Montale, Levi, and Brodsky." A fourth motive: "several times I thought, immodestly, that I could do better than previous translators." A fifth motive "was to say something about myself under the cover of a translation, a device I discovered in Pound. . . ." Thomas cites only two such imitations or cloaking device poems in this collection, one after Catullus's elegy for his brother and one after the Anglo-Saxon poem "Deor," both of which in their different ways work exceedingly well. Then there is the overriding motive, more like an impulse or an instinct, that one hopes all translators of poetry share: "I translated these poems because I liked them and wanted to convey that feeling and the emotions of the poems themselves in my language."

"Liked" is surely an understatement. *The Truth of Two* feels like a small anthology of poems that Thomas has loved; the title encompasses various kinds of face-to-face intimacy, from love or friendship to the way poetry reaches across time to engage in dialogue with the reader—or the translator. Not all the poems Thomas has included radiate that kind of intimacy, but enough do so that readers of this *Selected* should feel a compelling sense of correspondence across languages and centuries.

Though we also get strong tastes of Latin, Anglo-Saxon, French, Chinese, and Russian, most of the poems in *The Truth of Two* were originally written in either Italian (Leopardi, Saba, Ungaretti, Montale, and Levi) or Spanish (Sor Juana Inés de la Cruz, Salvador Díaz Mirón, Machado, Salinas, Borges, and Neruda). Is it too much of a stretch to claim that a crystalline Mediterranean clarity emanates from many of these two groups—a wrung-out, utterly unsentimental radiance? These poems are dry: etched, precise, wry. In the case of Levi, the dryness edges over into bitterness and despair but retains its *sprezzatura*, though in a poem like "The Elephant" this acerbic tone deepens to a trumpeting moan:

Would you like to hear my story? It's brief.
The clever Indian lured and tamed me,
The Egyptian shackled and sold me,
The Phoenician covered me with weapons
And built a tower on my back.
It was absurd that I, a tower of flesh,
Invulnerable, mild, and intimidating,
Confined in these hostile mountains,
Slipped on your ice that I'd never seen before.
For us, when we fall, there is no salvation.
Some blind hero kept on trying to find
My heart with the point of his lance.
To these mountaintops, lurid in the sunset,
I trumpeted my useless
Dying bellow: absurd, absurd!

Montale has been translated often; Levi, who is, of course, best known for his prose, less often, at least to my knowledge. But whether or not Thomas does better than other translators with these poems, his translations from Italian and Spanish are confident, precise, and graceful. Many of the poems by Levi (Thomas includes twenty here) I hadn't known, and I am grateful for all of them, whether Levi is writing about Passover, Pompeii (and Anne Frank and Hiroshima), an elephant, a dromedary, a mole, or a pedantic mouse.

I had read a good deal of Montale and always liked what I read. But this passage, from his "Sorapis, 40 Years Later," was a revelation. It would be tempting to quote entire poem, but here is how this poem about revisiting a lake concludes:

Then holding you by the hand, I guided you
up to the top, an empty hut.
That was our lake: a few spans of water,
two lives much too young to be old
and much too old to feel we were young.
We discovered then what age is.
It has nothing to do with time,
but is something that says, that makes us say
we are here, a miracle
that cannot repeat itself. By comparison,
youth is the vilest of deceptions.

I'm reminded of what a wonderfully ageless man in Jamaica said to my beloved and me a few years ago: "Hage [as he pronounced it] is just a number." Another Montale poem I didn't remember having read is the crusty and chewy "Venetian Prose," an account, presumably accurate, of the poet's interviewing Hemingway two months after false reports of the novelist's death: "He's still in bed. In his hairy head / the eyes and eczema are glistening holes."

"Venetian Prose" concludes "He lived for a few more years and dying twice / had a chance to read his obituaries." This sense of a second chance, of revisiting a place, a person, or a text, seems to be a recurrent one in *The Truth of Two*, though it is also probable that as I approach the age of seventy I'm growing more attuned to patterns of recurrence. Then, too, the devoted reading and rereading, writing and revising, that inhere in the process of translating a beloved poem, constitute another kind of recurrence. Sometimes the echo of a previous text or meaning is an uncanny one, as in Yves Bonnefoy's "Hopkins Forest," a poem that sounds at the outset like a simple description but melts or morphs into a phantasmagoric vision. Again, I'd read a good deal of Bonnefoy, but I didn't remember these stanzas:

I went back inside
and re-opened the book on the table.
Page after page
there were only indecipherable signs,
clusters of forms without any sense,
although vaguely recurring,
and beneath them an abyssal white

as if what we call the spirit
were falling there, soundlessly,
like snow.
Still, I went on turning the pages.

Many years earlier,
in a train at the moment when the day rises . . .
the passengers were reading, silent
in the snow that was sweeping the gray windows,
and suddenly,
in a newspaper open next to me –
a big photograph of Baudelaire,
a whole page,
as if the sky were emptying at the world's end
in recognition of the chaos of words.

This mysterious epiphany is composed, Bonnefoy tells us in the next stanza, partly from dream and partly from memory. But the moment of recognition transcends both dream and memory. The epiphanic experience is almost ineffable—it's neither simply an event that can be narrated nor an image that can be described. Still, the poets to whom Thomas is drawn can't help attempting to evoke what they have experienced. It's paradoxical that the dry precision I've referred to maintains its sharp particularity even when what's being evoked seems impossibly abstract. Yet these poets manage it—and Thomas delivers their vision intact. The following passage from the Spanish poet Pedro Salinas, whose work I hadn't known, is the source of this entire collection's title, which is also the title of Salinas's poem. "Error," "truth," "earth," "love," "destiny"—we might seem to be wallowing in a bog of unvisualizable abstractions. But in Thomas's rendering, the immediacy of a love poem lights up what might equally be allegory or prayer:

You, deceived
by clarity, and I by darkness,
so long as we walked alone,
have delivered ourselves, in exchanging
error for error, to the tragic truth
called the world, earth, love, destiny.
And the fatal face of it all we can see
in what I have given you and you given me.

At our love's birth there was born for each
the other's terrible, necessary side,
the light, the darkness.
The two of us go towards it. Never again alone.
The world, the truth of two, the fruit of two,
the paradisiac truth, the bitter apple,
attained only in the total tasting
when all innocence ends,
both of the day itself and the night by itself.

As I savor this book, a minor cavil remains, or a couple of inter-twined observations. The most successful (and often excellent) trans-lations here are usually of poems in free verse, which Thomas handles with great poise and subtlety. Rhymed, metered poems generally also work very well, but there are some notably awkward spots. In Sor Juana Inés de la Cruz's "Hope," for example, the second and third lines could surely have been rethought: "Mad hope! The gilded frenzy every man / Is swept away by day by day" calls for a second and third reading and still sounds odd. The final line of Leopardi's classic poem "The Infinite" also reads oddly, with what seems an unnecessarily awkward use of a con-traction: "And going under's easeful in this sea." Another obtrusive con-traction mars the entire final stanza of Montale's beautiful "To pass the noon, intent and pale":

And walking in the dazzling sun
to feel with sad amazement
how all we are and go through's in
this following a wall up on

the top of which jagged bits of bottles run.

Are these among the poems which Thomas "immodestly" (his word) thought he could "do better than other translators"? One wonders. After all, Leopardi and Montale have been much translated.

In fairness, Thomas does beautifully with some rhymed poems. I'm thinking in particular of the selections from Brodsky with which *The Truth of Two* ends, especially "The wind abandoned the woods," which has a distinctively Frostian ring, and the final piece in this volume, "What do the bushes say to the wind?"

The final couplet of "What do the bushes say?" might serve as an epigraph to this book which is so concerned with loneliness and communication, solitude and intimacy, silence and utterance: "The dialogue's incomprehensible / when you're alone." And the dialogue throughout *The Truth of Two* is a memorable one. Not every collection of translations of various lyric poems from various times and places has so thoroughly coherent and compelling a theme.

NAKEDNESS IS MY END

THE KEYNOTE OF *Nakedness Is My End: Poems from the Greek Anthology* is struck at the outset by Semonides of Amorgos, quoting Homer and reminding us to live, since "our end is near." This caution is never far away. But then I was taken, perhaps distracted, by several charming cameos of animals in the short Greek poems (dating from the seventh century B.C.E. into the Common Era) Edmund Keeley has selected, arranged, and translated. There is Nicias' grasshopper lamenting its captivity:

> I was captured cunningly while resting on green leaves,
>   And a boy's skinny hand takes delight in me now.

There are Ariston's mischievous mice, who have developed a taste for nibbling the poet's scrolls:

> . . . if you sharpen your teeth again on my books,
>   you'll quickly come to know, wailing,
>   a banquet not good for you at all.

There's Damocharis's "most evil cat," who, having devoured its owner's partridge, has lost its taste for humbler fare:

> And now there's nothing on your mind but partridges,
>   the mice are dancing, running off with your daintiest feast.

A particularly poignant vignette by Leonidas of Tarentum presents cattle heading back from a winter pasture:

> The cattle came home from the hill at dusk
>   by themselves, through deep snow.

The cowherd Therimachos sleeps an endless sleep under the oak
tree
where the sky's fire struck him down.

These poems also feature fruits, but an apple is seldom only an apple.

I'm an apple, tossed here by someone who loves you, Xanthippe,

writes Plato. And Paulus Silentarius also has apples on his mind:

> Stealthily, so her nervous mother wouldn't know,
> the lovely girl gave me a pair
> of rosy apples. Maybe she used magic
> to glaze those apples red and secretly
> torch them with love: miserably, I am
> entangled in flames, and in place of breasts,
> good god, my hands vainly caress two apples.

Each creature, plant, or object in these poems (a lance, a wine jug, a garland) is both vividly itself and also, effortlessly, a trope. On the edge of death, or (depending on one's angle of vision) from the other side of death, the voices in these poems cut through externals to speak to us here and now directly of the essential. And yet those externals are essential too. The mice's sharp teeth, a girl's dark hair "curly as parsley" (Philodemus)—each detail is backlit by impermanence. The passing sensation (irritation at the marauding mice; desire for the girl; enjoyment of wine) that occasioned each poem has been captured and preserved in the amber of the poet's medium.

It wouldn't be quite right to say that less is more. Less is what remains to us, and its richness in each poem here has to, and does, suffice. But it is certainly true that less is more when it comes to the elegantly slim sheaf of poems (*lepidum novum libellum*, as Catullus might have put it) selected by Edmund Keeley from the much more lavish offerings of the Greek or Palatine Anthology, a collection of Greek poems spanning many centuries. Most of the poems in the Greek Anthology are epigrams, many are epitaphs; all are brief, but they're numerous enough that reading them one after the other creates a sense of clutter and repetition. Keeley has solved this problem with his artful selection of sixty-one poems by about twenty-eight poets, including the prolific Anonymous.

Keeley's judicious choice of poems, and his elegantly limpid translations, offer some of the same poignant pleasures as does the group of elegies he published in 2015 for his wife of many years Mary (1926–2012). While the poems in *Requiem for Mary* are longer then the poems Keeley has translated in *Nakedness Is My End*, the poems from the Greek Anthology and Keeley's own poems share a striking family resemblance. In both groups of poems, the tonal range encompasses a rueful, gentle irony; occasional querulousness; and a pervasive tenderness shading into stoical acceptance of the inevitable. In "Acts of Nature," for example, Keeley complains to the "supervisor" at the cemetery where he is visiting his wife's grave that her headstone is "soiled by droppings." But this objection modulates by the end of the poem into a philosophical equilibrium, as he reflects on the supervisor's answer that the droppings on the grave "were a simple Act of Nature":

> I went home unhappy.
> But as I thought about it,
> the urn in that grave
> carries acts of nature
> from the beginning and the end
> as will the other beside it
> no time at all in the future
> waiting for its stain or blossom
> as the great gods of nature
> in their capricious wisdom
> choose to mark that grave.

A similar arc of feeling, from complaint or irritation to a wider view, recurs in "Grass," with the hope that after "a blank matted spread / of dried mud and weeds" around Mary's headstone, "a carpet of grass / will show up in its time / to circle her place of rest. . . ." As the poem "Animals" acknowledges, we are subject, as are all animals, to the laws of nature. And in "Hospice," the beautiful final poem in *Requiem for Mary*, Keeley comforts the frightened and hapless young hospice worker and in so doing gently reassures not only her but himself and us immediately after his wife's death that "there was nothing more to do." Having said which, he goes on himself "to do what had to be done / after kneeling to say goodbye."

The spirit of *Requiem for Mary* imbues *Nakedness Is My End*, and vice versa. Not all the poems Keeley has chosen to translate are tender elegies, any more than Keeley's own delightful poem "Molar" is a tender elegy—except that finally it is. Some of the poems in *Nakedness* are salty or comical; some are angry reproaches. But all are softened by their intense humanity, and all are lit by mortality. Written so long ago, they are fresh and ageless.

February 5, 2018 was Edmund Keeley's ninetieth birthday. This luminous collection is the latest addition to Keeley's long list of distinguished translations from Greek; it is also a labor of love. I suspect and hope that *Nakedness Is My End* is not yet the end, not the last we'll hear from this tireless writer, whose humanity and generosity have already given us so much.

WHITE POLKA DOTS

W HEN I DECIDE it's time to deaccession a book in order to make more shelf space, more breathing space, for other books both old and new; and when I'm therefore poised to put this particular book in a box—with other recently singled out books to take down to the Strand or up to Book Culture and possibly sell—when this happens, I pull the book in question down from a shelf and open it.

As I leaf through the pages, I come upon a passage I don't remember having read before. The book is *Against Wind and Tide: Anne Morrow Lindbergh's Letters and Journals, 1947–1986*. This passage isn't from a letter or a journal; it's from "Musical Chairs," a talk the author gave in 1981, when she was a few years older than I am now. Today that talk is rich for me with meaning it evidently didn't have when my friend Reeve Lindbergh, on one of her rare visits to New York, gave me a copy of her mother's book, which she had edited beautifully.

Mrs. Lindbergh, who died in 2001, has moved beyond aging. But I still inhabit the zone of the living, which is the realm of relentless change (even more than "relentless," I like the Virgilian adjectives "ineluctable" and "irremediable," more resonant expressions of the same general idea). In 2017, I am five years closer to understanding what Mrs. Lindbergh said that day at the Cosmopolitan Club than I was when Reeve gave me her mother's book. Five years older and perhaps at least intermittently paying more attention.

Should I copy my favorite bits of "Musical Chairs" into my commonplace book, as I sometimes do with prose, more often with poetry? No, the passages are too long, the whole talk is too long. Besides, now that *Against Wind and Tide* is on its way out, I seem to be finding many more irreplaceable passages. "Musical Chairs" is charming and wise on the theme of aging, but much else in this book is also charming and wise— on filing correspondence, on loneliness, on grief, on grandchildren. And the truth is that Anne Morrow Lindbergh's writing doesn't excerpt particularly well. She's no La Rochefoucauld or Heraclitus; she deals not in gnomic adages but in the ebb and flow, the back and forth, of human interchange. Still, as if she were a poet or aphorist, I do copy down a few passages. And only then do I feel free, at least notionally, to pass the book along to a friend who expressed interest in it last week at lunch, when I must have been talking about my discovery—or rather rediscovery—of the book. My friend: a person is a cozier destination than Housing Works or Book Culture or the Strand. To pass the book along to my friend—to give, to lend it—is not an abstract gesture but part of a conversation. I tell my friend to feel free to keep the book. She promises to return it. And at this point I finally realize that *Against Wind and Tide* is—at least for the foreseeable future—a keeper.

Was I wrong even to think of giving this book away? No. I would never have found the luminous passages had I not opened the book and leafed through it. I would not have opened the book had I not taken it off the shelf. I would not have taken it off the shelf had I not thought of giving the book away. (Many of Mrs. Lindbergh's reflections in "Musical Chairs" concern tidying up, passing on, giving away.) Loss and disappearance loom like specters, if the inevitable can be called spectral. The plausibility of even a partial, even a planned, intentional divestment—say, of one book—causes a pang that makes one pay attention, that stops one in one's tracks.

Eventually these shelves will all be emptied and carted away somewhere—not only the books, the shelves themselves. Eventually we'll all be carted away. "The better part of the man," writes Thoreau, "is soon ploughed into the soil for compost"—scoured of our contents, discarded, transformed. So maybe it lessens the shock if I now begin, gently, gradually, approaching the shelves, pulling out one book at a time and opening it, and finding or re-finding what had been invisible or forgotten, invisible because forgotten, spotting what had been hidden in plain sight. Is this gradual process cutting off the dog's tail by inches?

Possibly. I don't think so, any more than I think it was wrong to imagine getting rid of a book.

Some months ago, my mother-in-law lent me a bright red cardigan flecked with big white polka dots—a cheerful garment, baggy, comical, almost clown-like. She remembered where, though not when, she'd bought (it's always easier to remember where than when): on Lexington Avenue one cold winter day, on her way to or from the Ninety-Second

Street Y. What attracted her were those big bold polka dots, which reminded her of her friend Robert Rauschenberg, who liked polka dots. (Who knew that? Not me.)

A week later, as my husband and she and I were going out her front door on a chilly January morning, she lent me a crimson cloche hat and a rose and fuchsia scarf, both rich warm colors, both velvety to the touch. Lent me? Gave me. So as we made our way to the doctor's office—one of many doctors—there I was, gifted with wearable memories pulled from a full closet and passed along with the affection and intention that are the privilege of the living. This affection, this intention are only possible before the orphaned closet's doors are closed. When this happens, all the dresses, sweaters, skirts, and blouses, neutral and impersonal and numb, can only hang there, waiting to be boxed and moved from that crammed closet, that house, that life, that history to some unknown destination.

The principle applies like a refrain. She would never have picked out the sweater with white polka dots and remembered a piece of the story that went with it had she not thought of passing things along. And, poised at the threshold, leaving her house for the doctor's office, she would not have thought of passing things along unless, unless, unless.

Metonymy: something associated with the person or thing stands for that thing or person. Synecdoche: the part stands for the whole. These thrifty tropes do thrifty double duty; they can be easily repurposed from the realm of poetry to the realm of life. If the law of rhetoric ordains transformation, the law of impermanence requires divestment. Acquire, enjoy, forget, lose, rediscover, cherish, and pass on. To love that well which thou must leave ere long: the motto of the bookshelf or the bedroom closet; the lesson of the second half of life.

TRANSLATED OBJECTS

When my son Jonathan moved from our West End Avenue apartment to Brooklyn, he took a surprising amount of furniture with him—heavy, dark brown furniture mostly, from his late father's side of the family. Furniture I'd failed for years to notice I no longer needed. But once the dresser, table, chair and whatever else had been loaded into a van and taken away, on a rainy December night in 2014, the West End Avenue apartment where I now lived with my new love began to breathe. Corners of rooms, newly empty, stretched themselves, plumped themselves out with air.

Meanwhile, Jon's new place in Bedford-Stuyvesant began to take on the look of the apartment he had just moved out of: the apartment where he had grown up and where he'd periodically alighted between moves to college, Missoula, Kathmandu, Chicago, Portland, and now Brooklyn, where the new apartment also featured inlaid wood floors, a narrow winding corridor, bookshelves, and that furniture.

The West End Avenue apartment in its turn bore a striking family resemblance to the apartment a mile north, on Riverside Drive, where I had grown up: a dark apartment, a long corridor winding its obscure course from front to back; and furniture: a bentwood rocking chair and a loveseat from my mother's family in Virginia, a massive seminar table my father had somehow spirited from a Columbia classroom. Not all of this furniture was heavy and dark brown, but much of it was; the dominant DNA prevailed through three generations of apartments. But as if on an allegorical pilgrimage through purgatory, each of these three apartments commanded a bit more light than its predecessor. The Riverside Drive apartment on the first floor was darker than the West End Avenue apartment on the third floor; the Bed-Stuy apartment, a fourth-floor walkup, had more light still. Onward and upward.

And then another direction: south. Three years after his move from

Manhattan to Brooklyn, Jon moved to North Carolina to live with his girlfriend in a house by the Haw River, the house where, six months later, on a May day of rain and sun and rain, she and he got married on the riverbank. When he moved down, he brought with him much of that faithful, sturdy, well-travelled furniture, as well as tablecloths, bowls, mugs, a Greek rag rug, a framed manuscript sheet of his father's music, family photographs, *The Changing Light at Sandover*, a blown-up image of the Monroe Leaf cover of his grandmother's translation of *Ferdinand the Bull* into *Ferdinandus Taurus*, and more, much more that I do not remember—although each time we visit them there, I think I recognize a few more items transplanted from another life. Each book or bowl appears to have settled into its new riverine space. Each has its provenance: more stories than any one heir could possibly remember or pass on. How much, after all, does Jon ask me about these things? How much do I spontaneously tell him? How much of what he's told does he retain?

The invisible heirlooms encoded in our genes are wedding presents waiting to be claimed, unpacked, set in place, and then eventually moved. Both buried and superficial, family resemblances are written on our faces, legible to those who can read the signs. If all that we inherit could be identified (is the word earmarked?): this nose, that height, this high cholesterol, that love of puns, this overbite, that scoliosis, this perfect spelling—we'd recognize it even in transit from one incarnation to another. But what we see is only scraps; hints; clues. We pay more attention to objects than to bodies, let alone to souls.

Objects transported through time or space are translated, like Bottom in *A Midsummer Night's Dream* after his vision, or like the objects James Merrill spies in his poem "After the Fire." In that poem, visiting his Athenian cleaning lady Kleo, Merrill notices item after item once his own: "I seem to know that crimson robe. . . ."

> . . . Meanwhile
> Other translated objects one by one
> Peep from hiding: teapot, towel, transistor.

They've been—stolen? filched? borrowed? appropriated? by Kleo's son Panayoti. The best word is the one the poet has already used: translated. Not that my son and daughter-in-law have filched anything. Everything that has passed from me to them has been freely and joyfully, if sometimes absent-mindedly, given. Nevertheless, Jon and Julia are inevitably in the process of translating these new and also not new possessions into their shared new dialogue, a language still in process, still undergoing merging and revision.

It's a rhetorical law, and also maybe a psychological fact, that over objects moved into fresh contexts as lives unfold and change, metonymy and synecdoche settle like fine dust. So let me focus synecdochically on one object among many; let the part stand for the whole.

Take this rug. Now it lies on a dark red downstairs floor in a house on a riverbank in Saxapahaw, a hamlet near Carrboro, North Carolina. The rug was woven by a Samian lady on her inherited loom. The path by which it came to this house isn't simple. Many years ago, back in New York (or, summers, in Vermont) after my four years on the Greek island of Samos, I cut up old blue jeans, blouses, nightgowns—denim, batik, flowered flannel, gingham—into long strips. I rolled the strips up into balls the size of balls of yarn and mailed them from the States back to Marathokampos, a village on the southwest side of Samos. Here the weaver transformed the strips into colorful, durable, striped runner rugs which she then packaged and mailed back to me. All of which is to say that the rugs were translated, indeed re-translated: from Manhattan or Vermont (the house there was a great repository of eligible rags) to Samos and back to Manhattan again, and from there to Brooklyn and now, most recently, to Alamance County in North Carolina—which may, however, not be the rug's last stop.

Samos is in the news now for reasons that have nothing to do with rugs or wine or tourism and everything to do with the plight of refugees herded into overcrowded camps. My time there in the seventies now feels mythical. The rugs—there were quite a few of them, and for years I kept many of them in a closet, pristine, waiting like a dowry—abide.

Think of a villanelle or a pantoum, poems in which entire lines are recycled or repurposed. Think of a sestina, whose six end-words chime in a set pattern. These durable poetic forms both capture and accede to theme and variation, mutability and limits. But at this stage of my life, I seem to lack the patience to fit each iteration into a set pattern, even if it's a pattern that affords room for improvisation. I don't feel like fitting bowl, tablecloth, desk, mug, or rag rug, singly or in artful combinations, into the set space of the poem's container.

In James Merrill's dense dream poem "Childlessness," the word *plot* does double duty as a space and a story. "She" is the poet's "dream-wife": "I hear her tricklings / arraign my little plot . . ." If a flower or shrub can be transplanted, can a plot, as in "storyline," also accommodate this kind of change? Turning back to "After the Fire," the "translated objects" Merrill recognizes not only appear (or "peep from hiding") in a new place; they are themselves different, in this new context—this new garden plot or story plot. The poet's complicated feeling about this new disposition of his things resolves into a stoical shrug: "Life like the bandit Somethingopoulos / Gives to others what it takes from us."

Poetry is where I usually go to make sense of what Wallace Stevens calls "life's nonsense." And yet, despite this ingrained habit, poetic forms, such a reliable and generous and time-tested bulwark against chaos and randomness, can come to seem arbitrary, rigid, even falsifying in their imposition of order. Even as its duration gets shorter and shorter, life these days feels to me as if it's opening out—concentric circles? A river trickling (Merrill's word in "Childlessness") into various deltas? There's a sense of spreading and an attendant thinness—not too much in any one place. Poems by contrast, or some of my favorite poems, are dense, compact. They lend themselves to being memorized. They feel like permanent possessions that resist change. Closure, never my favorite word, makes more sense in the context of poetry than in a life's passage, or even the passing on of an object. Things don't usually come to an end; we do.

Pass it on. The bowl, the book, the dresser, that rug, its rainbow of soft much-washed color on color, the patterns of some of the original fabrics still visible—they have apparently come to rest, but it's an illusion. Whitman writes in "To Think of Time":

> To think how eager we are in building our houses,
> To think others shall be just as eager . . . and we quite indifferent.
> I see one building the house that serves him a few years . . . or seventy
> or eighty years at most;
> I see one building the house that serves him longer than that.

That longer-serving house, that little plot, could be a grave. Or maybe it could be a poem.

V

Poetic Knowledge

DON'T GET HYSTERICAL,
GET HISTORICAL—AND MYTHICAL

PRECISELY A WEEK before the dreaded inauguration, I found myself thinking about work written by Euripides, W. H. Auden, Walt Whitman, and—a couple of months ago—by some of my students at Rutgers-Newark. In however zig-zaggy and haphazard a fashion, allow me to try to join this constellation of dots—or as Auden put it in "September 1, 1939," these "ironic points of light."

A graduate seminar on myth in literature I taught this past fall met on Wednesday afternoons. On November 9, I walked the students through "September 1, 1939."

To the best of my recollection, not one of the dozen of them (both MA and MFA students) was familiar with Auden's work at all. Marilyn Hacker, in her trenchant essay "Poetry and Public Mourning," reminds us that "Auden wished to excise some of his early political poetry from his oeuvre because he had ceased to hold the convictions there expressed: many readers go on reading these poems, wherever they stand in their politics." It's well known that "September 1, 1939" was widely circulated on the Internet after 9/11. It's also the case that some people quickly began to refer to November 9, 2016 as "11/9."

The reading on our syllabus that week was Euripides' play *Iphigenia in Aulis*. And although for part of the afternoon Iphigenia yielded air time to Auden, her compelling and nightmarish story continued to preoccupy the students. In addition to *Iphigenia in Aulis* and *Iphigenia among the Taurians*, we'd read Barry Unsworth's hard-hitting 2003 novel *The Songs of the Kings*, also about the sacrifice of Iphigenia by her father Agamemnon and his henchmen, and we had seen Michalis Cacoyannis's 1978 film *Iphigenia*, which adheres closely to Euripides' language. An ambitious father, a nubile daughter, an angry mob: "Iphigenia? Ivanka?" asked my student Ariel. Logical? Not exactly. Compelling as a parallel? Undoubtedly. For her final project, Ariel, a poet, wrote a short play on the subject. Another student wrote a dialogue, another a sequence of poems—all works that took these young women (all women) outside their usual generic comfort zones and that considered the ugly but endlessly ambiguous story of the sacrifice from multiple angles. No myth has a single or simple meaning; to understand it, you almost have to retell it, and in retelling it you can't help changing it a little. "The forms of the tales that work survive, and the others die and are forgotten," writes Neil Gaiman of myth in *The View from the Cheap Seats*. True enough; but just think of all the teeming life forms stories take before they become (as some certainly do) extinct.

Are the classics irrelevant? Walt Whitman thought so. In "Song of the Exposition" (1871) he wrote:

> Come Muse migrate from Greece and Ionia,
> Cross out please those immensely overpaid accounts,
> That matter of Troy and Achilles' wrath, and Aeneas', Odysseus'
>   wanderings,
> Placard "Removed" and "To Let" on the rocks of your snowy
>   Parnassus . . .

Whitman calls for "a better, fresher, busier sphere, a wide, untried domain." But his breezy optimism, his airy dismissal of stale grievances, didn't seem to pertain to the world we found ourselves living in last fall. Instead, my students were mesmerized by the darkly compelling, ironic, and multi-faceted story, which varies in every retelling, about the ruthless father and his daughter and the political backdrop against which the drama plays out.

Myth, I tell my students over and over, presents not a lesson but a vision, and lets us make of that vision what we will. At the tail end of 2016, I was drawn back to Auden—not "September 1, 1939" this time, but to *New Year Letter*, a long and immensely eloquent poem Auden wrote a few months later, about politics, art, and much else. I'd remembered and sought out again the ominous notes this poem strikes at the start, his matchless evocation of global jitters leading up to World War Two. But I'd forgotten the wonderful passage, also quite near the beginning of the poem, in which Auden authoritatively puts the case that art offers neither realism nor an easy set of instructions but rather

An algebraic formula,
An abstract model of events
Derived from past experiments,
And each life must itself decide
To what and how it be applied.

What does all this have to do with the Trump era we're being pulled into? Well, that words matter; that the classics retain their relevance, even if only because (as Auden puts it in "September 1, 1939") "we must suffer [it] all again." That we have to keep thinking for ourselves; even great literature of the past presents no easy answers. That the insistent tweet of the present mustn't drown out the past or the future. Robert Frost reportedly said at a dinner party in 1960, "Don't get hysterical, get historical. If they get some sense of historical background they'll see how these things happen over and over again."

Writing, teaching, journalism—these occupations, these vocations and avocations are more important now than ever. In the immediate future, they may become endeavors that call for more courage than many of us have at our disposal. Maybe we won't need our courage; maybe we will. Some of us will find it. Time will tell—mythic time as well as the other kind; the past as well as the present.

POETIC KNOWLEDGE

Robert Frost wrote in "The Figure a Poem Makes":

> Scholars and artists thrown together are often annoyed at the puzzle of where they differ. Both work from knowledge; but I suspect they differ most importantly in the way their knowledge is come by. Scholars get theirs with conscientious thoroughness along projected lines of logic; poets theirs cavalierly and as it happens in and out of books. They stick to nothing deliberately, but let what will stick to them like burrs where they walk in the fields.

Like burrs . . . or maybe more like ticks, which are plentiful in the long grass this early July in Vermont. But we don't want burrs and ticks to adhere—we strip them off when we come in from the fields—whereas presumably we do want knowledge to stick. So that (as Frost observes in his talk "Education by Metaphor") at some point the analogy breaks down. Ticks and burrs don't nourish us (on the contrary); knowledge does.

"Knowledge" is a clumsy and imprecise term for the kinds of connections I find myself making when, every summer, we come up here and I find myself walking through the fields. One kind of connection is derived from poetry. In the silence as I walk or pick wild strawberries or weed the vegetable garden, a line from some neglected corner of my memory will suddenly detach itself and slot into place, lighting up the moment.

Last week I was fretting about the long-neglected flower gardens my mother dug and planted here half a century ago. If my mother, who died in 1992, is anywhere, I believe she is here in these gardens, now overgrown and bushy but still retaining more than a hint of their original beauty. And I think of E. E. Cummings's poem that begins "if there are any heavens my mother will (all by herself) have / one." But "all by herself" sounds lonely, solipsistic—even though Cummings then swiftly corrects that solitude by introducing the courtly ghost of his father into the paradisiacal setting the reunited lovers share.

When I think of my mother's gardens, when I think of this house, I think of people—family, children, grandchildren, friends, various connections rippling out from a center of, yes, spacious solitude and meditative silence. Gardens and houses create space both for solitude and for company. But as the Greek poet George Seferis notes, in another line that came back to me recently, "Houses, you know, grow resentful easily when you strip them bare." (The poem is "Thrush," translated by Edmund Keeley and Philip Sherrard.) Part of the furniture of this house, and of my mind, inheres in poems. So that's one kind of knowledge.

I'm also thinking of another kind of connection for which, again, "knowledge" isn't quite the right word. The idea is captured, though, in phrases my father, the classicist Moses Hadas, used in the titles of two of his books: *Old Wine, New Bottles* and the subtitle of his *Hellenistic Culture*, which is *Fusion and Diffusion*. For Moses, who had a strong impulse to democratize the study of the classics, those new bottles would be the fresh container of translation. According to the parable, new wine will burst the old bottles; but Moses saw that the old wine would benefit from a new delivery system. And *Fusion and Diffusion* aptly evokes both the transformation and the expansion that attend on cultural transmission. If fusion suggests a coming together of previous separate entities and the possible creation of something new, then diffusion evokes an opposing outward movement. In the twenty-first century, surely the digital world is both the new bottle and a powerful new diffuser.

The apple (as Frost might have said) doesn't fall far from the tree. I've recently completed verse translations of Euripides' two plays about Iphigenia, spellbinding dramatizations of war and politics, family dynamics and trauma. As I worked, and particularly when I was finishing the translations and teaching *Iphigenia in Aulis* last November, there was no need to underline the alarming yet also perennial relevance of a story which was already old wine when Euripides decanted it into the new bottle of drama.

Another recently finished project sprang into being in January 2017, when our granddaughter was born. As the family considered names, I thought of Camilla, the warrior maiden, the swift runner, in Virgil's *Aeneid*. The name met with approval, and soon I found myself returning to the *Aeneid*, particularly to the poem's dark second half, which one rarely reads in high school. It didn't hurt that I was on sabbatical and had no classes to prepare or papers to correct. Almost every day I'd read a few pages in Sarah Ruden's translation, moving to the Latin whenever something struck me. Here were extraordinarily vivid depictions of war fever and hysteria, anxiety attacks, sleepless nights, fearful mothers standing on the battlements watching their sons march past.

If the Cummings and Seferis poems cited earlier were already somewhere in my mind, the Aeneid was more like a field through which I found myself intentionally but unhurriedly striding, always ready to pause and pick up a treasure.

Poems for Camilla consists of twenty-nine poems written between January and May 2017. Some of their titles have a contemporary ring: "Poetry Out Loud," "Filing System," "Weaponized," "Special Effects," "Anxiety Attack"; some, like "Iron Sleep," go straight to their Virgilian source. Neil Gaiman and David Copperfield, Riverside Park and Central Park, all make appearances, and the unnamed menace of President Trump broods over several of the poems. Camilla is there—both Camillas—and my husband's beloved younger brother, his *fidus Achates*. Lavinia, Amata, Latinus, Euryalus, Nisus, the Sibyl, and, of course, Aeneas are recurring presences.

Poems for Camilla will be published around Camilla's first birthday. Will she read these poems when she's older? The intention is there, at the very least, the possibility. When and if Camilla is ready or curious, the poems will be available. I love this durability of the intangible. Last week, in the first reclamation project of this particular summer, we replaced the grubby old kitchen stove (had mice been nesting in the oven or in the burner coils? So it seemed, but who wanted to know?) with a new one. "This should last your time," said the cheerful Sears delivery man. The bittersweet expectation is that the next stove, the next roof repair, the next revisioning of the garden will be the task of the next generation. Whereas the beauty of poems, of the classics, of the kind of knowledge we accumulate without having to go to the appliance store, is that they never need to be replaced. By definition, they outlast our time.

WHAT GOOD WILL
THIS KNOWLEDGE DO YOU?
FOUR POETS ON ILLNESS

Charles Bardes, *Diary of Our Fatal Illness* (University of Chicago Press, 2017)
Cameron Conaway, *Malaria Poems* (Michigan State University Press, 2014)
Christine Stewart-Nuñez, *Bluewords Greening* (Terrapin Books, 2016)
Jennifer Franklin, *Looming* (Elixir Press, 2015)

An octogenarian has bladder cancer: two years of procedures, hospitalizations, home again, confusion, decline, and death. His son pays close attention throughout and writes about the experience.

A young boy with a seizure disorder develops aphasia. His mother, who also suffers several miscarriages, pays close attention throughout and writes about the experience.

A health care worker in Thailand and elsewhere acquires a great deal of scientific knowledge about malaria and encounters many people who are suffering from the disease. He pays close attention throughout and writes about the experience.

A poet's young daughter is profoundly autistic. The poet pays close attention throughout and writes about the experience.

Charles Bardes is a doctor. Christine Stewart-Nuñez is a professor of English. Cameron Conaway is an activist and writer. Jennifer Franklin is a poet and teacher. All four of them had written and published poems before the current crop of books. Nevertheless, the experiences that occasioned these books, and which the poems in them record and address, galvanized Bardes, Stewart-Nuñez, Conaway, and Franklin into a new intensity and focus. The death of a parent; a child's irreversible neurological condition; the ravages of a parasitic disease over whole populations—these are not passing aches and pains but irrevocably life-altering experiences, which one doesn't get over. "We never," writes

Franklin in her poem "Demeter's Decision," "appreciate anything until it is lost." And then we appreciate it with a vengeance.

In Keats's late epic fragment *The Fall of Hyperion*, the god Apollo proclaims that "Knowledge enormous makes a god of me." Even if their personal losses didn't make these four writers into poets, perhaps their experiences made them better or different poets than they were before. Losses, suffering—whose? Their own or the suffering of others seen up close, experienced over time? The pronouns blur. What's clear is that suffering focused their minds, made them pay attention—and not just attention to the symptoms or the hospitals or the medications, but to everything, including familiar myths or paintings, a train ride, a conversation. And not only pay attention, but keep a record of the dying father, the struggling boy, the malaria sufferer. A record for whom? Sharon Olds used to remind her students that it wasn't only a question of who they were writing *to*, but who they were writing, speaking, *for*. The mere act of bearing witness—of writing, of communicating the onslaught of details, diagnoses, medical lore—this act, if only temporarily and in flashes, clears the mind; with luck and skill, not just the writer's mind but sometimes the reader's mind as well.

All four of these books would have been beneficial to their writers even if they had never been published—to their writers and maybe to a small (or, given the Internet, not so small) circle of family and friends. But having been published, *Diary of Our Fatal Illness*, *Bluewords Greening*, *Malaria*, and *Looming* have entered willy-nilly into a busy national conversation about being a patient or a caregiver, a doctor or a parent or an adult child. Furthermore, these slender books have, of course, entered the clamorous world of American poetry. Every day, especially during National Poetry Month, one encounters self-congratulatory statements about the diversity and dynamism of American poetry, its generosity and inclusiveness. But if race or gender or class are no longer barriers to poetic utterance, being old or ill or disabled may be the next hurdles. Perhaps these hurdles have been vaulted over already—after all, isn't Disability Studies a new academic field? Still, there's an inherent isolation in the patient's or caregiver's experience, a loneliness that inflects all these books and relegates them to a quiet but crucial corner of the loud arena.

The very inwardness peculiar to poetry, its paradoxical combination of the personal and the universal, is what makes it distinctive and irreplaceable. Its essential trope of apostrophe makes poetry a perfect vehicle for addressing the sick, the dying, or the dead. Poetry has always offered a natural way to mourn or pray. If the poet's range of reference includes myth, as is very much the case with Bardes and Franklin, then the myth in question (Demeter and Persephone in Franklin's poems, a range of Homeric and other references in Bardes) springs into fresh life even as it deepens and enriches the poet's personal experience. If the poet's resources are scientific, as is the case with Conaway, then the science enriches the poetry and vice versa. The intersections and overlaps are both generative and beneficial. In "Uncivilised Poetics," a recent issue of the excellent new periodical *Dark Mountain Review*, Rob Lewis encouraged his fellow practitioners to "tear down the walls, break up the categories, open the channels. Allow poetry to flow into science, science into prayer, prayer into nature, nature into poetry, and around and around let it go. Interpenetration is in the nature of things." Channels are beautifully opened, interpenetration is in action, when Stewart-Nuñez writes a poem entitled "Lexicon for Landau-Kleffner Syndrome" or when Bardes writes,

> It must have been three in the morning when my father phoned. Son, he said, I travelled for days until I reached the center. I underwent purifications and slept in the temple, where incense and fumes wafted through the air, serpents slithered between the supplicants, and priests tiptoed about us. There I learned my cure in divine dreams and snaky whispers.

It's not as if Jennifer Franklin had to strain to reach for the myth of Demeter and Persephone; it was right there, ready for her use as she investigated maternal loss. Demeter's loss of her daughter, however wrenching, is less devastating than Franklin's permanent loss of the daughter who, trapped in the underworld of her autism, is neither physically absent nor personally present—a murky condition the psychologist Pauline Boss has dubbed ambiguous loss. Ambiguous loss also characterizes Stewart-Nuñez's interactions with her increasingly aphasic son, and Bardes's with his failing father. Ambiguous loss is hard to live with; it is also a fertile field for poetry. As Stewart-Nuñez puts it in "When My OB/GYN Said He Didn't Understand Poetry,"

> When I build a nest of words,
> paradox and ambiguity kiss each time,
> offspring running down the page.

In addition to apostrophizing the absent or unresponsive, in addition to braiding myth or science into their fabric, poems have a generic genius for asking unanswerable questions. Conaway and Franklin provide eloquently defiant examples:

> You know the names
> Of every Sicilian wildflower
>
> But what good will this
> Knowledge do you in this world?
>   (Franklin, "Wildflowers")

> Is the surface of life like the thin skin of stilled
> water or the water itself? Is it the brindle of *Anopheles*
>   or the mosquito being behind
> what we've wrapped in name and taped down with distance?
>   (Conaway, "Die Never Always")

Stewart-Nuñez is more declarative and descriptive, and Bardes oddly eschews question marks, so his work lacks an interrogative lilt. But the dispiriting flatness of the exchanges Bardes reports are no less unanswerable for the absence of question marks.

> My father said, I suffer pain. The doctor said, Where.
>
> Dad, I said, why do you now read only the history plays.

If myth and apostrophe ease the loneliness and solipsism of the sickroom, if questions open out the scene into larger vistas, then simile and metaphor, also native to poetry, have a similar function. They relieve the tedium and vary the scene of the sickroom or the waiting room, if not for the patient then at least for the observer, the one keeping vigil, who is after all often the poet. Listening to a reading of the *Iliad* some years ago, I was very struck by the sheer relief provided by the wonderful string of similes at the start of Book III. Released from the claustrophobic tent full of heroes shouting at each other, the audience stirred and breathed; we could, however briefly, imagine the scene from a loftier, fuller, and calmer vantage point. Poetry constantly offers such little respites.

Of these four poets, Franklin is the most formally accomplished. Her lush, controlled lyricism aches with an unrelieved sadness that might risk monotony, but her poet's eye and ear, and her probing honesty, seldom fail her. Conaway is more stylistically uneven, but his electrifying "Die Never Always" is worth the price of admission. Perhaps Conaway's "In Season," a trenchant tour of a "supermarket / in a six-story mall / in Bangkok," could have been a prose sketch, an article. Perhaps Bardes's "Diary" could have been (after all, it nearly is) a memoir. And yet in choosing what Auden called "a way of happening, a mouth," these poets all know what they're up to. For poems, with their contrasting textures, their brevity, the discontinuous energy of their juxtapositions, can be uncannily true to the hour-by-hour experiences of illness and caregiving—experiences that are at once painfully slow and endlessly unpredictable. There are conversations, doctors' visits, excursions, remissions, relapses, diagnoses, dreams, flashbacks, distractions, descriptions, lists, apposite quotations—the catalogue goes on. Prose risks smoothing out the gaps, papering over the bumpy passages with specious homogeneity.

These are books for which to be grateful. They were written under circumstances of varying but wrenching difficulty; all the authors did their best to bear witness while at the same time lifting themselves above their respectively problematic situations. In writing these books, Franklin and Bardes, Conaway and Stewart-Nunez have helped themselves. But we are their beneficiaries too. For in addition to learning from the courage and perspicacity with which all these poets face illness, one can be inspired by their ability to tap into the timeless realms of trope, metaphor, and myth. Bardes's dying father may now "only read history plays," but his son and these other poets know better.

AN ECSTASY OF SPACE

Jane Cooper, *Scaffolding: New and Selected Poems* (Anvil Press, 1984)
Rosmarie Waldrop, *Streets Enough to Welcome Snow* (Station Hill Press, 1986)
Rosmarie Waldrop, *The Reproduction of Profiles* (New Directions, 1987)

*S*CAFFOLDING, THE TITLE of Jane Cooper's *New and Selected Poems*, suggests a support system, a work in constant progress (scaffolding put up while repairs are made), and also a skeletal, stripped-down intensity—all apt figures for this poet's quest for clarity and impulse toward self-revision. Adrienne Rich refers on the back cover of *Scaffolding* to Cooper's "continuing inner growth," and Cooper herself, in her Foreword, speaks of "the continuous journey the work has been for me all along." Cooper's oeuvre indeed refuses to stand still, which may be one reason critics have tended to detour around it. Nevertheless, the image of scaffolding is more evocative than that of a journey when one considers Cooper's career. It's as if the inner growth Rich mentions is achieved by continually peeling away layer after layer; what once was essential now seems superfluous and is calmly or exuberantly discarded to make room for the new.

What's that new like? The spareness of Cooper's recent work cuts both ways:

> For the last few years, particularly, we have all lived with the threat of nuclear holocaust. I want just to suggest it through images of all-consuming light, rooms with only a few sticks left in them, and a stripped-down landscape that is both the joyous, essential condition of truth telling and an almost unbearable vision of the future. (From the Foreword)

So the bright, bare room is both a joyful vision and a frightful glimpse of a bleak wasteland. Once the scaffolding is finally dismantled, we will have arrived at both heaven and hell.

One way to look at Cooper's work as *Scaffolding* presents it is to chart her progress toward that dangerous bright edge. We can note what has happened to the lineation, the prosody, even the punctuation between a poem from *Mercator's World* (1947–51) and one from *The Flashboat* (1975–83).

> Head first, face down, into Mercator's world
> Like an ungainly rocket the child comes,
> Driving dead-reckoned outward through a channel
> Where nine months back breath was determined
> By love, leaving his watery pen
> —That concrete womb with its round concrete walls
> Which he could make a globe of all his own—
> For flatter, dryer enemies, for home.
>
> (from "For a Boy Born in Wartime")

> The future weighs down on me
> just like a wall of light!
>
> All these years
> I've lived by necessity.
> Now the world shines
> like an empty room
> clean all the way to the rafters.
>
> . . .
>
> To live in the future
> like a survivor!
> Not the first step up the beach
> but the second
> then the third
>
> —never forgetting
> the wingprint of the mountain
> over the human settlement—
>
> (from "The Blue Anchor")

The tightly packed pentameter lines of "For a Boy" tend to split in "The Blue Anchor" into pairs of shorter lines with two or three stresses apiece, creating greater speed even as the syntactical texture is thinned out. The eight quoted lines from "For a Boy" are less than a complete sentence; "Blue Anchor" is almost breathlessly simple by contrast. Alliteration and assonance foster teeming connections within almost every line of "For a Boy" but are sparse in "Anchor," true to the poetics of the empty room. "For a Boy" is altogether more clotted, ponderous, and rich to read; one could liken the very different beauty of "The Blue Anchor" to that paradoxical wall of light, both shining and disembodied.

But careful chronological tracing seems the wrong tactic when we encounter a single (and crucial) poem, "All These Dreams," which is dated 1967–83. How do you disentangle the styles on a palimpsest? And it's also discouraging to an historical approach that Cooper has chosen to put her memorable 1974 essay, "Nothing Has Been Used in the Manufacture of This Poetry That Could Have Been Used in the Manufacture of Bread," between *Mercator's World* and *The Weather of Six Mornings*—that is, between groups of poems dated respectively 1947–51 and 1954–65. Why, for that matter, include an essay at all in a Selected Poems? "Nothing Has Been Used" is less an aesthetic manifesto (if it were, surely it would have been placed first or last in the collection) than an invaluable guide to Cooper's fluid but distinctive sensibility and style. The essay gives us an extended hearing of a voice that is necessarily curtailed in Cooper's usually short poems. Honest, self-critical, vehement without bravado, that voice comes through, for example, when Cooper remembers that

> during one of my interviews [at Sarah Lawrence] I was asked, "And why do you think you can teach poetry?" and I answered, "Because it's the one place where I'd as soon take my own word as anybody else's," though I went on to say that that didn't mean I thought I was always right!

Too shifting to be summarized without distortion, the argument of "Nothing Has Been Used" is faithful to the growth and change that are Cooper's theme. Like Emerson, Cooper is hard to paraphrase, but inspiring to read, and—as she leaps from autobiographical incident to piercing aphorism—tempting to quote from. Some of the comments about poetry in "Nothing Has Been Used" are worth pondering for any lover of the art.

> For what poetry must do is alert us to a truth, and it must be necessary; once it exists, we realize how much we needed exactly this.

A poem uses everything we know, the surprising things we notice, whatever we can't solve that keeps on growing, but it has to reach beyond autobiography even to stay on the page. Autobiography is not true enough . . .

I have a very old-fashioned idea of what poetry should do. It is the soul's history and whatever troubles the soul is fit material for poetry.

T. S. Eliot long ago pointed out that when poets make general statements about poetry, it is their own work they have in mind. Any reader of these passages can infer that Cooper has a lofty yet grounded notion of the nature and mission of poetry, as derived from facts but needing to transcend them. Despite a protean multiplicity of styles and indeed of subjects ("whatever troubles the soul is fit material"), poetry is marked for her by its high seriousness, its power and obligation to tell the truth.

A problematic part of that truth, for Cooper, is her earlier work. The poems from the 1940s and 1950s may seem to her insufficiently genuine, influenced by other (and largely male) poets; yet she concludes "Nothing Has Been Used" by saying she has learned to accept those poems "as part of whatever I now am . . . For if my poems have always been about survival—and I believe they have been—then survival too keeps revealing itself as an art of the unexpected."

I love the way that sentence twists in one's hands, refusing to end until it has completed its thought in an unexpected way. And the thought, like the entire essay, is complicated. To put it crudely, Cooper is both endorsing and condemning her early work. Her tone seems generous; yet a reader can easily be swayed into agreeing with what is perhaps implied: that her more recent poems are in some way more valuable than the early work. (Or *is* that implied? Cooper's delicacy of tone leaves us room to wonder.)

It is characteristic of Cooper that she relegates a recurrent theme of her work to a subordinate clause. The poems may indeed be about survival. The question, though, is less what Cooper writes about than how she writes. Has her style been crucially changed by the progressive simplifying we can discern between the full lines and complex syntax of "For a Boy Born in Wartime" and the almost hectic immediacy, and greater emphasis on the self, that we see in "The Blue Anchor?"

My answer would be that a family resemblance is discernible between most of the poems in *Scaffolding*, and that the shared features include concision and exactness; careful attention to details both of appearance and of mood; a strong sense of the line, and finally, a rejection of facile endings. These are not easy qualities to describe in literary terms. Grace Paley has well expressed what many of Cooper's admirers must feel: "This is a beautiful and stubborn book of poems. The poems say only what they mean." Is this a negative virtue? It's true that Cooper can be praised in negative terms: She avoids sloppiness, sentimentality, and—perhaps most unusual for a poet of her generation—obscurity. Following her own precept that poetry must go beyond autobiography, she speaks of large matters without sacrificing personal experience or an intimate voice.

In fact, Cooper's voice may be the most distinctive feature of her work. It reminds me of "the low tones that decide" (Emerson's phrase in "Uriel"), and also of the two aunts in *Swann's Way*, helplessly well-bred and subtle, who thank M. Swann for his gift of wine in such discreetly veiled terms that no one but their family understands them. Not that Cooper is cryptic; it's just that she's incapable of raising her voice or putting things coarsely, whether she's writing in the forties about World War II or in the seventies about a dream of communality. Words such as "delicate" and "nice" have become terribly suspect: Adrienne Rich has written (and Cooper cites her) of the pressures on women writers of their generation to be "nice." As for "delicate," that adjective was applied to the present writer in a recent magazine article, evoking derision from all kinds of friends and acquaintances. Some other word must be found to convey both the finely wrought and modulated character of Cooper's work from first to last, and her unremittingly ardent set of standards for both the style and the substance of her poetry.

An early poem that Cooper includes in *Scaffolding*, "Long View from the Suburbs," is a dramatic monologue in which Cooper attempts to "invent how it might feel to be the old Maud Gonne, whose extraordinary photographs had appeared in *Life* magazine" (from "Nothing Has Been Used"). So much for the poem's provenance; as for its style, Cooper says that "the rhetoric remains heavy (that need to write long lines, to have a battery of sound-effects at my command—like a man?)" She fails to do justice here to the originality and, yes, delicacy of her own effects. Yeats may have contributed to something in the poem's conception, and Auden, surely, to phrases like "A streetlight yielded to the sensual air." But the searchingly quiet mode of the poem is already Cooper's alone:

Once for instance
He begged to meet me under an oak
Outside the city after five o'clock.
It was early April. I waited there
Until in the distance
A streetlight yielded to the sensual air.

Then I walked home again. The next day
He was touchy and elated
Because of a new poem which he said
Marked some advance—perhaps that "honest" style
Which prostitutes our memories.
He gave it to me. I said nothing at all

Being weary. It had happened so often.
He was always deluding himself
Complaining (honestly) that I spurned his gift.
Shall I tell you what gifts are? Although I said
Nothing at the time
I still remember evenings when I learned

The tricks of style.

The poem hovers between the figure of Gonne and a probable accu-
mulation of personal experiences as nimbly as its sentences cross stanzas.
With a charming authority the tone glides between rueful amusement,
amused anger, and weary exasperation at male grandiosity and importunate enthusiasms. Note the eloquent sigh ("it had happened so often")
and the barbed parenthetical "honestly." No wonder many poets sacrifice
such subtleties for more unmixed rhetorical effects, for reading "Long
View" we can neither wholly sympathize with nor wholly condemn the
wry and ghostly resonance of a speaking voice that both is and is not a
persona. Cooper moves beyond biography here. We don't need to know
about Maud Gonne to savor the subtleties and ironies—and the aside (the
low voice dropping still lower?) about that "honest" style that prostitutes
our memories is surely a reflection of Cooper's own feeling about the
kind of desperately autobiographical poetry, exemplified by Lowell and
Berryman, that was coming into vogue around the time "Long View"
was written.

If the "I" in "Long View" both is and isn't a persona, there is no "I" at all in "For a Boy Born in Wartime." Cooper moves closer, as the years pass, to some center from which that skinny pronoun can authoritatively issue; yet her use of the first person is mostly exploratory, tentative, low-key, until the pivotal "All These Dreams" (dated 1967–83). Even that poem, with its unusual aposiopesis and exclamations, is full of questions.

> Where have I escaped from? What have I escaped to?
> Why has my child no father?
> I must be halfway up the circular stair.
> To shape my own—
> Friends! I hold out my hands
> as all that light pours down, it is pouring down.

In very general terms, the shift of emphasis in Cooper's work is from more public poems (of war) to more private poems (of love, family, dreams, work). Yet one must immediately qualify. The "public" poems were inward in their questing, and the "private" poems open out to speak to concerns as far-flung as nuclear holocaust, or what it means to be a woman, or—in the latest poem here, "Threads"—what it felt like to be Rosa Luxemburg in prison. Indeed, in "Threads" Cooper presents Luxemburg in a way that forces us to revise any pat notion of this woman as a merely political figure:

> We live in the painfulest moment of evolution,
> the very chapter of change, and you have to ask,
> *What is the meaning of it all?* Listen,
> one day I found a beetle stunned on its back,
> its legs gnawed to stumps by ants; another day
> I clambered to free a peacock butterfly
> battering half dead inside our bathroom pane.
> Locked up myself after six, I lean on the sill.
> The sky's like iron, a heavy rain falls, the nightingale
> sings in the sycamore as if possessed.

Imprisoned for her radical beliefs and opposition to World War I, Luxemburg tries to shed the weight of despair by passionately studying nature, especially birds and geology and insect life. But she cannot help seeing—and mourning—the painful struggles of historical change that have their deadly counterpart in the laws of evolution. Her intervention to save the peacock butterfly comes too late.

But just as Cooper's controlled tone is a pretty dependable constant, so we come to count on the images that surface throughout *Scaffolding*, images that help to shape the soul's troubling into art. One image is clearly signaled by the title of the 1970–73 poems but can also be seen elsewhere: dispossessions. Cooper is working her way toward what, as we've seen, she calls "rooms with only a few sticks left in them . . . a stripped down landscape." We see the inner and outer bareness in the problematic "All These Dreams":

> All these dreams, this obsession with bare boards:
> scaffolding, with only a few objects
> in an ecstasy of space, where through the windows
> the scent of pines can blow in . . .
> . . .
> O serenity
> that can live without chairs . . .

It took many readings for me to connect this passage with Thoreau's ecstatically ascetic mysticism, with Andrew Marvell's withdrawing mind in "The Garden," and perhaps also with some of George Herbert's plainly furnished rooms. But "All These Dreams" doesn't feel literary in the way that "Long View" or "For a Boy Born in Wartime" evidently came to feel to Cooper; it is a disembodied vision that is also a joyful *cri de coeur*, as familiar and strange as the dream state it invokes.

Less elated than the vision in "All These Dreams" is this fuller account of the same impulse toward spring-cleaning in "Souvenirs," the second poem in the splendid three-poem title sequence of *Dispossessions*. I quote "Souvenirs" in full:

> Anyway we are always waking
> in bedrooms of the dead, smelling
> musk of their winter jackets, tracking
> prints of their heels across our blurred carpets.
>
> So why hang onto a particular postcard?
> If a child's lock of hair brings back
> the look of that child, shall I
> nevertheless not let it blow away?

Houses, houses, we lodge in such husks!
inhabit such promises, seeking the unborn
in a worn-out photograph, hoping to break free
even of our violent and faithful lives.

Every detail of these expert lines seems to throw poetic light on a domestic dilemma, and vice versa. (The muse as pack rat or housecleaner; as the superego from whom we hope "to break free," or the magical link with the past?) As its title indicates, "Souvenirs" is no mere list of totems but concerns the act of remembering; yet part of the poem's persuasiveness surely derives from the reader's certainty that these carpets, jackets, locks of hair, and postcards are real, that Cooper is writing from abundance, not decorating emptiness with synthetic images.

The emblem of the house full of relics, that postcard especially memorable, reminds me of similar concerns in the work of two of Cooper's contemporaries, Adrienne Rich and James Merrill, whose different approaches to divesting themselves of the weight of the past are discussed in the late David Kalstone's illuminating book *Five Temperaments*. Rich's "Meditation for a Savage Child," writes Kalstone, juxtaposes "indignation [with] a residual attraction to familiar objects and the habit of cherishing." In Merrill's "The Friend of the Fourth Decade," the past is epitomized (as for Cooper in "Souvenirs") by postcards, but throwing them out—or as the friend suggests, rinsing the ink off—doesn't work: "the memories [they] stirred did not elude me." Ruefully Merrill acknowledges the power of what Cooper calls worn-out photographs:

I put my postcards back upon the shelf.
Certain things die only with oneself.

One wishes Cooper had found a place among Kalstone's temperaments.

The voice in "Souvenirs" is vehement but not angry. "So why hang onto a particular postcard?" sounds to me like an honest question, not a rhetorical posture; and "shall I / nevertheless not let it blow away?" is similarly a thought, not—or not yet—a dismissal. The same rapt, feeling-its-way intuition toward a desired space makes itself felt in "Rent," from the 1975–83 group *The Flashboat*:

I don't want your rent, I want
a radiance of attention
like the candle's flame when we eat,

I mean a kind of awe
attending the spaces between us—
Not a roof but a field of stars.

Notice the poem's rapid zoom from couple at the candlelit table to the
"field of stars"—a change of weather indeed, and scale, and tone, and light.

Such an outdoor space is also the scene of "Praise." The decks have
been cleared, and work/play is in progress, beyond the norm:

Between five and fifty
most people construct a little lifetime:
they fall in love, make kids, they suffer
and pitch the usual tents of understanding.
But I have built a few unexpected bridges.
Out of inert stone, with its longing to embrace inert stone,
I have sent a few vaults into stainless air.
Is this enough—when I love our poor sister earth?
Sister earth, I kneel and ask pardon.
A clod of turf is no less than inert stone.
Nothing is enough!
In this field set free for our play
who could have foretold
I would live to write at fifty?

Who could have foretold I would set the field free? might be another way
of putting it. The poem is a kind of psalm to (re)creation; mere dispos-
session has yielded both to a more sublime blankness and to a different
kind of construction—a creation not of domestic interiors or of kids,
but of architecture—more scaffolding! I myself feel more at home with
the Cooper of "Souvenirs," but the elation in *The Flashboat* comes from
somewhere; it feels honest and earned.

Companion to the successive strippings in Cooper's work is an
image a little harder to describe. It might be called recognition, or self-
scrutiny, or looking into a mirror, or meeting someone else's eyes—or
meeting one's own. The self, after all, cannot be thrown away like a "particular postcard" or a lock of hair; it changes, and we can keep track of
the changes by focusing from time to time on the latest manifestation
of what we are. As early as "For a Boy Born in Wartime" Cooper refers
to "the concrete / Unmalleable mirror world we live in." The mirror
slowly clears:

Feelings aside I never know my face;
I comb my hair and what I see is timeless,
Not a face at all but (besides the hair)
Lips and a pair of eyes, two hands, a body
Pale as a fish imprisoned in the mirror.

(from "The Knowledge That Comes Through Experience")

That fish-pale body is unsettlingly reminiscent of Sylvia Plath's image of a woman looking in a mirror and seeing an old woman rise in it "like a terrible fish," though as we might expect Cooper is more controlled in her distaste for what she sees.

One solution to the problem of appearances, in *The Weather of Six Mornings*, is to address oneself as another. Indeed, the self presented by an old photograph (which has evidently not yet been discarded) *is* an other. "Leaving Water Hyacinths" (subtitled "from an old photograph") begins "I see you, child, standing above the river" and moves, at the start of each successive stanza, to a closer identification of speaker with image: "I know—because you become me" and finally "I know—because you contain me."

In two remarkable poems—apparently about her mother but actually, I think, about the double layering of selves (younger and older mother; younger and older daughter)—Cooper is true to the difficulty not only of liking images of ourselves, but of reconstructing the appearances even of those we love:

Why can I never when I think about it
See your face tender under the tasseled light
Above a book held in your stubby fingers?
Or catch your tumbling gamecock angers?
Or—as a child once, feverish by night—
Wake to your sleepless, profiled granite?

But I must reconstruct you, feature by feature:
Your sailor's gaze, a visionary blue,
Not stay-at-home but wistful northern eyes;
And the nose Gothic, oversized,
Delicately groined to the eyesockets' shadow,
Proud as a precipice above laughter.

A curious cubism supplies us with more visual details than we can well assimilate; the reconstruction is no more "realistic" than a Picasso portrait, and yet (or therefore) communicates powerfully what struggles to find a niche in memory. These lines, which splendidly render back what the speaker says she can't see, are from a poem entitled "For My Mother in Her First Illness, from a Window Overlooking Notre Dame"; yet at the poem's close it is the daughter who is ill: "Alone and sick, lying in a foreign house, / I try to read. Which one of us is absent?"

A similar pentimento gives an uncanny doubleness to "My Young Mother," quoted here in full.

My young mother, her face narrow
and dark with unresolved wishes
under a hatbrim of the twenties,
stood by my middleaged bed.

Still as a child pretending sleep
to a grownup watchful or calling,
I lay in a corner of my dream
staring at the mole above her lip.

Familiar mole! but that girlish look
as if I had nothing to give her—
Eyes blue—brim dark—
calling me from sleep after decades.

Mother and daughter, past and present: The successive embodiments merge with a fluency reflected in Cooper's supple and sparing use of the first person. A poem about her mother, for example, twists into one about her, rather as a letter that begins by politely eschewing the writer's concerns manages gracefully to arrive at some personal news. Survival, Cooper has said, keeps revealing itself as an art of the unexpected; the unexpectedness of some of Cooper's shifts of emphasis surely has the spryness and resilience necessary for survival.

Cooper is able to invest poems that almost or completely suppress the first person with a searching intimacy that constitutes a kind of mirroring at a remove. "Waiting" and "A Circle, a Square, a Triangle and a Ripple of Water," neighboring poems from *Dispossessions*, look at, and into, not only the eyes but the entire body, both in itself and, especially in "A Circle," in relation to others.

> My body knows it will never bear children.
> What can I say to my body now,
> this used violin?
> Every night it cries out strenuously
> from its secret cave.
>
> (from "Waiting")

> Seemingly untouched she
> was the stone at the center of
> the pool whose circles
> shuddered off around her.
>
> (from "A Circle")

It wouldn't be hard to rewrite this pair of passages so that "Waiting" was in the third person and "A Circle" in the first person, so precise is Cooper's intimacy, and so passionate her observation.

At about the point in Cooper's work where she reaches the ecstasies of empty space, the images of self-searching drop. The overlay of one's parents *is*, by middle age, a thing of the past—still there, no doubt, but no longer news. And a new kind of mirror can be found in the gaze of like-minded companions and other variants of reflection. In "All These Dreams," there is no mirror—after all there are no rooms, and presumably no walls—but "light poured down through the roof on a circular stair / made of glass." And at the poem's close, which I have quoted earlier but must return to, Cooper interrupts herself in the midst of shaping . . . what?

> I must be halfway up the circular stair.
> To shape my own—

My own image? self? work? Her word does double duty as the object of "to shape" and as a glad apostrophe: "Friends!"

That circular stair is a good emblem for Cooper's work. It may recall Yeats's winding stair, but it has its own radiance; and the poet is halfway up it, not in a dark wood but in a group of friends, laughing. The most rewarding thing about *Scaffolding* is the way Cooper's scrupulous and profoundly serious art moves toward joy.

If Cooper strains toward sparseness, Rosmarie Waldrop, in *Streets Enough to Welcome Snow*, is a chatelaine of spaces whose spareness is deceptive. Like a resourceful city dweller, Waldrop hoards images in narrow quarters that manage to seem neither cramped nor chaotic. One of the pleasures her work offers is its dovetailing of disparate items, memories, sensations into almost invisibly small corners:

> Once
> I've got something
> I lie
> down on it
> with my whole body.
> Goethe quotations, warm
> sand, a smell of hay,
> long afternoons.
>
>   (from "Remembering into Sleep")

The verticality these short lines create fosters a nimble rapidity of motion that deftly mimics the mind's associative hoppings. For Waldrop is above all a poet of thought; her lines abound in sensation, but the movement of consciousness underlies and informs remembered scents, crackling combs, puffing pipes. The passage just quoted, for example, is followed by an immediate moving away from simple remembered sensation:

>   But it
> would take a road
> would turn, with space,
> in on itself,
> would turn
> occasion into offer.

Author of five previous books of poems, a novel, an unclassifiable collection I'll come to in a minute, and many translations, Waldrop is an accomplished writer who seems comfortable with her own style. The short lines so much in evidence throughout *Streets* can become wearying, but the contents of the poems are less simple and restricted than the look of the pages might suggest. At best, the short lines contain vitality; more often they are used with telegraphic effectiveness:

> Distant boots.
> Black beetles at night. A smell
> of sweat.
> The restaurant,
> yes. You've no idea
> how much my father used to eat.
> Place thick with smoke.
> Cards. Beer foaming over
> on the table.

At times, Waldrop's mini-lines fragment annoyingly what my ear wants to perceive as a fine iambic line. Two examples: "For all her beauty / worshipped / but unloved" and "the burn / and the bandage both / making memory." Is the assumption here that the reader is incapable of processing a paradox—or indeed any kind of complexity—unless the contrast it embodies is separately packaged by the lineation? An occasional foray into the landscape of long lines would give Waldrop a far greater range of effect.

Nor do these poems always benefit from the fragmentation of their syntax. Try to follow the grammar of "On Being Forgotten," from a sequence called "Actaeon: Eleven Glosses on an Alibi":

> How does it happen
> like thin rain
> a look that
> takes too long to arrive
> endless passage from eye
> to eye
> but what does forgetting precisely
> forgetting is now thin rain
> it gnaws at his skin
> with beginning of fear
> fear of water
> it might
> give to the touch
> a look was drowned

in a wound
an eye all pupil all open which bleeds.

Should we say simply that the syntax here imitates the putt-putting looseness, the repetitious stammer of lost memory? I don't like to ascribe simplistic motives to a writer of Waldrop's intelligence; she probably knows what effect she wants, but the style can become a tic all the same, albeit a mildly witty tic:

once upon
a time
once upon the impatient sea
once
in the kitchen
get me out please
I want
I want
the rain the river the morning balks at the cold

    (from "Providence in Winter")

At other times, Waldrop achieves not only elegance but a sense of remarkably luxuriant leisure in the narrow confines of the framework she has constructed for herself. I've seldom seen a more economical description of falling asleep (falling into sleep? diving?) than:

Castles in sand.
Or Spain. Space
of another language.
Sleep
is a body of water.
You follow your lips
into its softness. Far down the head finds its level.

    (from "Remembering into Sleep")

Robert Peters has written that Waldrop has "taken up residence in the abyss between signified and signifier." Assuredly she is not afraid of silence; but even more eloquent than blankness is what one uses to garnish it. Not surprisingly, Waldrop has a striking description of stifled utterance, indeed of general paralysis:

The cat
can't lift its paw,
its leg longer and longer
with effort.
A crying fit
is cancelled. An aria jelled
in the larynx.
Nothing moves in the cotton
coma

    (from "Remembering into Sleep")

It is entirely characteristic of Waldrop that the larger context of this passage is a consideration of how dreams, memories, language itself baffle: "A dream, like trying / to remember, breaks open words for other, hidden meanings." Perhaps what Peters's stylish-sounding formulation means is that Waldrop is an explorer of those meanings. If so, I'd agree.

Streets Enough to Welcome Snow offers many pleasures, but these pale in comparison with the dense, inscrutable little blocks of text that constitute Waldrop's wonderful collection *The Reproduction of Profiles*. So far as one can tell from the publication dates, *Streets* and *Profiles* were written at about the same time. If the latter volume came later, it would be interesting to try to apply David Kalstone's template in reverse: is Waldrop moving toward a kind of formal constraint, buttoning what had previously been unbuttoned? Not that either of Waldrop's books is disheveled or self-indulgent; but *Profiles*, the more uniformly shaped of these works, radiates the confidence of an achieved style. Here, in Stevens's words, Waldrop's anima seems to have found its animal. Underneath the bleakness of some of the profiles' surfaces pulses the exuberance of power, the power of exuberance.

I've never been comfortable with the term "prose poem," since samples of the genre often seem to combine the worst features of both parents. Waldrop's paragraph-long profiles, though, manage to unite the intense suggestiveness, and often the rapid pace, of lyric with what Barbara Guest has called the "unnerving leap of suspended narrative."

Of course, shreds of story float in the broth of many poetic sequences: works like *The Waste Land, Paterson, The Bridge*, and Seferis's *Mythistorema*, which share a discontinuous narrative progress, a halo of suggestiveness, and disappearing and reappearing snippets of character and event, have a vague affinity to *The Reproduction of Profiles*. Closer to

Waldrop's particular preserve here, however, are (as she has said) Wittgenstein's anti-metaphysical dicta. I think also of the quasi-scientific, precisely lush aphorisms of Malcolm de Chazal's *Sens Plastique*; of the Ashbery of *Three Poems*; and of the miniature (not minimalist!) stories of Lydia Davis (Davis has translated Maurice Blanchot; Waldrop has translated Edmond Jabès and many Austrian poets).

It's easy, in short, to think of *Profiles* as the sort of literary form that comes more easily to Europeans: are these *petits poèmes en prose* in English? But Waldrop's beautifully turned—and turning; writhing—sentences are translations, not from French or German, but from pure thought; like her poems, but in a more distilled and masterful mode, they delineate the movements of the mind. What Bruce Andrews has called Waldrop's constant retrieval from one plane to another is nowhere more in evidence than in these compactly flexible, subtly pithy paragraphs, each of which does indeed execute some kind of bringing back.

Behind Wittgenstein or Baudelaire, I sense in *Profiles* the master of aphorism whose crabbed and enigmatic utterances retain an astounding modernity in their fragmentary state, a state that some scholars argue was never anything other than fragmentary. The following meager sampling of Heraclitus ought to show both the laconic imagistic elegance of his style, and the bite of a complexity that imagist poems are too simple to achieve:

The name of the bow is life, its work is death.

The fairest order in the world is a heap of random sweepings.

Death is all we see awake; all we see asleep is sleep.

Not comprehending, they hear like the deaf. The saying
  is their witness: absent while present.

Eyes and ears are poor witnesses for men if their souls
  do not understand the language.

This tragicomedy of the mind's gymnastics Waldrop dons like a leotard and proceeds to bemuse us with gestures that keep changing. Paradox now defuses, now signals desire; speculation thickens into argument; denial shucks off its erotic guise and puts on dialectic.

From Heraclitus to Wittgenstein, from Proust to Stevens, philosophical writers have taken language as their medium and mirror. Waldrop is no exception; yet she somehow avoids the solipsistic taint which so often imbues ponderings on language, time, and the self. (The alternative to avoiding solipsism is to soak oneself, like Proust, in the destructive element.) Her narrative force, like bursts of fresh air, intermittently clears away the curling ground fog of *me me me*; in these paragraphs there is nearly always an other—one other, often a lover/other, so that although language is a constant preoccupation, it is demystified by context.

> If I fail to deposit a coin, everyday language produces the most fundamental confusions, but what pleasure in getting lost if it is unavoidable? (p. 20)

> Your face was alternately hot and cold, as if translating one language into another—gusts from the storm in your heart, the pink ribbon in your pocket. Its actual color turned out to be unimportant, but its presence disclosed something essential about membranes (p. 26).

> I was afraid we would die before we could make a statement, but you said that language presupposed meaning, which would be swallowed by the roar of the waterfall (p. 28).

A "profile" worth quoting in full uses a narrative strategy to limn both a relationship and a frontal assault on the ungraspable sinuosity of language:

> In order to understand the nature of language you began to paint, thinking that the logic of reference would become evident once you could settle the quarrels of point, line, and color. I was distracted from sliding words along the scales of significance by smoke on my margin of breath. I waited for the flame, the passage from eye to world. At dawn, you crawled into bed, exhausted, warning me against drawing inferences across blind canvas. I ventured that a line might represent a tower that would reach the sky, or, on the other hand, rain falling. You replied that the world was already taking up too much space (p. 33).

Observe how stealthily we've crossed the border from a temporal to a spatial sense of language. Looking back, one notices that the larger section from which this profile is taken is entitled "If Words Are Signs."

The palpable pleasure Waldrop's elegant constructs bestow is at ironic odds, now and then, with the hesitancy of the voice—a voice always supremely articulate, often suave in a deadpan way, yet sometimes querying if not quite querulous, obsessive, nagging. Not that a voice is the same as a self—should one hazard the weary term persona? Yet it won't do, either, to think of the voice as a disembodied emanation. It issues from a body that can feel sleepy, for example:

> I felt sleepy, no doubt because I have a long past and don't speak foreign languages (p. 47).

> In the middle of rainy weather, sleep was pinning me down on the bed, lids barnacled shut with adjectives in color. Sleep, which cannot be divided from itself or into parts of speech, pushing a whole sea at my body so unable to swallow its grandiose and monotonous splendor (p. 80).

The self has distinctive characteristics and reactions:

> Being late is one of my essential properties: Unthinkable that I should not possess it, and not even on vacation do I deprive myself of its advantages (p. 37).

> I had always resented how nimble your neck became whenever you met a woman, regardless of rain falling outside or other calamities (p. 27).

It can even manage—temporarily—the last word:

> You said there was still time, you could still break it off, go abroad, make a movie. I said (politely, I thought) this wouldn't help you. You'd have to kill yourself (p. 26).

That the mind's and body's lapses and eclipses are finally unimportant—or rather are important but not disabling—is reassuringly demonstrated by the way the tics and contretemps, the interruptions and cul-de-sacs of daily life find their way into, and enhance, the glinting fabric of the words. This is the paradoxical consolation of *Profiles*. The sleepiness Waldrop evokes is akin to the states of drowsiness or incapability conjured up by two poets who have a similarly rueful mastery at turning their liabilities to assets. Listen to Ashbery in *Three Poems*:

> . . . You see that you cannot do without it, that singular isolated moment that has now already slipped so far into the past that it seems

a mere spark. You cannot do without it and you cannot have it. At this point a drowsiness overtakes you as of total fatigue and indifference; in this unnatural, dreamy state the objects you have been contemplating take on a life of their own, in and for themselves. It seems to you that you are eavesdropping and can understand their private language . . . ("The System")

And here is David Lehman in the title poem of his collection *An Alternative to Speech*, where a supremely articulate poet gesticulates in an elaborate dumbshow that is both frightening and funny:

> Sudden attack of aphasia, I hold my breath like smoke
> And take credit for the brutal gifts
> The darkness bestows. Do you have a friend
> To lend me? . . .
>   From whom I may learn an alternative
> To speech, recipes for staying hungry,
>   instructions on staying awake,
> If death isn't everything.

These protestations of incapability, drowsiness, and aphasia are both ironic and truthful; being alive and awake is often a sleepy business, shot through with occasional gleams of insight and energy. The paradoxical consolation, as I've said, is that these confessions of dumbness are not only close to experience but actually enhance our awareness. Our drowsy thoughts glide gratefully through such stimulating labyrinths as Jane Cooper's scrubbed white rooms and the unsettling nooks and crannies of Waldrop's multi-dimensional profiles. All praise is due to the creators of both.

SUBTERRANEAN FORCES

Edward Baugh, *Black Sand: New and Selected Poems* (Peepal Tree Press, 2013)

Erica Dawson, *Big-Eyed Afraid* (Waywiser Press, 2007), *The Small Blades Hurt* (Measure Press, 2014), and *When Rap Spoke Straight to God* (Tin House Books, 2018)

Ishion Hutchinson, *House of Lords and Commons* (Farrar, Straus and Giroux, 2016)

Rowan Ricardo Phillips, *The Ground* (Farrar, Straus and Giroux, 2012) and *Heaven* (Farrar, Straus and Giroux, 2015)

IN THESE JITTERY TIMES, writing about literature is an enterprise pocked with pitfalls. Translate a text from a language spoken by relatively few people into one of the global tongues and you can be accused of colonializing, appropriating, privileging, and all the rest of the moralistic litany of blame. Closer to home, as I, an aging white woman, sit down to write about four wonderful poets of color three of whom are young enough to be my children, it would be terribly easy for me to feel paralyzed between bad choices. Should the skin color of Edward Baugh, Ishion Hutchinson, Erica Dawson, and Rowan Ricardo Phillips make a difference? If not, then why mention it? Why group these very different poets, why herd them into this particular pen, at all? Yet ignore the fact of race and you may be called complicit in the silence. Ignoring race is a privilege of white people. No wonder the late and much missed Tony Hoagland referred, in a recent essay, to "the double or triple bind of power, apology, and hazard that hamstrings white writers when they attempt to deal with race." Confronted by this complicated maze, it's easy to choose silence as the graceful way out. And yet how silent is that silence, really? It's troubled, murky, roiling with history. Hoagland again: "In matters of race, subterranean forces always seem to be actively coexistent with those explicable by rationality."

What to do? Two voices from decades ago resonate now. In *Three Poems* (1989), John Ashbery posited the dilemma: "I thought if I could put it all down, that would be one way. And next the thought came to me that to leave it all out would be another, and truer, way." This sweeping statement can be understood as including politics as part of "it." And politics is unquestionably at issue in a poignant conversation recalled by the artist Zoe Leonard about a conversation she had with David Wojnarowicz at his 1990 show "Tongues of Flame." "I felt guilty and torn. I felt detached—my work was so subtle and abstract, so apolitical on the surface. I remember showing these pictures [small prints of clouds] to David and talking things over with him and he said—I'm paraphrasing—Don't ever give up beauty. We're fighting so that we can have things like this, so that we can have beauty again."

The dilemma, the dichotomy, the unforgiving choice, the swerve in a career—they're everywhere you look. They're not new; two penetrating and authoritative books (important? forgotten? both?) about twentieth-century poetry, Richard Howard's magisterial *Alone in America* (1969) and David Kalstone's *Five Temperaments* (1977), both trace, in some of the poets they consider, a stylistic trajectory from more formal to more open, unbuttoned, bold. And in the powerful 2017 anthology *Resistance, Rebellion, Life: 50 Poems Now*, editor Amit Majmudar comments in his introduction that beyond "the obvious go-to poets for political engagement, I could see the ruptures that an aroused political consciousness seemed to precipitate" in other poets' oeuvres, "that transition from filigree to in-your-face." That filigree-to-in-your-face unmasking isn't merely a matter of doffing one persona and putting on another. It's a matter of vision. Not just how but what: what do you see, what do you say? What do you put in or leave out? What can you bear to include or to ignore?

If silence is a guilt-provoking thought for me, then I can only begin to imagine how it feels to be a poet of color. In a poignant but confusing passage in her memoir *Ordinary Light*, Tracy Smith has paired the consciousness, the silence, and—if I understand her rightly—also the impulse to transcend the burden of knowledge. She writes:

> I don't think we ever truly forgot about whites, even when we were alone among ourselves in the thick of family. I doubt any blacks do. There's always a place in the mind that feels different, distinct; not worse off or envious but simply aware of an extra thing that living in a world that loathes and fears us has necessitated we develop. Perhaps

that thing is the counterbalance to the history of loss I often tried to
block out with silence . . .

Edward Baugh, Ishion Hutchinson, Erica Dawson, Rowan Ricardo
Phillips: by choosing these four poets, of course, I am passing over many,
many others—a critical problem even where race isn't at issue, but again,
a more fraught one these days.

My justification, if one is needed, is that to write about a poet one
admires is always to learn more, to dig a little deeper. And the more I
think about these poets' work, the more I see how elegantly, in their very
different ways, each of them has, from the beginnings of their respective careers, found ways of negotiating the racial labyrinth—has, in a
sense, managed to have their cake and eat it too: to speak the truth without sacrificing elegance and wit. Perhaps this achievement—all their
achievements—is one way to (in Smith's phrase) transcend the burden
of knowledge. Just such a transcending is what Tony Hoagland is calling
for when he writes: "the poems of grievance and testimony written by
poets of color will become tiresome unless they motivate their own consciousness." And Hoagland quotes the late Reginald Shepherd: "Identity
poetics is *boring*, giving back the already known, in an endless and endlessly self-righteous confirmation of things as they already are . . . the
greatest literature has always engaged in the generation of new realities,
not the reiteration of the same old given reality." Of course, in literature,
as in the other arts, new realities are composed of carefully chosen and
combined strands of old realities.

The poet Edward Baugh, born in 1936, whose distinguished academic
career has unfolded in his native Jamaica, eludes simple classification.
Baugh's new reality is a thoughtful, endlessly nuanced, sometimes quiz-
zical probing of the parameters and possibilities of poetry, of Blackness,
and of how these two intersect. It took me a while to discern the persis-
tence of these entwined themes; Baugh's work is always elegantly subtle.
But *Black Sand* (2013), Baugh's New and Selected, can be construed as an
ongoing argument: a dialogue between speech and silence, between presence and invisibility, even between one dialect and another. The poems
keep returning to fundamental questions: not only what to write about
but how to write about it. Even if these questions are sometimes posed by
clueless interlocutors, they're important questions, and not easy to answer.

Sometimes Baugh addresses the unaccountable ebb and flow of inspiration. In "The Comings and Goings of Poems," he writes, "Interview-

ers ask me how the poems come. / Do they need some special frame / of mind, some auspicious hour / of night, and where? So this one / is to pull out of my hat the next time / some interviewer asks. . . ." In a deft twist, the poet's attempt to answer seems to turn into a poem: "and I couldn't even pinpoint when the flow began / or why; and then, right there, while that one / was coming, this one came, to tell / how the first had come. And isn't it worth / a poem to explain, how many a time / things come together, without reason or rhyme?" The title poem, "Black Sand," is a beautiful unfinished gesture, an extended clause of what sounds like a contrary-to-fact condition. Too long to quote, it begins: "If the poem could open itself out and be wide / as this beach of black sand. . . ." What then? Baugh doesn't say, but we're invited to finish the thought, which is inflected by the spellbinding and poignant image, in the lines just before the poem trails off into silence, of "the largo of sunset spreading over the city / as the jagged, wounding edges of our unworthiness / are worn down by forgiveness, wave after untiring wave . . ."

Perhaps it's the same importunate interviewer who asks "how the poems come" who wants to know "So, what would you say that poetry is for?" ("What's Poetry For?") Such questions may be well-meaning, but Baugh loses patience. He does not, however, forget his manners: "I mouthed well-meaning platitudes, / and then we slunk away, the poem and I, / to nurse our dream of heaven: a place / where no one asks what poetry's for." Baugh's unfailing urbanity allows him to see the humor in a reviewer's comment that "A few of the poems are, admittedly, slight and ornamental"—a phrase the poet transforms into a "slight and orna- mental / butterfly that flew across the morning." The ham-handed ques- tions or comments are transposed into another key in a poem entitled "To the Editor Who Asked Me to Send Him Some of My Black Poems." Even here, Baugh's delicate touch doesn't desert him. But the poem has an edge, and even the faintest hint of half-humorous threat, that might be useful to all poets of color who receive such request:

> Friend, at first I thought
> you had exposed me quite,
> found out in me a lack:
> I had no colour-coded verse!
> But then a thought flashed back:
> truth is, my poems are so black
> they are invisible to even me,

you wouldn't be able to see them
were I to send them;
moreover, what is worse,
their gravity is so intense
that any light that ventures close
to them just disappears; you too
would be forever lost to view;
and so, in consequence,
not wishing to put you
and your safety on the line,
I beg, respectfully, to decline.

The poem as black hole? Not quite. Yet there is indeed darkness in Baugh's poems—different tonalities of ethical darkness, shadow, and evil. Baugh's urbanity doesn't fail him, but neither does his sensitivity to the injustice and tragedy lurking not far below various kinds of surfaces. In "A Nineteenth-Century Portrait," the shadow is cast by both nature and history:

"How well the boy's / dark visage serves design, / matching the dark of the trees to cast / in relief the pale, proprietorial white. / Those were the good days; they didn't last." Yes, but good for whom? In a poem about a friend's death, there is always, even as "our talk steps precariously round it," a dark hole in the garden. In "Sunday Afternoon Walks with My Father," a richly evoked and apparently gentle memory tunnels deeper to the poem's haunting finish, as the little boy glimpses an enormous turtle: "primeval otherness / under the glint and surfaces of weekday / worlds, Sunday's obstinate, slow / disquieting underside, the lap and suck / of black water, the compelling undertow."

Would it be pushing too far to be reminded by this passage, as well as by others in *Black Sand*, of Hoagland's comment (already cited above) that "In matters of race, subterranean forces always seem to be actively coexistent with those explicable by rationality"?

Not that most of Baugh's poetry is exclusively or overtly concerned with either poetry or race. History runs through these poems like an underground stream; it's as if Baugh can't help peering below "the glint and surfaces of weekday worlds," or of the present day. "Soundings," dedicated to Kamau Brathwaite, recalls a 1983 reading by that poet. As much as the reading itself, Baugh recalls a woman in the audience weeping, presumably because what she hears reminds her of home—Jamaica.

So a remembered poetry reading and a remembered fellow member of the audience awaken yet another memory, as Baugh himself is transported back in time and space, "connection / of spirits across oceans, across deserts, grounds / of resistance, resilience. The spirits approve." Something like this complex layering and cultural recovery is also evident in "Yabba," a tribute to pottery, to a particular potter, to the Jamaican cultural doyenne Miss Lou, and even to the word "yabbam" which turns out to derive from a West African language, Twi.

I've neglected to point out that Baugh's poems are also deeply literary. Milton, Larkin, Shakespeare, and T. S. Eliot can all be heard here, as well as Brathwaite and Derek Walcott—Baugh is a Walcott scholar. To ponder the subtleties of Baugh's allusions is to come to terms with the poet's own (always subtle) recognition of the inevitable presence and pressure of the public sphere, be it history or race—as if those two could be disentangled. "Choices," which begins with a quote from Milton, segues almost imperceptibly into Jamaican patois, the language which is coterminous with fidelity to one's place. The poem ends: "I wouldn't say I would never leave, / but if that's what they calling ambition, / then for now I sticking with love, / River mullet still running in Grandy water, / and the busu soup simmering, / keeping warm 'til you come." "Truth and Consequences" begins with a reference to Cinna, the unfortunate poet murdered by a mob in *Julius Caesar* because they confuse him with Cinna the conspirator. But it makes no difference to the mob which Cinna he is:

It was then he learned,
too late,
there's no such thing as *"only* literature".
Every line commits you.
Those you thought dead will rise,
accusing. And if you plead
you never meant them,
then feel responsibility
break on you in a sudden sweat
as the beast bears down.

Baugh's delicate poems, often ornamental but rarely slight, acknowledge and engage in dialogue with an omnipresent shadow, whether the poet encounters that shade in nature, history, memory, or literature. Only the rare poem in *Black Sand* relaxes into a moment of sheer crystalline beauty—beauty which is, tellingly, usually unpeopled, as in "The Arrival:"

> That morning as usual,
> the mountain-witch birds
> practiced their beauty
> in the secret places
> of the high forest.
> In tree-shaded pools
> the minnows took life
> at their ease. The hillsides
> were a concert of green.
> And then the miracle of
> white sails erupting
> like whispering thunder
> out of the blue.

Baugh, too, practices his beauty in secret places. With a wholly characteristic subtlety, his poetry reveals its richness and strength. It took me too many readings to recognize "The Arrival" as a gemlike *ars poetica*.

Like Baugh, Ishion Hutchinson (born 1983) was born and raised in Jamaica, though unlike Baugh, Hutchinson hasn't stayed on the island. And like Baugh's, Hutchinson's work is imbued with literature. But where Baugh is subtle, fastidious, almost feline in the delicacy with which he approaches the fraught shadows of history and race, Hutchinson, though his work is far from simple, is louder and more emphatic; his poetry can boom with the somber sonority of a tolling bell. Hutchinson is master of a rhetoric whose thundering cadences are occasionally knotted and clotted to the point of near-incomprehensibility:

> I credit not the genie but the coral rock: I man am stone.
> I am perfect. Myself is a vanishing conch shell speeding round
> a discotheque at the embassy of angels, skeletons ramble to check out
> my creation dub and sex is dub, stripped to the bone, and dub is the heart
> breaking the torso to spring, olive beaked, to be eaten up by sunlight.
>
> ("The Ark by 'Scratch'")

. . . for I, tristes-tropiques-man,

ice-pick raconteur, who love the spondee of the furnace,
feared a knife sliced my throat, chipped over an imaginary
moat; an anachronistic river sighed below the asphalt,

I heard a man yell in his cell: "Get the fucking money, Pete!";
I lowered my head, holy, as daylight paled into a horse
pluming towards me; I laughed; it halted, "O my chevalier!"

    ("There")

Even in its most orotund opacities, Hutchinson's verse is rich and
often beautiful. And he can write with a powerful clarity whose honesty
feels not only eloquent but also hard-won and persuasive.

Hutchinson is a poet who demands and rewards rereading—the
poems require a second look to yield up a richness which is reliably there.
They're always serious poems; one sees the point of William Logan's
comment that "In a landscape of younger American poets increasingly
shy of language rich with responsibility, . . . Hutchinson is like fresh air."

Where Edward Baugh slyly slides lines from Milton or Shakespeare,
Larkin or Eliot into his poems, Hutchinson, though his work is rife with
echoes and allusions, is more likely to describe the act of reading itself. I
was going to say "celebrate" the act of reading; but like much in Hutchinson's work, the tone is as complicated as the power dynamics of a colonial education.

Reading, after all, happens in a particular place and time. A powerful
sequence entitled "The Lords and Commons of Summer" begins:

I circled half-mad a dead azalea scent that framed
my room; I licked anointed oil off a sardine tin,

opened *Being and Time*, perplexed myself, then picked up
and blew a clay bird whistle, silence came scratching,

the same way it did at the funeral of Heidegger,
when no silence came.

I love that sardine tin and its pungent oil, whose scent mingles uneas-
ily with the fragrance of the azaleas and the rebarbative abstractions of
Heidegger. Another poem, "Reading Late: *Anabasis*," takes us (arrestingly
in the second person) from reading Xenophon—and reading him with
intense imaginative engagement—to the bed where the reader is lying:

> You read the ripples of their sandals
> and armours dragged in dust, the anagram
> of crows following them. . . .
>
> So you pulled the cord on the light, to wade
> the sepia sheets, trouble on the road . . .

That trouble on the road can be ancient or contemporary or both. In between the imagined sandals and armor and the light cord, trucks rumbling down a highway intervene.

In "The Orator," a scaldingly magniloquent poem too long to quote in full, the solitary reader has become a bemused student (perhaps a graduate student at that) listening to "a tweeded rodent scholar" "harping in dead metaphor / the horror of colonial heritage." In a more mordant version of Baugh's "Soundings," the listener's mind leaps back to the island of childhood: "There I remembered the peninsula / of my sea, the breeze opening the water / to no book but dusk; no electricity, just stars pulsing over shanties. . . ." Less dependable than starlight, the power in the lecture hall fails:

> . . . thunder shocked
> away Edison's filaments: a dead watt.
> Inarticulate at the dead lectern,
> he stood grasping what he had learned
> in all the colleges, but went hollow
> and I heard his breath in shallow
> bursts the way a firefly's ticks amplify
> a lonely room, each tick signified
> his mother back home, who still,
> after many years, her only skill,
> cleans uptown houses to knuckle
> out a living; another tick, his supple,
> ever-ready sister, breeding at the first attention. . . .

Eventually the light goes back on, but what the darkness has revealed doesn't fade. At the end of "The Orator": "'Applaud the fluorescence!' he cried. / I couldn't, those bulbs hurt my eyes."

Another powerful poem not so much about reading as about its aftermath, how a text and a place stratify and coalesce, is "Marking in Venice." The indignation that inflects "The Orator" is here more inward and reflective. The poet is visiting Venice: "My first time, yet a return (islands have that trick / about them, Jamaica, Cyprus) . . . In the Ghetto," the sight of "an old man and a girl . . . walking to, or from, synagogue" evokes the tragic reflection with which the poem ends:

Their exile infects and reminds me this is no

vacation, just hate's old transfiguration, language's
treason, the savage cause carved in stone.
A lamp blows out in his beard, gravels of nimbus

reconvene; God grumbles in his mirrored palace,
for he knows he has loved wisely but not well.

Never oversimplifying, eschewing sentimentality, always eloquent, Hutchinson is a great poet of education. The maps and globes conspicuous in some of his earlier poems, poems that memorialize his school days, are iconic presages of the future traveler's explorations of culture and geography, even if every voyage only leads to "hate's old transfiguration." The voyages and memories, the love of learning and the rage at the conditions under which that learning took place, are beautifully realized in a recent, still uncollected poem about an old professor's ambivalent and ungracious gift of a book:

. . . his book, offered abruptly,
taken, stowed away, now posthumously examined:
fragile pencil webbings of flickered exclamations,
impatient the way he paced the blackboard,
erased a word ("meteors"), hurled glances
somewhere far off, beyond me. . . .

He died. His pupil flowered later into
the voltage of self-alienating poetry,
away from that moribund grammarian's
blind reluctance. Still, as moving iron
will fuse and repel, by his book, I am
the unspared prodigal of his abuse.

I don't know a more eloquent, and more excoriatingly honest, account of a gifted pupil's wrenchingly ambivalent response, than that "fuse and repel," that sense of unspared prodigality. Gratitude and resentment meet without precisely blending, and the memorable result is at once an elegy, a tribute, an accusation, and a reflection whose gaze is trained both inward and outward. Hutchinson may not be easy on anyone, and that includes himself. But his knotty conflicts, his faithfulness to the complex darkness of history, do not prevent him from writing wonderful poems.

Edward Baugh's characteristic tone is one of rueful private reflection; while his poetry is absolutely alive to the public sphere, he tends to look inward and backward, and there's an interiority to the voice. The more declamatory Ishion Hutchinson frequently reflects on his past, and the effect is a nuanced, layered consciousness: the poet is in Venice or in a university lecture hall, but also and simultaneously in Jamaica. Any important text is a passport to memory—and never a sentimental or simple memory, but often a memory of wrenching conflict.

Born in 1979, Erica Dawson is a few years older than Hutchinson and a generation younger than Baugh; and her remarkable poetry's relation to race and to the past has a different flavor from either of theirs. Dawson is more performative; with a nervous, jumpy, juicy energy that's both exhilarating and exhausting, she makes each poem into a kind of shtick or dance or revue (in fact a wonderful poem in Dawson's second book, *The Small Blades Hurt*, is entitled "La Revue Nègre"). Perhaps what I'm fumbling to evoke here is best described as pace. Where Baugh's ruminations gently glide, where Hutchinson broodingly tunnels inward through strata of culture and memory, Dawson is all over the place, flailing yet succinct, bubbly yet controlled. Particularly in her first two books, *Big-Eyed Afraid* (2007) and *The Small Blades Hurt* (2014), she packs her lines with so many cultural, geographical, historical, and personal references that we zip from Josephine Baker to Puccini, Johnny Cash, the Alamo, the battle of Jericho, and Pinocchio in a single stanza— and no, it's not a coincidence that so many of those names rhyme. Dawson is in love with form, its effects and its control, not excluding rhyme, which she wields with wit and panache. She excels at shaping her exuberant lines with their capacious references into sonnets or ballades; her energy comes in small but powerful packages that are all the more dynamic for being contained.

Big-Eyed Afraid, Dawson's debut volume, can be read as a sort of family album; many of the poems begin "I was born, Mom says. . . ." Here's history as familiar, genetic, personal, embodied. Dawson has unflinchingly witty poems about hair, legs, breasts, feet, puberty. It's hard to know what to quote, but here are a few stanzas from "High Heel":

I line

My ankles up and, see,
They propinquate. They roll until
They collapse. The missing insteps spill
From the slingbacks' nudity

And barest ties. So call
Me Mary Jane with a turf toe fetish.
I'm stacked. With three-inch-high coquettish
Stilettos, I'm Belle o' the Ball

And socket joint. *There goes
High Heel.* I've heard my ankles crack
And traced the point where I go black
To white on all ten toes

(Top brown to bottom peach)
As if my foot's biracial. In
The lady's pump, I'm genuine
Sunday best (Praise Jesus! Preach!).

When we leave Dawson's skin with its range of hues and her bones and hair for something harder to see, her mind or soul or psyche, the poems remain pulsingly in the realm of the physical. One of the most mesmerizingly memorable poems in *Big-Eyed Afraid* is "Disorder," a hummable ballade about an elusive diagnostic code. The first stanza should give the flavor:

I'm systematically deranged.
Two. Nine. Six. Three. I've multiplied
The digits, switched them, disarranged
The code, prognoses side by side.
And I begin. I'm certified,
Depressed, no symptoms to decode.
The signifier signified
In this recurring episode.

Fast-forward to the envoy:

Yet I wake up, always inside
This room, writing the palinode—
Two. Nine. Six. Three—identified
In this recurring episode.

Few poets writing now whom I can think of—male or female, Black
or white, young or old—are so deft and witty when it comes to putting
forms to work, fitting all kinds of chaos into the elegant box of a stanza
("*This room*") ticking and crackling with energy. Among the living, Alicia Stallings comes to mind; among the departed, James Merrill. But
Dawson's voice, diction, and preoccupations are indelibly her own. For
one thing, Blackness is a constant, no less in her thoughts than her body.
Later in *Big-Eyed Afraid*, the speaker, now grown, discerns Africa and
slavery imprinted on her body:

I'm wearing Africa
On my brown stomach: a birthmark
Dotted with freckles, nevus dark
And ticklish. *Laugh 'Rica,*

Mom says. *The master stoles*
Himself a spotty people. I see
A darker reef and symmetry
In her black island moles.

The hectic pace, the capacious diction bubbling with unruly puns,
and the unrelenting candor of Dawson's poems can make reading her a
challenge. How to keep up with a poet whose vocabulary alone is a salutary workout? Poetic form is an anchor, a handle, a railing, no less for the
poet herself than for the panting reader. "Bees in the Attic," a crown of
sonnets in *Big-Eyed Afraid*, a poem that encompasses suburbia, a house, a
garden, an attic, girlhood, depression, and, yes, bees, among many other
things, is an island—not precisely of calm, since the language buzzes, but
of an achieved tranquility. Like Dawson's bees, the seagulls at the end of
"Intermission," a poem in *The Small Blades Hurt*, offer a respite, a breath
of air, a momentary stillness—even though, in Homeric fashion, the
seagulls inhabit and animate a simile:

The treble S is slung

    From the conductor's wrists.
There, in the faltering high C,
The alto's note, sad symmetry
    And syllable, subsists

    Like absent seagulls who,
Ashore, leave tiny fleeting prints,
As markers of their sustenance,
    And hover in the blue.

I'm reminded not only of Baugh's gemlike little poem, cited earlier, "The Arrival," but also of David Wojnarowicz's poignant advice, also cited above, "Don't ever give up beauty." It may be that in the chaotic clutter—to call it nothing worse—of human history, a glimpse, a memory, a simile may be all we can hope for in the way of respite.

To the degree that it encompasses more history than *Big-Eyed Afraid*, Dawson's second book, *The Small Blades Hurt*, is, despite the unmistakable family resemblance between the two collections, altogether darker. We move away from early memories to the realm of history and literature, always under the shadow of racial violence. "Griot" revisits Robert Hayden's poem "Night, Death, Mississippi" and tries to imagine the lyncher's wife. "I, Too, Sing America" is an eerie and haunting fantasy/dream/nightmare about the execution of Mary Surratt, who was hanged in 1865 together with the other accused conspirators who had plotted Lincoln's assassination. "I, Too, Sing America"—the title is taken from Langston Hughes. And the penultimate poem in *The Small Blades Hurt* links Hughes with John Brown; its title is "Langston Hughes' Grandma Mary Writes a Love Letter to Lewis Leary Years After He Dies Fighting at Harper's Ferry." The historical link is a tragic reminder—as if we needed one now, in the days before the fraught 2018 midterm elections—of how recent and how terribly relevant and alive the days of slavery still are.

Dawson's new book, *When Rap Spoke Straight to God* (2018), also rooted in history, is heightened by an apocalyptic urgency which moves beyond the personal and historical to the spiritual, the ethereal, the diction of gospel but also—as per the title—of rap. Church has always played a role in Dawson's memories and references, but the organ notes in this new book have an unsettling way of modulating into rant or gunfire.

As it so often can be, poetry is truer than history. Or maybe it's simply prophesying.

> Get it right, Jesus. Get you a gun.
> This is your chance at vigilante.
>
> Bring this shit home and fucking ante
> up your omnipresence. Because
> in the beginning there was
> it good?
>
> It's not. Where is your free-
> for-all? What of that jealousy?
>
> This is your chance to be a man
> who keeps the shells because he can;
> and, when he shoots, he always cocks
> his head up toward his shadow-box
> shiny with carbon-copied gods
> and gutted animals. Thy rod's
> useless. The good word cannot make
> morning beget another take
> on mourning.

Anywhere you dip into the extended rhapsody (rap-sody?) that is *When Rap Spoke Straight to God*, you'll come upon something old and new, familiar and alarmingly fresh at the same time. To revisit Majmudar's formulation, Erica Dawson (and a poem from this book is her contribution to Majmudar's anthology *Resistance, Rebellion, and Life*) never loses her natural affinity for filigree, but the extended riff that is this book is also, and eloquently, in-your-face.

Where Dawson is speeded up, Rowan Ricardo Phillips (born in 1974) is deliberate: measured, calm, sometimes elliptical. His poems offer up a lot of space—between words and lines, between thoughts. "Nature," a poem in Phillips's 2015 collection *Heaven*, consists of a single line: "This is what I sound like when I'm thinking." This spaciousness, this room for silence, doesn't make the poems feel discontinuous or fragmented; rather, it's as if we're being enfolded in a mantle of quiet at the same time as we're being encouraged, even challenged, to follow the poet as he thinks or feels his way from line to line. An apparent hesitation or tentativeness is matched, in Phillips's work, by an underlying confidence, and along with that confidence is the sense of an underlying energy. Not that Phillips is poised to pounce, exactly. He's not agonized or tormented, and he has tremendous trust in the renewing and sustaining power of poetry. But his heaven would be less heavenly if he didn't allow for darkness.

"Tonight," the opening poem in Phillips's debut volume *The Ground* (2012), is an *ars poetica* worth quoting in full.

> In the beginning was this surface. A wall. A beginning.
> Tonight it coaxed music from a Harlem cloudbank. It freestyled
> A smoke from a stranger's coat. It stole thinned gin.
> It was at the edge of its beginnings but outside
> Looking in. The lapse-blue façade of Harlem Hospital is weatherstill
> Like a starlit lake in the midst of Lenox Avenue.
> Tonight I touched the tattooed skin of the building I was born in
> And because tonight is curing the beginning let me through.
> And everywhere was blurring halogen. Love the place that welcomed you.

We have Harlem, music, smoke, night stars, Gwendolyn Brooks. An unearthly light seems to hover over some mysterious birth. The poem is too vatic to be entirely intelligible, but what comes through the rapt hush is the poet's instruction, his note to self to "love the place that welcomed you." I think of other loopings back in memory, as Baugh listens to Brathwaite, hears an audience member weeping, and is transported back to Jamaica; or as Hutchinson, traveling in Venice, is tugged by a bitter undertow: "no / vacation, just hate's old transfiguration, language's / treason." For Phillips, it's as if, however high toward heaven he ascends, he's never really left home. And for him that sense of groundedness is a blessing—it's the gift that keeps on giving. The juxtaposition of cultures, what Lucie Brock-Broido calls the marriage of the formal with the demotic, is everywhere in Phillips's work once you look. Consider his recasting, or rather re-hearing, of the appearance and voice of Arnaut Daniel in *Purgatorio* XXVI. The troubadour who sings in Provencal has become Bob Marley:

> And slowly a bright starfield fell to the sea,
> Fell all about the one my guide had pointed out.
> And he said, *Rastaman. Higher man. Angel*

Seven-sealed . . . No. But I smell some of the smoke
Of Babylon on I. Come closer. Closer.
So I-man have some ital veneration.

I am Bob, who weep and strum and gather and
Love all tings lickle and small. Jah left I lung
And guitar to sing to everyone. All dem!

But I nah know ting bout dem but what I sing.
And I nah wan know ting. I nah wan know ting!
So when I complete I uphill trip to I

Sing some of I soul you see ere so close peeled
From I-man structure. . . .

Evie Shockley has rightly pointed out that Phillips asserts his affinity with Walcott, Stevens, and Dove, to which we need to add Dante and Shakespeare. "Measure for Measure," in *Heaven*, is a wonderful poem about falling asleep ("in Woody Creek, Colorado," of all places) reading *Measure for Measure* and waking up, and *Hamlet* is omnipresent. And as we see in his Arnaut Daniel/Bob Marley, Phillips engages these canonical presences not only by reading and rereading them, but by rewriting them. In an interview with fellow Farrar Straus Giroux poet Lawrence Joseph, Phillips quotes a line from Catalan poet J. V. Foix, *"M'exalta el nou I m'enamora el vell,"* or "I'm exalted by the new and in love with the old." And he continues in response to a question about his "formal strategies": "Form is an invisible map. It leads you from poet to poet, century to century, country to country, language to language, culture to culture. . . . My one formal strategy consisted of two elements: to enjoy making the poems and to follow their folds, like a finger tracing the skyline. . . ." That almost intuitive following where the poem leads accounts for some of the hesitancy that makes reading Phillips's poems an experience at once tranquil and gradual. I can't think of another poet whose work changes so much for me from reading to reading, as I follow the poems' folds. We've seen that Dante's Arnaut folds over into Bob Marley. In another poem in *The Ground*, the second part of "Two Studies of Derek Walcott," Walcott folds over Spenser (or is it vice versa?). Furthermore, the poem's title, appropriate for a painting, and its opening lines strongly recall Wallace Stevens. But if we uncrumple this much-crumpled thing, as Stevens put it in *"Le Monocle de Mon Oncle,"* we also find Phillips himself somewhere among the folds.

> The sea is blue, the sea is green, the sea
> Is yellow when the sea is both sea and sun.
> It erases. The seasons erase. A mirror erases its subject
> And asks the vanished subject to love itself whole again.
> Great, skymaking shepherd. Allegorist and allegory. What did you begin
> With painted birds dotting your painted island in curatorial iambics;
> And then the length, the length, the length: your ambition
> Strong like Spenser's, who politicked in Ireland, while courting epic,
> And caged his dark exilic woe behind lines burned black and lambent?

Ambition: Phillips's often rapt tone, at once focused and sublime—one eye, as it were, on the ground, one scanning the skies—isn't at all incompatible with ambition. He's a writer to be reckoned with: a critic (*When Blackness Rhymes with Blackness*), translator from Catalan and Spanish, and screen writer, and now a sportswriter, whose *The Circuit* I look forward to reading. There's an ease and confidence in Phillips's ability to make one part of his career nourish another, and the resulting unfolding is a pleasure to watch.

I've so far failed to mention love and rage. Phillips's love poems—"Golden" in *The Ground*, and the beautiful "Vall de Nuria," which closes out *Heaven*—are praise songs of the first order, often located at the dreamy edge between sleep and waking, and suffused with light:

> The white rose. The celestial silence.
> The lake of light. The bed-like inner thigh
> Of empyrean buttermilk and gold,
> Call it what you will, it wakes me tonight.
> Heaven reheavens. And the mind's prelude
> To the touch of your lips on my forehead,
> On my neck, our drowned silences celloing
> In the dark like flames drawn on the ocean,
> Is not the mind's prelude but its heaven.

And then there is the darkness: of race, of our moment, of every moment. Phillips has several poems about what it's like to venture into, say, a store as a Black man; but I'm thinking in particular of his contribution to *Resistance, Rebellion, Life*, a poem entitled "Dark Matter Ode." The very title marries science and classical poetics, and the poem, addressed to Phillips's young daughter, marries tenderness and rage:

> leaning in, inspecting you like a crook,
> I am the poet in his pillory.
> I see you as free. I sing of the wood.
> And I sing of the bars. I am the dunce
> Of the stars who sings of the bars.
> Poets know time is a dead man walking. . . .

Phillips mentions Chidiock Tichborne, the sixteenth-century poet whose beautiful poem on the eve of his execution is all we have of his work. We can think also of Yeats's "Prayer for My Daughter" or the glimpse of the daughter in Robert Lowell's "Memories of West Street and Lepke." But finally the voice is Phillips's own. It is the voice of any parent loving the child they know will forget this moment. But it is also the voice a Black father addresses to his Black daughter now, in this time, and also in an alarming future.

> I love that you sleep so softly despite
> The virus of my verbal flailings flowing
> Through your veins. One day you will be facing
> It, the reflective black immensity
> Of it all, and you will seethe and set out
> Into a world of science and anger
> That I just can't imagine. Today won't
> Matter to you because today to you
> Won't be by then today, which went like this:
> There was an IMAX movie about Dark
> Matter and the protests about how Black
> Lives matter, but then for you the same sleep
> And then a million years from now somewhere
> Discovering that something like this one
> Moment could have happened, could have mattered,
> That you asleep in your crib were a god
> In the machine and that poem your father
> Wrote you was a fucking living weapon.

The reflective black immensity of it all. This phrase, like the dark matter in Phillips's title (itself a reference to, among other things, the IMAX movie he's just seen), encompasses but also transcends human skin color. The dark matter here dwarfs any human dilemma. And yet the unforgettable image sequence of the loving father musing over his child's crib, the bars, the song as a weapon—this chain of association and trope effortlessly and inevitably brings the dark matter out there in the cosmos home to one bedroom, one baby asleep in her crib, one father/poet/Black man. The dark matter, that is, is not only outside us; it's also inside.

In many ways, Rowan Ricardo Phillips is the calmest, the least fraught and tormented, of these four superb poets, all of whom, to be sure, artfully balance the tensions of history and heritage. But given Phillips's gift for love and awe and calm, his ability to express sheer grace and joy without sentimentality or shame, the final three words in "Ode to Dark Matter" enact the leap from filigree to in-your-face with a salutary shock: *fucking living weapon.* Not that Phillips is ever merely filigree; but he would surely agree with David Wojnarowicz that we should never "give up beauty." Phillips's poems give us beauty over and over. But—as he muses over the crib—Black Lives Matter. There's a "reflective black immensity" beyond any one poet's, father's, person's power to grasp. And in this condition of partial helplessness, poems are better weapons than guns.

The dialectic, the struggle, the subterranean forces—they all continue.

VOICES OF ELDERS

THE LAST TIME I spoke to my brother David was in 2004. I was in Athens. Europe was awash in Euros. I'd been invited to participate in a writers' conference in Delphi, for which I'd been flown from New York first class and put up at the Grande Bretagne Hotel before being bussed to the conference center in Delphi the next day. It was another world.

David was in St. Louis, dying of colon cancer but alert and funny. Our phone connection, as I unpacked in the hotel room, was as clear as if he were in the next room. "Remind me again, what are you doing in Greece?" he asked. "Reading your poems?" I admitted that I'd been invited to talk about how my poems had been influenced by Greece and Greek writers, but that nothing had been said about actually reading them. "Aha!" said David triumphantly. "I'm not surprised. People would always rather hear poets talk about their work than listen to them read it."

What was true for poetry in 2004 seems to have held equally true for fiction in 2016. Not that I never read novels, but given the choice of reading a novel by a distinguished writer of a certain age (say a novel by Joyce Carol Oates or Shirley Hazzard or Ursula K. Le Guin) or reading what that writer has to say about her craft, her career, or the general state of the literary culture, I tend to opt for the latter. Should I be ashamed of this preference? All I know is that now I'm of a certain age myself, I would usually rather learn something about the art of writing or the whys and hows, the ins and outs, of a particular career, than be told a story—so long as the person writing about the art has earned the authority to pronounce.

In reading such pronouncements, one also learns, if only inadvertently, something about the art of civility, the mannerliness (or not) with which a seasoned writer responds to questions she has surely heard dozens of times before or reviews stories or novels that aren't always as accomplished as the stories or novels she herself has written. What kind of octogenarian might I be? I wonder, reading these collections. If I live so long, who would be my role model?

The book I found least engaging of these three was also the most enticingly titled: Oates's *Soul at the White Heat* (the phrase is borrowed from Emily Dickinson). Oates's book, despite its promising subtitle ("Inspiration, Obsession, and the Writing Life"), is essentially a collection of book reviews, with a lecture or two thrown in, most of which appeared in the *New York Review of Books* and which were therefore at least faintly familiar to me. Who was the intended audience for this book—readers of the *NYRB*? Fans of Oates's fiction or of her other criticism? Oates always writes well, with fluency and perspicacity. But had I not been aware of the gothic nature of her fictional world, the bleakness and savagery of her imagined landscapes, I wouldn't have guessed them from the workmanlike, even-tempered writing here. For despite its breathy title, *Soul at the White Heat* seems on the whole rather lukewarm. The reviews gathered here, of writers ranging from H. P. Lovecraft to Louise Erdrich, and from Larry McMurtry to Margaret Drabble, are bookended by two pieces which are not reviews. The first of these, entitled "Is the Uninspired Life Worth Living? Thoughts of Inspiration and Obsession," strings together quotes from Yeats, Woolf, Wittgenstein, Henry James, Emily Dickinson, Plato, and many others—all eminently worth revisiting, but none surprising, at least not to this jaded reader. Again, one wonders about the intended audience of this hefty collection. *White Heat* ends with "A Visit to San Quentin," which is vivid, disquieting, and also utterly predictable. On leaving the prison, Oates feels "a surge of relief and joy." Yup.

If I want Oates really imaginatively engaging with writers, if I want her to catch me up with something unexpected, I'd turn to her unforgettable and indeed unclassifiable little 2008 book *Wild Nights!* (another Dickinson-derived title) with its perfectly captured stylistic tonalities and its wicked riffs on biography, on temperament, on the lonely weirdnesses of Poe or Hemingway or Dickinson. *Wild Nights!* combines imagination with scholarship to produce a distinctive brew. By contrast, there's nothing very weird or wicked in *Soul at the White Heat*. It may or may not be germane to observe as well that these pages offer few hints of Oates's many decades as an expert practitioner in the world of literature. She's knowledgeable, even authoritative; she is extraordinarily well read and, as noted, she writes very well. But she doesn't seem interested in claiming the authority that is one of the pleasanter features of being an elder. The voice in these reviews, if not girlish, is ageless and finally somewhat anonymous.

Shirley Hazzard's voice on the page is distinctive and consistent: magisterial, thoughtful, deliberate, always formal. If *Soul at the White Heat* is a generous serving of leftovers, *We Need Silence to Find Out What We Think* is conscientiously compiled, edited, footnoted; Brigitta Olubas has gone to a lot of trouble to disinter essays, reviews, and also some brief opinion pieces, some dating from the 1970s and 80s. A review of some stories by Muriel Spark was published in the *New York Times Book Review* in 1968. One feels that every sentence Hazzard writes is carefully weighed and tasted beforehand; what emerges isn't light, but it lingers. Still, some pieces were more worthy of exhumation than others.

We Need Silence braids together three contrasting thematic strands: thoughts about literature and culture; brief essays or opinion pieces about the United Nations; and a few short sections of memoir which double as travel pieces. In "Canton More Far," Hazzard recalls a remote time and locale: her own youthful experiences in Hong Kong, where she was employed in "an office concerned with the colony's security." The sense of place is always strong, but equally vivid and evocative is the memory of what Hazzard was reading at the time. "Canton" is a very rich little piece of writing; details recalled decades later add pieces to a still unsolved puzzle.

> The following morning, I sat on the living-room floor and read *Rebecca*. The weather, very usual for the time of year, was an alternation of glowering sunshine and sudden downpour that sent up a steamy odor of vegetation from the garden. The Jarvises' apartment had its own contrasting smell—a shuttered smell of mildew and insect spray, of furniture polish and face powder, the smell of colonial houses in the Orient. There was about this, as about the apartment in general, something so true to form, so representative of the British community, as practically to exonerate the Jarvises there and then from any suggestion of foul play. Someone operating against his country's interests would, one imagined, hardly have found it possible to align himself so uncompromisingly with its attributes, might even have introduced a note of interest, some telltale innovation of taste or atmosphere.

One sees what Willard Spiegelman meant when he wrote recently that every sentence of Shirley Hazzard's affords him pleasure. Her judicious gravity here accommodates a something lighter and more slippery, an almost feline irony; her retrospective insight is so elegantly shaped to her perceptions of the time that the entire passage takes some pleasurable unpacking.

Icy and damning, the pieces about the United Nations have a different kind of authority, but one recognizes the measured voice, the care in constructing sentences, the well-earned authenticity (Hazzard was a UN employee for years):

> There is no such thing as official cowardice. All cowardice—like all true courage—is personal.
>
> I know of no setting where idealism is ridiculed as at the U.N., where "realism" and "the possible" are so often equated with conformity and fearfulness, where the personal initiative and public engagement from which all human advancement proceeds are less nurtured or esteemed, no place more remote from acts of intellectual and moral courage, more incapable of distinguishing between discretion and poltroonery. The patron saint of the U.N. is Pontius Pilate.

In the brief final section poignantly entitled "Last Words," Hazzard—perhaps under pressure of failing health or flagging energy—is both more succinct and also more openly emotional. Accepting the 2005 National Book Award, she said: "I do not . . . regard literature as a competition. It is so vast. We have this marvelous language. We are so lucky that we have a huge audience for that language." And in the latest of the pieces gathered here, in a discussion at the New York Society Library in 2012, she has a wonderfully suggestive (and now, in October 2016, a yet more ominously relevant) phrase:

> I feel very much—I have felt increasingly in recent years—that the world has a kind of Vesuvius element now, that we're waiting for something terrible to happen, and we do have an idea of what it might be like, but maybe we're pleasing ourselves with that because it might be much more terrifying.

It's too bad that so scrupulously edited a book should contain errors that make nonsense out of entire passages. The UN is surely "impotent," not "important" (see p. 111); and on p. 155 the word "not" has fallen out of a crucial clause, reversing Hazzard's intended meaning. But this is a quibble. We should be grateful for the existence of this book, occasional typos and all, for its insights into Montale and Vergil, Leopardi and Kurt

Waldheim. Hazzard doesn't shy away from history and ethics; indeed, they're inseparable from her thoughts about literature. She writes memorably that

> ... immense evils are impossible to hold in the mind. One's own contemplation of them can carry dangers of posturing, of easy vehemence, and of claims of unearned morality. By contrast, acts of goodness—even of 'public' goodness—can only be properly discussed or understood in their individual manifestations.

What Hazzard calls the Vesuvius element manifests differently—more bluntly—in Ursula Le Guin's language. In her acceptance speech to the National Book Foundation on the occasion (November 2014) of having been awarded the foundation's Medal for Distinguished Contribution to American Letters, Le Guin didn't mince words:

> Hard times are coming, when we'll be wanting the voices of writers who can see alternatives to how we live now, can see through our fear-stricken society and its obsessive technologies to other ways of being, and even imagine real grounds for hope. We'll need writers who can remember freedom—poets, visionaries—realists of a larger reality.

Ursula Le Guin died in 2018. Did she, in 2014, foresee Trump? Le Guin was nothing if not a visionary writer; nothing's impossible. *Words Are My Matter* is a wonderful collection, full of crunchy and surprising nuggets, pieces introducing me to books I had never heard of (H. L. Davis's 1936 novel *Honey in the Horn*) or writers I'd never gotten the hang of (Philip K. Dick). Sometimes, as if tossed off in passing, there is a beautiful moment of reflection on—well, in the following example, on beauty itself. In an essay about the house she grew up in, "Living in a Work of Art," Le Guin muses:

> I keep talking about comfort, practicality and impracticality, stairs, smells, and so on, when what I want to talk about is beauty; but I don't know how to. It seems you can only describe beauty by describing something else, the way you can only see the earliest star after sunset by not looking at it.

And this essay ends by wondering "if much of my understanding of what a novel ought to be was taught to me, ultimately, by living in that house.

If so, perhaps all my life I had been trying to rebuild it around me out of words."

This unregenerate nature of words as a medium, this struggle—by its very nature unfinished and unfinishable—to construct something permanent and true, is the burden of the eloquent little poem which serves as the book's epigraph and which also gives this collection its title. The second stanza will have to suffice here: "Words are my matter. I have chipped one stone / For thirty years and still it is not done, / That image of the thing I cannot see. / I cannot finish it and set it free, / Transformed to energy."

Le Guin can sound crusty and acerbic. Her sometimes spiky impatience in this artfully edited collection is enormously appealing, as is her candor. In a 2004 talk, she spoke passionately about an abortion she had in her youth. One doesn't find the likes of that in either Oates or Hazzard—or, for that matter, of a reflection like this:

> The New York/East Coast literary scene is so inward-looking and provincial that I've always been glad not to be part of it; but when I lived in London I was positively terrified by the intensity of British literary cliques, the viciousness of competition, the degree of savagery permitted. That bloody-mindedness may have lessened somewhat, but still, whenever I review a British book for the *Guardian*, I'm glad I live in Oregon.

Wherever we live, we're lucky to have Le Guin's thoughts on, among other things, genre. "Genre: A Word Only a Frenchman Could Love" is the title of her admirably clear and illuminating essay on that subject. Later on in *Words Are My Matter* one comes upon a wonderful two-page riff on being attacked by "the decaying corpse of genre fiction." "Genre breathed its corpse breath in her face, and she was lost. She was defiled. She might as well be dead. She would never, ever get invited to write for *Granta* now." Another piece I'll return to, "Teasing Myself Out of Thought," manages to avoid cliché and sanctimony even as Le Guin, not shying away from the sublime, is unafraid to echo Keats repeatedly, first in her title and then again—and again:

> A poem or any story consciously written to address a problem or bring about a specific result, no matter how powerful or beneficent, has abdicated its first duty and privilege, its responsibility to itself. Its primary job is simply to find the words that give it its right, true shape.

That shape is its beauty and its truth.

A well-made clay pot—whether it's a terra-cotta throwaway or a Grecian urn—is nothing more and nothing less than a clay pot. In the same way, to my mind, a well-made piece of writing is simply what it is, lines of words. . . .

Writing about what we find in the pots (or words) others have made, Le Guin summons Keats again, as well as her beloved Lao Tzu, whom she has translated (and isn't Cleanth Brooks lurking somewhere in the vicinity of that well-made urn?):

Keats is on my side in this, if I understand his principle of negative capability, and so is Lao Tzu, who observed that the use of the pot is where the pot is not. A poem of the right shape will hold a thousand truths. But it doesn't say any of them.

I'm reminded of Le Guin's thought, which I've already cited, that beauty can only be described by describing something else. That kind of indirectness, which leaves a connection to be made, a space to be filled, also animates "Teasing Myself Out of Thought," as Le Guin refuses to fill the empty vessels in her audience with comfortable pieties about literature. She teases not only herself but her audience (at least, her readers now, or this reader); she challenges us to think, makes us fill the shape with meaning, makes us exert ourselves. Le Guin's strenuous energy and wiry wit come through clearly, whether she's being attacked by the corpse breath of genre or creating an alternative universe or talking about the art of writing or reviewing a book or recording with candor and clarity her experience of a week at Hedgebrook. Le Guin's honesty is occasionally rebarbative. She wasn't afraid to sound like a sage; but rather than predictably wise, her well-earned opinions are passionate and sometimes prickly.

THREE STEPS DOWN

THREE STEPS DOWN. In the small dim room where I will soak for an hour, I'm sitting naked on the bottom of three steps that lead down into a square tank. Through a triangular notch at the bottom of the closed door, I can see a piece of the yellow door of the opposite room, lambent as with a concentrated dose of sun from some unseen source. *Little patch of yellow wall, little patch of yellow wall*, Bergotte kept dizzily repeating when, despite feeling ill, he ventured out to an exhibition to see Vermeer's *View of Delft*. "Little patch of yellow wall" were his last words.

Three steps down. In this square little room, half in, half out of the oblong tank of blood-warm water, I look up at the small high windows just under the low ceiling—windows not to look through but to look at, roughly painted on smeary glass in black, gold, and russet strokes. In what I first took to be abstractions, figures reveal themselves: an Indian warrior face up in a flowing river; a horse's head in profile; a woman's torso, sharp breasts pointing forward. A bearded prophetic figure in a thundercloud leads the pack, all of them slanting, surging forward, all borne up in a stormy swirl of sky. Were these forms always there or did they need my gaze to awaken? Later, on the way back to Albuquerque, red rock formations on one side of the highway enclose the form of a woman—tall, statuesque, enfolded in the element and struggling to get out. She does not move or try to catch my eye; she does not step forward and wave to me. But there she is. Was she always there, or did my gaze create her?

Three steps down to the mildly briny, amniotic water. Half my hour is gone; I'm nearer to the end than the beginning. In this soft bag of skin, or in other guises, how many lives have I lived? In the dim subaqueous light, as if even my eyes were under water, I look at myself from a distance. I can see how I have linked my life with my beloved's, can almost touch the link and feel the astonishing ease and lightness of the leap from nothing to something. And then the gentleness, the softly lapping waves of the gradual acclimation, days and nights, then weeks and months and years speeding up as he and I moved forward, linked. But in this bath I am alone.

The blood-warm water, the three small steps down. Collarbone-deep now, do I see the pattern, so clearly because it no longer holds, because it is broken? Or is it that I am so infused with the pattern, so watermarked, that I can step outside myself and see it? It's not the pattern blurring, it is me. Gravity dissolves in this dim tank; age and identity melt in the neutral tea in which I'm steeping. Attachments drift like lily pads moored deep beneath the surface, rooted how and where no one can see. Something submerged, forgotten, flickers and rises like a gentle fin, tugs, vanishes again.

My time is up. Three steps out of the water, and drying off and getting dressed. Out on the back veranda, solar gain, though I'm shivering a little. Clouds cycle, sky changes. We, not the sun, are moving. Shadows lengthen. Slow minutes, swift years, the body's dissolution, sharp edges blurring, blunting. I think of stepping back into that waiting water, but no, the little door has closed behind me, the mystic soak is done, at least for this year. What is there to fear? Nothing. Everything. It is time to face the daylight, though now shadows are lengthening. Afternoon is turning into evening.

CREDITS

Edward Baugh, excerpts from "The Comings and Goings of Poems," "What's Poetry For?," "To the Editor Who Asked Me to Send Him Some of My Black Poems," "Sunday Afternoon Walks with My Father," "Soundings," "Choices," "Truth and Consequences," and "The Arrival" from *Black Sand: New and Selected Poems*. Copyright © 2013 by Edward Baugh. Reprinted with the permission of Peepal Tree Press.

Elizabeth Bishop, excerpt from "The Moose" from *The Complete Poems 1927–1979*. Copyright © 2008 by Alice Helen Methfessel. Reprinted by permission of Farrar, Straus & Giroux, LLC.

Yves Bonnefoy, excerpt from "Hopkins Forest" from Harry Thomas, *The Truth of Two: Selected Translations*. Copyright © 2017 by Harry Thomas. Reprinted with the permission of The Un-Gyve Limited Group.

Jane Cooper, excerpts from "Long View from the Suburbs," "All These Dreams," "Threads: Rosa Luxemburg From Prison: 1. Wronke, Spring 1917," "The Knowledge That Comes through Experience," "For a Boy Born in Wartime," "The Blue Anchor," "Rent," "Praise," and "Souvenirs" from "Dispossessions" from *Scaffolding: New and Selected Poems*. Copyright © 2000 by Jane Cooper. Used by permission of W. W. Norton & Company, Inc.

Erica Dawson, excerpts from "High Heel" and "Disorder" from *Big-Eyed Afraid*. Reprinted by permission of The Waywiser Press (Oxford & Baltimore). Excerpt from "Intermission" from *The Small Blades Hurt*. Copyright © 2014 by Erica Dawson. Reprinted with the permission of Measure Press. Excerpt from *When Rap Spoke Straight to God: A Poem*. Reprinted with the permission of Tin House Books.

Moses Hadas, excerpts from *Old Wine, New Bottles: A Humanist Teacher at Work*. Copyright © 1962 by Pocket Books Inc., renewed 1990 by Simon & Schuster, Inc. Reprinted with the permission of Simon & Schuster, Inc. All rights reserved.